THE THREE BEARS ARE DEAD!

(INFLATION, INTEREST RATES, GOVERNMENT SPENDING)

ROBERT J. FROEHLICH

FORBES / AHCP

A Division of Forbes Inc.
60 Fifth Avenue
New York, New York 10011

CIP Data is available.
Printed in the United States of America
10 9 8 7 6 5 4 3 2 1

ISBN 0–8281–1143–X

to the three most important people in my life

My Wife

My Lover

My Best Friend

who all happen to be the same wonderful person...

Cheryl Froehlich

ACKNOWLEDGMENTS

Many persons, both knowingly and unknowingly, have assisted me in development of this book. My business associates and colleagues over the past twenty years have unwittingly been subjected to many of my investment philosophies, strategies and beliefs and their reactions have aided considerably in the development of my thoughts.

Special thanks to my outstanding assistant, Michelle Pilota, for her assistance in tasks which ranged from typing the entire manuscript to proofreading, to researching, and even an occasional editorial change to make sure that I was paying close attention.

From the deepest part of my heart I would like to thank my parents, whom have both passed away, for their constant encouragement and support. I hope that they can see me now and are as proud of me as I only wish I could tell them that I am of them.

As a parent myself I am so very fortunate to have two wonderful teenage daughters: Marianne and Stephanie. I cannot thank them enough for listening and caring as I ramble on at the dinner table always giving them the long version of "the world according to Dad." If they only knew how much their inquisitive looks and innocent comments actually helped shape my opinions. Thanks also for letting me still win when we play tennis even though I know that you both have passed me by. I am so very proud of both of you.

And finally, my loving wife Cheryl, who is without a doubt my most valuable asset. Not only is she an understanding wife and a caring mother but she is my most sensitive and meticulous critic as well. It was Cheryl who made sure that I never lost sight of "Main Street" when I was trying to explain what was happening on "Wall Street." I love and respect you more than words can express.

TABLE OF CONTENTS

Dedication   iii
Acknowledgments   v
Introduction   ix

Chapter One
General Investment Perspective   1

Chapter Two
Economic Perspective   21

Chapter Three
Stock Market Perspective   75

Chapter Four
Bond Market Perspective   121

Chapter Five
Currency Market Perspective   143

Chapter Six
Commodity Market Perspective   163

Chapter Seven
Global Perspective   179

Chapter Eight
Political Perspective   201

Chapter Nine
Commentary on Key Investment
Issues that Evolved in 1997   225

Chapter Ten
Brady Commission Reform   247

Chapter Eleven
Top 10 Investment Themes for '98   257

Chapter Twelve
The Greatest Investment Idea for the Next
Millennium . . . Boomernomics   263

INTRODUCTION

The market's focus in recent years has been on our new paradigm economy that has been fondly referred to as the "Goldilocks'" economy, meaning it's not too hot or not too cold; but rather, it's just right. The real story in the investment world, however, is not about Goldilocks, but rather it's about the three bears who are dead!

In the story-telling world of Goldilocks, the enemies were papa bear, mama bear and baby bear. In the investment world the three bears who are our enemies have a different name. They are called inflation, interest rates and government spending. These are the three bears that cannot only turn our Goldilocks' economy upside down; they can throw the entire investment world into chaos.

I am happy to inform you that these three bears all died in 1997. The year started out like many other years in our markets; however, by Tax Day, April 15, it became quite obvious that we were embarking upon a year unlike any other before it, into uncharted waters on every front. In the first eight chapters of this book I will explore and recap the driving forces of the markets beginning on Tax Day and progressing throughout the entire year of 1997—a year which will go down as a landmark one in which the Brady Commission's stock market circuit breakers were triggered for the first time ever and we witnessed first hand what it's like to invest in a global marketplace. The events in Southeast Asia have proven that all of the financial markets of the world are interconnected either economically, politically or psychologically. Southeast Asia proved that it is impossible for any market to isolate itself from the major events that dominate the global market.

Each of these eight chapters will include a collection of my weekly investment strategy commentaries from various times throughout the year between Tax Day and the end of the year. These insights will enable you to see the market trends through my eyes as together we see how these issues evolved over time.

1 GENERAL INVESTMENT PERSPECTIVE

OVERVIEW

Let's begin by clearly understanding why the three bears—inflation, interest rates and government spending—all died in 1997.

First regarding the inflation bear, two powerful factors have combined to kill inflation: the global economy and productivity. Our global economy and global competition really kicked into full force with the end of the Cold War. All markets are becoming more competitive globally as trade barriers continue to fall. The ultimate collapse of the Iron Curtain has created the largest global market in the history of the world. This intense global competition keeps a lid on prices. What the "Industrial Revolution" did to manufacturing, the "Global Revolution" will do to inflation. Now the second powerful factor is productivity improvements, driven by technology. You see, the technology revolution is already here. These technological improvements allow us to do everything faster and with more flexibility than ever before. Think about this: ten years ago most libraries in the United States still used a manual index card catalogue system. Today, almost all are computerized and many libraries are connected to the internet, where you can look up a book, check it out and have it mailed to you without ever leaving your living room. I'm not sure where we will be ten years from now, but I can guarantee you that it will make today's high-tech library internet system seem as much in the dark ages as a manual index card system in a library seems today. When you overlay these technological driven productivity improvements with corporate restructuring, deregulation and privatization, there is simply no way to get inflation; that bear is dead. The death certificate was issued when the annualized increase for the Consumer Price Index (CPI) came in for all of 1997 at 1.7%. That's the lowest level since 1964!

Now the interest rate bear is also dead. Interest rates will continue to trend lower because of a combination of two factors. The first is the continual rise in our savings rate which is largely being driven by an aging population and the second is a higher emphasis toward private supplemental savings as baby boomers continue to lose confidence in both their public and private retirement plans. This renewed focus on savings is very bullish for interest rates; thus, I'm declaring this bear is dead as well. To accept that this bear is dead, however, we must first overcome a problem I call "Generational Conditioning." Investors are still convinced that interest rates will rise and once again the yield on the benchmark 30-year Treasury Bond will be above 10%. Some investors are even waiting for the yield to break the 14.8% record level it set in 1981. Well, they are going to have a long wait because it is never going to happen. The problem with investors waiting on the sidelines for interest rates to rise and yields to cross 10% again is Generational Conditioning. Here's what I mean: If you look back 200 years from today at the yield on the Long Treasury Bond, and before that, the railroad bonds, and before that, the highest grade taxable bonds, here is what you would find. The yield on the highest grade, prime taxable bond over the last 200 years has only been over 6% yield 14% of the time. The problem is, all 14% has been since 1968! In essence, our generation has been conditioned to expect bond yields that are unreasonable. Interest rates aren't supposed to be over 6%; they're supposed to be under 6%.

The third and final bear is not only dead, it is disappearing as well. Simply put, government spending is not a problem and neither is our deficit now that we have adopted our balanced budget agreement. Let me put this in perspective for you. While keeping track of our deficit, it is important not to look at it in isolation; the deficit should be looked at as a percentage of Gross Domestic Product (GDP). This is the most important way of looking at the deficit because it reflects our economy's ability to absorb the federal deficit. This is one reason why one of the key economic measurements for a country to become eligible for membership in the European Monetary Union is that their deficit as a percentage of GDP must be 3% or less. Our deficit as a percent of GDP stands at less than ½ of 1%. To give you some historical perspective, the highest our deficit ever was as a percentage of GDP was back in 1943 when it was an unbelievable 31.1% of GDP. The highest level that our deficit has reached in the last 50 years as a percentage of GDP was in 1983 when it stood at 6.3%. While all of Europe is struggling to find budget gimmicks, asset sales, gold revaluation or whatever to be able to reduce their deficits to 3% of GDP, our deficit stands at ½ of 1% and is drastically falling; this bear is really dead!

Sit back now and enjoy the ride as I recap with you how the issues and events that drive my investment outlook evolved on a week by week basis from Tax Day (April 15th) through the end of 1997.

For the Week of April 14, 1997

There is no change in my asset allocation recommendation. The stock market should take center stage this week as earnings season is now in full swing. Look for the market to rebound nicely fueled by strong earnings reports. The bond market will continue to be under pressure as economic releases will likely build a case for another rate hike at the Federal Open Markets Committee meeting on May 20, 1997.

ASSET ALLOCATIONS	
STOCKS	70%
BONDS	25%
CASH	5%

For the Week of April 21, 1997

There is no change in my asset allocation outlook this week. All eyes should remain focused on earnings reports as they will continue to dominate all of the financial markets this week. I expect earnings to continue to surprise on the high side which should mean that the rebound will continue in the stock market. The quiet economic front means the bond market may even stage a little rally of its own, the last one before the Federal Open Markets Committee meeting on May 20, 1997. The single greatest risk to the financial markets this week could be the fear that Japan will intervene to weaken the U.S. Dollar.

ASSET ALLOCATIONS	
STOCKS	70%
BONDS	25%
CASH	5%

For the Week of April 28, 1997

There is no change in my asset allocation outlook this week. The economic release calendar will take center stage and dominate the markets' concern. This week will also provide us with the most important clues regarding what the markets can expect from the

Federal Reserve Board at their next meeting on May 20th. Hold on, I expect it to be a very volatile week for both the stock and bond market.

ASSET ALLOCATIONS	
STOCKS	70%
BONDS	25%
CASH	5%

For the Week of May 5, 1997

There is no change in my asset allocation outlook this week. I expect the stock market to continue to outperform the bond market. Both markets will feel their greatest impact from the economic releases again this week, which by the way, should show that the economy is not ready to slow down. The wild card of the week comes from Washington where any progress on a balanced budget deal could provide the markets with an unexpected lift.

ASSET ALLOCATIONS	
STOCKS	70%
BONDS	25%
CASH	5%

For the Week of May 12, 1997

There is no change in my asset allocation outlook this week. Economic releases will continue to rule the day again this week as both the bond market and stock market look for the final clue regarding where interest rates are headed. Both markets are nervous and I expect this to be a potentially volatile week where any piece of economic information will cause the markets to overreact.

ASSET ALLOCATIONS	
STOCKS	70%
BONDS	25%
CASH	5%

For the Week of May 19, 1997

There is no change in my asset allocation outlook this week. The waiting game is finally over. The May 20th Federal Reserve Board meeting is here and I expect interest rates to be moved up (maybe 50 basis points). This increase will not only rock the stock and bond markets, it will be the key driver of the currency markets (especially the dollar) as well.

ASSET ALLOCATIONS	
STOCKS	70%
BONDS	25%
CASH	5%

For the Week of May 26, 1997

There is no change in my asset allocation this week. All eyes will be focused on the economic releases. They will serve as a report card on whether the Federal Open Markets Committee (FOMC) made the right decision leaving interest rates alone. The FOMC will soon find out it is almost impossible to please both Wall Street and Washington. Given the choice between bad news (interest rate hike) and no news (uncertainty), Wall Street will pick the bad news every time. (Just raise rates and get it over with.) The only thing that Wall Street hates more than bad news is no news or uncertainty. On the other hand, given the same choice, Washington will pick no news over bad news all day long. After all, uncertainty is a way of life in Washington. Stay tuned, the May 20th FOMC meeting was the start of something, not the end of anything.

ASSET ALLOCATIONS	
STOCKS	70%
BONDS	25%
CASH	5%

dollar. It has become an excellent short-term leading indicator of which direction the markets may head.

ASSET ALLOCATIONS	
STOCKS	70%
BONDS	25%
CASH	5%

For the Week of September 1, 1997

There is no change in my asset allocation this week. This Labor Day holiday shortened week might be short on days but it will not be short on volatility. The sentiment in our markets has shifted and market expectations are now looking for an interest rate hike sometime this year. Economic releases now take on even greater importance as the market tries to determine which release will trigger the next rate hike. The markets could not have picked a worse time to focus on economic releases. The United Parcel Service strike will completely distort most of the economic signals in the coming weeks. This will only add to the confusion and uncertainty already in the market. Remember, confusion and uncertainty always lead to volatility. Maybe we should issue these upcoming economic releases with an (*) asterisk, just as we did to Roger Maris's home run record.

ASSET ALLOCATIONS	
STOCKS	70%
BONDS	25%
CASH	5%

For the Week of September 8, 1997

There is no change in my asset allocation this week. It is a rather light week from an economic perspective; however, when markets are nervous as they are today, it only takes one release to turn them upside down. When you combine our light economic calendar along with few earnings' releases, the real forces in the markets this week may very well come from outside of the United States. Leading candidates to throw our domestic markets a curve are Japan, Thailand, Germany or Washington D.C. (I can't help it, I still consider Washington D.C. a foreign land, from both a Main Street and a Wall Street perspective.)

ASSET ALLOCATIONS	
STOCKS	70%
BONDS	25%
CASH	5%

For the Week of September 15, 1997

There is no change in my asset allocation this week. The closer we get to a Federal Open Markets Committee (FOMC) meeting, the more volatile the market's reaction is to economic releases. As such, this week's releases will certainly move the markets. The markets will remain very nervous about Thailand and the Pacific Rim meltdown. I continue to feel that we have not seen the worst of this crisis. Keep one eye on Washington D.C. I'm getting a real sense that something big is about to finally break on one of many scandal-gates.

ASSET ALLOCATIONS	
STOCKS	70%
BONDS	25%
CASH	5%

For the Week of September 22, 1997

There is no change to my asset allocation this week. It should be a rather quiet week. Think of it as the calm before the storm, with the storm being the following week's Federal Open Markets Committee (FOMC) meeting. The storm has lost speed however, and the FOMC will not take any action at their meeting. What a great way to start the fourth quarter.

ASSET ALLOCATIONS	
STOCKS	70%
BONDS	25%
CASH	5%

13

For the Week of September 29, 1997

What a way to start the fourth quarter. This week is shaping up to be one of the more volatile weeks of the entire year. With eleven major economic releases, including the bellwether employment reports on Friday, I am sure that there are at least a few surprises to move the markets. Add to that the nervousness that always grips the markets the week of the Federal Open Market Committee's meeting, and you have a formula for major market swings. As if this is not enough, there is still time for a few companies to throw in their pre-earnings' disappointments before earnings season begins. Hold on, this week is shaping up to be a wild one.

ASSET ALLOCATIONS	
STOCKS	70%
BONDS	25%
CASH	5%

For the Week of October 6, 1997

There is no change in my asset allocation this week. It will be a very quiet week from the economic front as well as the pre-earnings disappointment front as most pre-announcements are now behind us. I expect this to be the beginning of a strong earnings season that will fuel the stock market to new record levels. When the biggest risk to the market is El Niño, count your blessings and grab an umbrella.

ASSET ALLOCATIONS	
STOCKS	70%
BONDS	25%
CASH	5%

For the Week of October 13, 1997

I am changing my asset allocation this week for the first time this year by increasing stocks to 75% from 70% and decreasing bonds to 20% from 25%; cash remains at 5%. A stronger than expected earnings season this quarter combined with next quarter's annual first quarter ritual of the baby boomers fully funding their 401(k)s, IRAs and other retirement vehicles as they receive the bulk of their annual compensation in first quarter bonus and commission checks, should combine to drive the market on its way to 10,000 by December 31. (That's December 31, 1998, not 1997; even I'm not that bullish.) The single greatest risk the markets face this week is the newest Washington scandal I've dubbed "Speakers-gate." With six different Federal Reserve Board officials speaking on four different days all across the United States, someone, somewhere, sometime is going to throw the markets a major curve this week; we just don't have **CLUE** who, when or where (my daughter's favorite guess is Mr. Green, in the kitchen with a lead pipe).

ASSET ALLOCATIONS	
STOCKS	75%
BONDS	20%
CASH	5%

For the Week of October 20, 1997

There is no change to my asset allocation this week. It will be an extremely light week from the economic front as the story in the market this week is likely to be the 2 Ps . . . Profits and Politics. Profits and earnings will determine the direction of the markets, not just for this week but for the remainder of the year. I expect profits and the market to go up. The second P, Politics, will be focusing on trade wars with Japan and illegal political contributions from foreign contributors. I expect these political influences to have the same impact on our markets as Alan Greenspan's "irrational exuberance" speech, it may slow the markets down but it won't stop them. I'll take Profits over Politics any day of the week.

ASSET ALLOCATIONS	
STOCKS	75%
BONDS	20%
CASH	5%

For the Week of October 27, 1997

This very well might be the "scariest" week of the entire year for the markets; it's only fitting that it falls on Halloween week. Just when you thought it was safe to get back into the markets, you realize that this week the markets will be spooked from every front. There are several economic releases that could scare the markets and who knows what gloom Alan Greenspan will deliver in his testimony to Congress. Also, the continued concern with the Asian currency and economic meltdown is far from over. It's a week like this that investors have to remember to have a long-term investment perspective.

ASSET ALLOCATIONS	
STOCKS	75%
BONDS	20%
CASH	5%

For the Week of November 3, 1997

I expect the markets to remain volatile with more movement to the upside than downside (remember, volatility moves both ways). This week will mark a very hectic economic schedule; however, this schedule will have to take a back seat to international events. All financial markets have been connected globally by the recent crisis in Southeast Asia. It doesn't matter whether the fiber that holds the markets together is economic, earnings or psychological; the fact is, all markets are interconnected in some way and no market, not even the United States, can isolate itself from other markets. The biggest event of the week is the fact that October is finally behind us and we lived to see another November. When we close the week on Friday, there will only be 47 shopping days till Christmas and 354 days till the one-year Anniversary of Gray Monday.

ASSET ALLOCATIONS	
STOCKS	75%
BONDS	20%
CASH	5%

For the Week of November 10, 1997

This slow week should be a welcome relief to the markets. With Veterans Day on Tuesday, many offices will be very thin that day and a light economic and earnings' calendar simply add to the calm. Come to think of it, most traders don't even care about the Federal Open Markets Committee meeting on Wednesday as the consensus feels the Southeast Asian crisis has removed any chance of a U.S. rate hike anytime soon (this time the consensus is right). When the market's attention slips to a check from 1982 made out to President Clinton that was found in an abandoned car, you know we are in for a slow week. It certainly puts new meaning to the phrase "the check's in the mail."

ASSET ALLOCATIONS	
STOCKS	75%
BONDS	20%
CASH	5%

For the Week of November 17, 1997

This week the markets will be driven by politics, not earnings or economic releases. The source of this political volatility is both here and abroad. Internationally, the "soap opera" in Iraq will continue to keep the markets on edge. Meanwhile, the financial summit in Manila regarding the Southeast Asian currency crisis could turn out to be the most important event of the entire year. Back here at home, the combination of the recent defeat of President Clinton's Fast Track Trade authority along with the rising trade deficit number on Thursday just might bring out all of the Ross Perot political "wannabes" talking down the benefits of free trade.

ASSET ALLOCATIONS	
STOCKS	75%
BONDS	20%
CASH	5%

For the Week of November 24, 1997

On this Thanksgiving week, investors who stayed in the market have a lot to be thankful for. Back in 1987 it took 463 days for the stock market to recoup its losses from "Black Monday." This year it took us exactly 26 days to recoup all of the losses from Gray Monday. It's the investors who got out of the market, not the ones who stayed in it, that lost money. The combination of a heavy economic calendar and light staffing on most trading desks due to the holiday week could result in a more volatile market than the releases would dictate due to the "B Team" over-reacting to any issue that comes across the screen. Happy Thanksgiving!

ASSET ALLOCATIONS	
STOCKS	75%
BONDS	20%
CASH	5%

For the Week of December 8, 1997

This week has all the "makings" for a very quiet one, maybe that's why I'm so nervous. It's an extremely light economic calendar; however, an economic "bombshell" is not out of the question. The stock market should continue its search for leadership while the bond market continues its strong rally. Attorney General Reno's Independent Counsel decision could have global ramifications this week and the New York Stock Exchange's decision to leave the market triggers at 350 and 550 points instead of moving them to a percentage basis will go down in history as the dumbest decision the NYSE has ever made. Look out Wall Street, you are about to hear the wrath of Main Street.

ASSET ALLOCATIONS	
STOCKS	75%
BONDS	20%
CASH	5%

For the Week of December 15, 1997

This week will be a very volatile one for the financial markets. There are numerous economic releases that have the potential to move the markets. Meanwhile, I expect the parade of pre-earnings' disappointment releases to continue as we struggle to digest the impact of the Asian crisis. Meanwhile, international events in South Korea and Japan will continue to dominate our domestic market. Oh, and I almost forgot; the Federal Open Markets Committee meets on Tuesday to decide what to do with interest rates. Who cares? The events in Asia virtually guarantee no rate hike.

ASSET ALLOCATIONS	
STOCKS	75%
BONDS	20%
CASH	5%

For the Week of December 22, 1997

It will be a slow week for the markets in this holiday shortened week. Few economic releases and even fewer "traders" actually working to react to these releases should combine to make this a rather quiet time for investors. Any shock to our markets will most likely come from some global event or an Alan Greenspan "holiday toast."

ASSET ALLOCATIONS	
STOCKS	75%
BONDS	20%
CASH	5%

2 ECONOMIC PERSPECTIVE

OVERVIEW

The real story in our surprising economy can be found in four different components: employment, manufacturing, capital spending and the consumer. It was these four components that combined to catch economists off guard and deliver another very strong year of economic growth. Let's briefly look at the driving forces behind each of these components starting with employment. The employment or labor markets remained very tight the entire year with the unemployment rate breaking and then staying below the benchmark 5.0% level. Everyone was watching to see if the combination of a tight labor market and the carry over of the UPS strike will lead to higher wages. First, regarding the UPS strike—It did not shift the balance of power back to unions. Union membership has been on a steady decline for the last 15 years and currently represents less than 15% of the total work force. In addition, the UPS strike was very unique. There are very, very few, if any companies that enjoy as dominant a role over their industry as UPS does over the Parcel Post Delivery Industry. Second, regarding tight labor markets. Even though labor markets are very, very tight, employees understand that in this very competitive global business environment you not only have to worry if you have a job, you have to worry if your employer will stay in business. That's why there were little, if any, signs of wage inflation. Let's move on to the second component, manufacturing. We had a vibrant manufacturing sector. Lead by automobile production and the continued push for productivity and technical improvements; the manufacturing sector was a real driver all year. Business continued to look to improve and enhance their manufacturing operations. We find ourselves in an almost perfect competitive marketplace. Three things make up a perfectly competitive marketplace. First, there are no barriers to entry; any new firm can enter an industry at any time. Second, there is no protection from failure. Failing businesses can't rely on government subsidies or intervention to bail them out. Third, no firm in any industry can set the price. Think about this for a minute. Firms can't increase profits by raising prices. They can increase profits only by cutting costs, boosting productivity and through innovation. Manufacturing enhancements became the order of the day which bodes well for the manufacturing sector.

Third, capital spending remained very strong all throughout 1997. One of the reasons that the economy was supposed to slow down is that most economists were calling for a major drop-off in capital spending in 1997. Most economists were wrong, and here is why. There was a major capital spending boom in 1995; in fact, this was one of the keys that fueled the strong bull market in 1995. Well, according to economic theory, when you have a major spike up in capital spending like we did in 1995, you typically do not see another major spike for four or five years. The theory is based on the principle that once a business makes a major capital expenditure on something like a new computer system or an enhanced manufacturing process, it can reap the benefits of this new expenditure for at least four to five years. This out-dated economic theory has been passed by because of the technology revolution. The life cycle of how long you can now reap the benefits of your major capital expenditure is no longer five years but it's ½ of that. You see, our technology revolution is moving so fast that by the time you order a major capital expenditure, have it delivered, installed and have your employees trained on how to operate it, it is almost obsolete because another piece of equipment is about to come off of the assembly line that does it better, faster, longer, with more flexibility and—guess what—it's cheaper. When you find yourself competing in a global marketplace, you have to have every competitive edge you can find. You cannot compete globally with equipment that is being made obsolete by the technology revolution. The new life cycle for capital spending is two years, not five, and that is why we had strong capital spending in 1997.

Finally, the consumer remained king throughout all of 1997 and was the real driver of our economy. Every single year for the past five years someone makes the forecast that this is the year that the high-debt burdened consumer will finally stop spending. Let me tell you something, the consumer's debt burden is not as bad as everyone makes it out to be and that is why the consumer did not stop spending. It seems like every month a new statistic comes out to show how bad off and how much in debt the consumer really is. Credit card delin-quencies are at the highest level since 1974; credit card debt as a percentage of disposal income is at the highest level in ten years; credit card debt as a percentage of an individual's net worth is also at an all-time high. Thus, it is easy to see why most people feel that this credit card debt crisis could stop the consumer. It can't; and the reason it can't is because we don't have a credit card debt crisis. Let me give you the one credit card debt number that no one talks about. In 1996 almost 40% of all credit card holders paid their credit card debt down to a balance of zero every month. Think about this for a minute: if 40% of all credit card holders are paying their credit card debt each month to a balance of zero, how can that be a crisis. The answer is—it's not. The crisis is that economists need to come down out of their ivory towers and realize people don't use credit cards to go into debt; they use them for the points. Depending on the type of card that you have, you can get points for frequent flier miles, points toward the purchase of a new car, points toward free long distance calls, etc., etc. In addition, if any of these Wall Street economists would ever go into a store to return some merchandise, they would quickly realize why everyone uses a credit card. If you find yourself returning something to a store that you bought with cash, you are about to begin the great negotiating return process that probably will end up with you receiving a store credit, not cash. Not so when you return something that you purchased with a credit card. You simply walk into the store, say "I am not paying for this, I don't want it" and if by chance the store clerk is dumb enough to cause you a problem, all you have to do is call Master Card or Visa or whatever, and they will credit your account and fight with the store clerk on your behalf. Credit cards aren't about going into debt—they are about shifting the balance of power away from store clerks to the consumer. It will not stop.

Because the consumer makes up ⅔ of the Gross Domestic Product of our economy, there is not a more important component. There were three reasons why the consumer did not slow down in 1997.

First, unemployment continued to hover in the low 5% and below. We are at full employment. Every single person in the United States who wants a job can get a job. It may not be the job that they want and they may not get paid exactly what they want; but they can get a job. Think about it, everyone that has a job has more money, everyone that wants a job can get a job, both of these are very positive for the consumer.

Second, consumer confidence is at the highest level it's been in the last decade. It's no surprise when you consider the low unemployment and low inflation rate environment that we have had—consumers are confident. Guess what, when consumers are confident they spend money.

Third, consumers are happy. That smile that you see on their face is because of the stock market. You see, since late 1994, the stock market has created trillions of dollars worth of household wealth in this country. When investors get their monthly or quarterly investment statements, it shows them that the stock market is making them rich;

that makes them smile. Remember, happy consumers spend money, which is exactly what they did in 1997.

All right now, sit back and enjoy the ride as I recap with you how the issues and events that drive my economic outlook evolved on a week by week basis from Tax Day (April 15th) through the end of 1997.

For the Week of April 14, 1997

This will be a rather light week for economic releases as only five major economic releases are scheduled to hit the street this week. In addition to being a light week, it will also be a very consolidated one as all five releases occur on just two days, Tuesday and Wednesday. Because the markets and the Federal Reserve Board continue their "witch hunt" for inflation, the most important release will be the Consumer Price Index which will be released on Tuesday. *The Consumer Price Index could surprise on the high side* as some temporary inflation pressures show up in the index this month. Even though I firmly believe that global competition will keep inflation under control in the long run, in the short run, there will be some months where inflation appears to be a problem; unfortunately, I think this could be one of those months. A move upward in the Consumer Price Index will be driven by a slight increase in food prices and airfare prices (with some of the airfare price increase due to the re-establishment of the 10% surcharge tax), and continued steady upward pressure from residential rents. The magnitude of the rise of the overall index will most likely be driven by two components that are actually falling, not rising. Energy prices and electronic supply and equipment prices must continue to post strong declines or this month's number could really catch the markets off guard with a big surprise. . . . *Look for Housing Starts to also surprise on the high side.* Housing starts remained strong all last year due to low unemployment and solid wage growth. When people who didn't have jobs get jobs, and when people who have jobs see their wages increase, the housing market ultimately benefits. In addition, there is another technical factor that will continue to support strong housing starts. That technical factor is that the inventory of unsold new homes has remained below historical averages. When this occurs, we almost always see strong housing starts to replace the weak inventory. Finally, the recent rise in interest rates will not have any immediate impact on the housing market. This should not be all that surprising when you consider all of the innovative, flexible financing tools available to potential new homeowners that can make a new home purchase look advantageous no matter where interest rates are or where they have been.

ECONOMIC RELEASES				
Economic Indicator	Period	Release Date	Previous Actual	Consensus
Consumer Price Index	March	4/15 - T	+0.3%	+0.3%
Business Inventories	Feb.	4/15 - T	+0.1%	+1.0%
Housing Starts	March	4/16 - W	+12.2%	+5.0%
Industrial Production	March	4/16 - W	+0.5%	+0.3%
Capacity Utilization	March	4/16 - W	83.3%	83.2%

For the Week of April 21, 1997

This will be one of the slowest weeks of the entire year for economic releases as only two major releases are scheduled for distribution this week. It is also a book-ends week for major economic releases, one at the beginning of the week, one at the end of the week and no major economic releases in between. The week's first release is on Monday when the Treasury Department releases its March budget statement. ***The March Budget report will show progress continues on the budget deficit.*** I expect the March report to mirror the consensus of Wall Street economists, which would be a decline of between $25B to $35B. This comes on the heels of last month's $44B budget decline. The spending patterns of the Federal Government have clearly changed; and programmatic policy shifts over the last few years on Welfare, Medicare, Medicaid and even Social Security continue to add up and help to present a positive, short-term budget deficit picture. Also, most of the "political timing" expenditures have already worked their way through the previous budget reports. You see, the Clinton Administration put a great deal of political pressure on all government departments to hold back on spending until after the election in order to report the lowest possible deficit just prior to the election (which they did). Thus the first part of the new fiscal year showed an expenditure "pop" as a result of Political Accounting 101. Those games are behind us (for now). . . . ***Existing Home Sales could throw the markets a curve.*** While the consensus on Wall Street is looking for a major decline, I think the markets could really be caught off guard with another strong Existing Home Sale number, driven in part by a measurement glitch. When you buy a home, whether it is a new home or existing home, you follow the same process. First you sign a contract, then several weeks or even months later you "close" on the purchase. New Home Sales are counted when the contract is signed, while Existing Home Sales are not counted until contract closing. Thus, Existing Home Sales tend to lag New Home Sales due to this measurement "glitch." The continued strength the past few months in New Home Sales could mean that Existing Home Sales are stronger than we think. . . . Both the Mitsubishi Bank/Schroder Wertheim report and the Johnson Redbook report, tracking weekly retail sales, will take on greater significance this week due to the light calendar of major releases. ***Look for both Weekly Retail reports to show solid retail consumption levels.*** With average hourly earnings rising and unemployment falling, consumers have money to spend and their first stop is usually at the retail level.

ECONOMIC RELEASES				
Economic Indicator	Period	Release Date	Previous Actual	Consensus
Budget Report	March	4/21 - M	$-44.0B	$-31.2B
Existing Home Sales	March	4/25 - F	+9.0%	-1.9%

For the Week of April 28, 1997

Run for cover as this will be one of the busiest and most important weeks of the entire year for economic releases. If there are any economic triggers that will influence the Federal Reserve Board's policy direction at its May 20th meeting they will most likely be unveiled this week. ***The scope and breath of these releases almost assures that we will receive mixed signals regarding the economy*** as some of the economic releases report on economic activity for April, others report on economic activity for March and some will even report on economic activity for the entire first quarter. Even though there are thirteen major economic releases, the markets are clearly focused on the employment reports: The Employment Cost Index, the Unemployment Rate and the Change in Non-farm Payrolls. . . . *I expect the Employment Cost Index to surprise on the high side.* Three issues are converging to drive this Employment Cost Index higher. First, there has been clear evidence in recent weeks of some wage creep occurring across various industries. Even in a global competitive economy, it's tough to keep a lid on wages when the CEOs continue to pull down multi-million dollar pay packages laced with stock options and other incentive plans. Second, there has been a shift to enhance the jobs that many workers perform; thus, many workers are getting more money because they have better jobs with expanded responsibility and authority. Even though these enhanced jobs have sometimes resulted in combining two or three positions into one—which is actually disinflationary in the long run—in the short run, it will show that employees wages are now higher. The third and most significant cost pressure will come from the benefits component of the index. Remember the Employment Cost Index is the only economic measurement we have that gauges true employment costs (wages plus benefits). After two full years of health care and insurance costs trending down, we now find ourselves in a period of moderate increases in health care costs. These increases will appear extreme because they will be compared to the recent declining trends. Don't underestimate the importance of this economic release. Alan Greenspan has made it known that he views the Employment Cost Index as one of the economy's most important releases. And what is important to Alan Greenspan will also be important to the markets . . . . I also *look for the Change In Non-farm Payrolls report to surprise on the high side*. For the past several weeks we have been receiving clues from all aspects of the economy that it is simply not ready to slow down yet. A healthy economy usually means healthy job growth.

ECONOMIC RELEASES				
Economic Indicator	Period	Release Date	Previous Actual	Consensus
New Home Sales	March	4/28 - M	-0.7%	-0.7%
Durable Goods Orders	March	4/29 - T	+1.5%	+0.1%

continued

27

ECONOMIC RELEASES				
Economic Indicator	Period	Release Date	Previous Actual	Consensus
Employment Cost Index	1st Quarter	4/29 - T	+0.8%	+0.9%
Consumer Confidence	April	4/29 - T	118.5	118.1
Gross Domestic Product	1st Quarter	4/30 - W	+3.8%	+4.0%
Chgo. Purch. Mgrs. Index	April	4/30 - W	57.5%	57.0%
Personal Income	April	5/1 - Th	+0.9%	+0.4%
Personal Spending	March	5/1 - Th	+0.3%	+0.5%
Nat'l Assoc. of Purch. Mgrs. Index	April	5/1 - Th	55.0	55.0
Construction Spending	March	5/1 - Th	+2.3%	0.0%
Unemployment Rate	April	5/2 - F	+5.2%	5.2%
Change in Non-farm Payrolls	April	5/2 - F	175,000	180,000
Leading Economic Indicators	March	5/2 - F	+0.5%	+0.6%

For the Week of May 5, 1997

After last week, it will actually seem like a vacation from economic releases, as only four are scheduled and none after Wednesday. I expect these releases to show a consistent economic theme of strong growth. Remember all of the releases this week are for the exact same reporting period, March. Unlike last week, when the releases covered three different reporting periods (March, April, 1st quarter). With so much anecdotal evidence already in regarding how strong the economy really was in the first quarter, the risk with these March numbers is clearly on the high side. . . . *The Housing Completion's release should show that the housing market is not ready to slow down just yet.* I expect this number to surprise on the high side. The fact of the matter is even with the recent twenty-five basis point interest rate hike imposed by the Federal Reserve Board, mortgage borrowing costs are not much higher than they were at the start of the year. In addition, the economy continues to add jobs and wages continue to improve. This powerful one-two combination of job growth and wage growth have kept consumer confidence levels at or near all-time highs. When consumers are confident, they are not afraid to commit to a "big ticket" purchase. And the big ticket purchase most frequently committed to is housing. . . . *I look for the Consumer Credit number to continue to creep higher as well.* The recent, very strong earnings reports of the Automobile Industry for the first quarter have provided us with the first clue to March automotive demand. I think that the demand was very strong, which means that unit automotive sales should increase, which in turn, will show up as an increase in consumer credit. The cost of vehicles these days just doesn't lend itself to paying cash, so it's credit all the way for most automotive consumers. Add to that the expected strong showing of non-auto retail sales and it will become apparent that the consumer is not ready to slow down. A strong consumer usually equates into an increase in consumer credit.

ECONOMIC RELEASES				
Economic Indicator	Period	Release Date	Previous Actual	Consensus
Housing Completions	March	5/5 - M	+10.8%	+2.0%
Factory Orders	March	5/6 - T	+0.8%	-1.5%
Wholesale Inventories	March	5/7 - W	0.0%	+0.4%
Consumer Credit	March	5/7 - W	$6.7B	$6.8B

For the Week of May 12, 1997

There will be a heavy calendar of economic releases this week, which is the last "full" week of releases prior to the Federal Open

Markets Committee meeting on May 20th. In times of uncertainty regarding what the FOMC may or may not do, the economic releases leading up to that meeting take on even greater importance as the market interprets each number as the one that will finally influence the Fed's next move. This week should be no exception. Any surprise in these economic releases could create dramatic moves in the markets. . . . *I don't look for any surprises from the Price Indexes this week.* Inflation watchers will have plenty to worry about this week as both the Producer Price Index and Consumer Price Index will both be released this week. The overall market consensus is for these numbers to remain flat, and I think the markets are probably right. While there has been some indication of inflation pressure from the energy component, most other components continue to be in a downward mode. Apparel prices are not spiking up as feared. Retailers know that their buyers are very cost sensitive and in order to stimulate demand, they must keep prices in check. Also, we continue to have mini "Air Wars" so I expect a slight pullback in that component as well. The real key may be coming from the technology sector where computer prices for both hardware and software are once again renewing a downward trend as the competition in this industry remains intense. Overall, we should receive an excellent inflation report card from both of the Price Indexes. . . . Retail Sales may hold the biggest surprise of the week as unique and conflicting circumstances could drive this number to either extreme. To begin, I think the market consensus of "flat" Retail Sales (+0.3% up slightly from last month's +0.2%) is wrong. One can make a compelling case why this number will be very weak. First of all, the early Easter this year pushed that holiday from April into March. Thus, retail sales for April will not show any of the traditional surge from Easter shoppers. In addition, the severe flooding and weather problems across the United States will also have a short-term, negative impact. On the flip side, there are two strong indicators that bode well for a rebound in Retail Sales. First of all with the unemployment rate at only 4.9%, we are truly at "full employment." When people are newly employed, their first stop with their first paycheck is usually at the retail level. Second, over the past year and a half, the housing market has been on a tear. Don't forget that when consumers are buying and building homes, it is usually only the first step in a very predictable buying pattern. The next stop is appliances and home furniture. When people have a new home, they want to fill it up with new "stuff." Thus, the recent strength of the housing market will also have a very positive impact on Retail Sales. *I look for weaker Retail Sales to rule the day.* The combination of no one buying any Easter bonnets in April and everyone paying their tax bill on April 15 probably delivered a deadly one-two punch to retail sales.

ECONOMIC RELEASES				
Economic Indicator	Period	Release Date	Previous Actual	Consensus
Retail Sales	April	5/13 - T	+0.2%	+0.3%
Producer Price Index	April	5/14 - W	-0.1%	0.0%
Business Inventories	March	5/14 - W	+0.3%	+0.1%
Consumer Price Index	April	5/15 - Th	+0.1%	+0.1%
Industrial Production	April	5/15 - Th	+0.9%	+0.2%
Capacity Utilization	April	5/15 - Th	84.1%	84.0%
Housing Starts	April	5/16- F	-6.3%	+0.4%

For the Week of May 19, 1997

It will be an extremely light economic calendar this week which means that there is very little to take the attention off of the Federal Open Markets Committee (FOMC) meeting. *I think that the FOMC will raise interest rates by 50 basis points this week.* Here's why. First of all, as the markets continue to try to figure out what Alan Greenspan was implying in his speech two weeks ago, let me add some insight. He was telling the markets that he is going to raise rates. You don't have to prepare the markets for good news, you prepare markets for bad news. Greenspan revealed that he didn't see any inflation in the economic numbers leading up to the March interest rate hike, yet he raised rates anyway. Thus the fact that the inflation numbers were tame last week is irrelevant. The only number that Greenspan sees is 55 (and it's not the 55¢ price tag for a big Big Mac that many economists point to as proof that there is not inflation). The first 5 is for the economy which broke through the 5% level in the first quarter with 5.6% Gross Domestic Product (GDP). This level is more than double the Fed's target of 2.0 to 2.5% GDP. The second 5 is for unemployment which broke through the

5% level down to 4.9% (the lowest rate since December 1973). This level puts us at or near full employment which will create tight labor markets. And in addition to my 55 theory, remember that the stock market's recent rise will re-instill consumer confidence. The Fed's concern is that a confident consumer may go on a spending spree and drive this economy even higher down the road. Don't forget that the consumer makes up over ⅔ of GDP, as the consumer goes so goes the economy. . . . In case you are interested, *I expect the Merchandise Trade number to come in below expectations.* This improving trade balance picture is being driven primarily by the lower prices that we are paying for importing oil. . . . *I expect the Budget Statement to surprise on the high side with a record surplus.* Washington appears to be falling all over itself finding new money here and there to balance the budget. Remember, this budget statement release is for April; thus, it will catch the last and biggest wave of tax receipts. The all-time record for a monthly budget surplus is $72B which was registered at tax time last year in the April 1996 statement. Records were made to be broken and this one surely will. . . . *The hidden gem of the week could be uncovered on Thursday. That is the day that the FOMC releases its detailed minutes from the March 25th FOMC meeting* when interest rates were increased. These minutes may hold the secret to what will happen at the next FOMC meeting which is July 2nd. . . . One final thought, if Alan Greenspan does raise interest rates, look for someone in Congress to propose abolishing the FOMC and replacing it with IBM's Deep Blue super-computer. If it can beat the world's greatest chess player in Garry Kasparov, maybe it can do a better job at setting interest rates than the world's greatest financial figure, Alan Greenspan. I wonder if it's possible to wipe "irrational exuberance" from a computer's memory?

ECONOMIC RELEASES				
Economic Indicator	Period	Release Date	Previous Actual	Consensus
Merchandise Trade	March	5/21 - W	-$10.4B	-$10.6B
Budget Statement	April	5/21 - W	-$21.3B	+$92.6B

For the Week of May 26, 1997

The only thing that was resolved at last week's Federal Open Markets Committee (FOMC) meeting was the fact that the FOMC has truly become politicized regarding the reality of economic growth and balanced budgets. The Balanced Budget Plan could make preemptive strikes (without any signs of inflation), a thing of the past. The only thing that has changed is that instead of the markets fearing May 20th (the last FOMC meeting), the markets are fearful of July 1st and 2nd (the next FOMC meeting). ***I would not rule out the possibility of Alan Greenspan moving rates between FOMC meetings in order to avoid all of the media and new-found political focus on his agenda.*** . . . The week will be shortened by the Memorial Day holiday on Monday; however, there will not be a shortage of economic releases. There will be five major economic releases and so compared to last week's very, very light calendar, this shortened week may feel like economic release overload. . . . ***Both housing releases: Existing Home Sales and New Home Sales should remain flat.*** If there are any surprises to these numbers, it will be on lower side. Weakness in these numbers has more to do with the weatherman that it does the economy. Both of these housing releases are for the April reporting period. And the April reporting period was dominated by severe weather conditions all across the United States. In addition, the strongest regional housing market in the United States, namely the Mid-West, was hit the hardest by the severe weather, which will further add to the potential weakness of the overall housing numbers. Don't let one month's worth of numbers lull you to sleep on the strength of the overall housing market. With unemployment levels at record lows, solid wage growth and no inflation, consumers remain confident; and confident consumers will ultimately fuel the housing market . . . . Speaking of consumer confidence, ***one of the big surprises of the week will be the Consumer Confidence Index will catch the markets off guard and surprise on the high side.*** I don't know what else consumers could ask for to make them more confident. With employment levels where they are, any consumer who wants a job can get a job. The Federal Government is on the threshold of balancing the budget by the year 2002. The stock market has regained all of its losses from the March 11 to April 11 mini-correction, IBM, the bellwether of the stock market has finally completed its ten-year climb back to the top, not to mention the fact that their computer "Deep Blue" crushed the World Chess Champion. Life is truly good and the Consumer Confidence Index numbers are about to show that. . . . ***This holiday week will end with a bang as first quarter Gross Domestic***

Product (GDP) will be adjusted to 6%. With the FOMC targeting economic growth at 2% to 2¹/₂%, crossing the 6% threshold could turn the markets upside down. Two components will drive this adjustment upward from the initial 5.6% level that was previously reported. First, the final sales component of GDP should remain solid as the recent retail sales numbers point to continued strength in the retail consumer sector. Secondly, last week's March trade deficit number (which surprised on the low side) has become a great leading indicator as to where the adjustment to GDP is heading. When the trade deficit goes up, the first adjustment to GDP is heading down. When the trade deficit goes down (like our most recent release) look for the GDP adjustment to go up, this time from 5.6% to 6.0%.

ECONOMIC RELEASES				
Economic Indicator	Period	Release Date	Previous Actual	Consensus
Existing Home Sales	April	5/27 - T	-2.8%	-1.0%
Consumer Confidence	May	5/27 - T	116.8	117
Durable Goods	April	5/28 - W	-3.0%	1.4%
Gross Domestic Product	1st Quarter (Adjusted)	5/30 - F	5.6%	5.8%
New Home Sales	April	5/30 - F	-2.5%	-2.1%

For the Week of June 2, 1997

It will be a book-ends kind of week for economic releases, as there are eleven major releases scheduled for this week, with four of the eleven falling on Monday and another four falling on Friday. . . . I look for the week to begin by receiving mixed signals on the economy with *Construction Spending coming in lower than expectations, while the National Association of Purchasing Managers (NAPM) Index will surprise on the high side.* It is very important, however, not to read too much into either of these economic surprises because they are both driven by unique circumstances. *Construction Spending will appear much weaker than it actually is because the reporting period is April, and April experienced very severe weather conditions all across the United States.* No region of the country was spared from this weather slow-down, while some regions of the country, due to the floods, almost stopped completely. On the other end of the spectrum, I look for *NAPM's surprise on the high side to be driven by one factor, and that is the striking Chrysler workers showing up at the assembly line again.* With employment staying strong, this Chrysler rebound could actually push NAPM above 55 which would certainly catch the markets off guard. . . . The most important release of the week will be Friday's Employment Releases, specifically the Non-farm Payrolls number. Be prepared, this number could hold the biggest surprise of the week and could actually approach 300,000. *Three factors could converge to cause the Non-farm Payrolls number to spike over 300,000.* First, the Non-farm Payroll numbers in the manufacturing sector were deeply depressed the last two months because of several strikes. The majority of those strikes were resolved and as a result there will be a big jump in the manufacturing sector. Second, the floods of April are behind us now and construction jobs which were negatively impacted by the flood will also show a nice upswing. The third and probably the most dramatic force, (and the one the market's are missing) is the unanticipated spike in flood damage clean-up, again in the construction area. These are not casual room additions to someone's house, we are talking about the immediate need to make someone's flooded home "livable" now. I think that the markets have underestimated the severity of the floods and will also underestimate the employment surge that will happen short-term in order to quickly clean up after the flood. The on again, off again, on again interest rate hike fear will clearly be "on again" if the employment number comes anywhere near 300,000.

ECONOMIC RELEASES				
Economic Indicator	Period	Release Date	Previous Actual	Consensus
Personal Income	April	6/2 - M	+0.6%	+0.1%
Personal Spending	April	6/2 - M	+0.5%	-0.1%
Nat'l Assoc. of Purch. Mgrs. Index	May	6/2 - M	54.2	54.6

continued

35

ECONOMIC RELEASES				
Economic Indicator	Period	Release Date	Previous Actual	Consensus
Construction Spending	April	6/2 - M	-0.2%	+0.2%
Leading Economic Indicators	April	6/3 - T	+0.1%	-0.1%
Factory Orders	April	6/4 - W	-1.6%	-0.8%
Housing Completions	April	6/5 - Th	-10.4%	-5.0%
Change in Non-farm Payrolls	May	6/6 - F	142,000	238,000
Unemployment Rate	May	6/6 - F	4.9%	5.0%
Wholesale Inventories	April	6/6 - F	+0.7%	+0.4%
Consumer Credit	April	6/6 - F	$2.0B	$4.1B

For the Week of June 9, 1997

After last week's very hectic schedule of economic releases (eleven in all) this week we get a reprieve with only three major economic releases scheduled to hit the market. From an economic perspective, you can even come in late this week as we won't see our first release until Thursday. . . . *I expect Retail Sales to surprise the markets on the high side* by beating expectations. It's the culmination of five independent factors, none of which individually would have the market influence to impact Retail Sales; however, their combined impact could truly through the markets a curve. First is the "Easter Bounce." The reason Retail Sales were so poor last month (April's release) was because our early Easter pulled traditional April Easter Retail Sales into March. We typically see the consumer take a breather after the Easter shopping season and then come back even stronger the following month. This Easter bounce will show up in this month's Retail Sales release. Second, I expect a rebound in Vehicle Sales. The labor strikes have been resolved and there are very few inventory bottlenecks to dampen retail supply for vehicles. Third, the cooler weather across the country has actually helped Retail Sales, not hurt it. While there was some initial concern that the cooler weather would negatively impact seasonal sales, that is simply not the case. The cooler weather kept consumers from working in the yard and playing outside and instead, sent them to the mall. While at the mall, the consumer actually tried to jump start the summer season by buying seasonal merchandise despite the cooler weather. Fourth, consumer confidence readings continue to remain very high. Remember, consumer confidence shows up first in retail sales. Fifth and finally, don't forget about the impact the floods will have on retail sales. I look for the terrible floods to provide a spike in the home repair and improvement component as victims continue to scramble to get their homes back to where they were before the floods. . . . *I don't expect any surprise from the Producer Price Index, there simply is no inflation.* Computer and electronic equipment prices continue to come down. Meanwhile, energy prices will also continue their steady march downward, although at a slower pace than recent months. There may be a slight increase in the food component; however, this pressure is clearly not enough to move the Index. . . . *Because it is such a light week, some of the second tier releases could generate some market attention.* On Tuesday, we have both the Mitsubishi Schroder weekly Retail Sales report and the Redbook Research Retail Sales Index. Then on Thursday, the Federal Reserve Bank of Atlanta releases its monthly national production index for May.

ECONOMIC RELEASES				
Economic Indicator	Period	Release Date	Previous Actual	Consensus
Retail Sales	May	6/12 - Th	-0.3%	+0.4%
Producer Price Index	May	6/13 - F	-0.6%	0.0%
Business Inventories	April	6/13 - F	+0.3%	+0.2%

For the Week of June 30, 1997

This will be a very busy, hectic and short week (due to the July 4th holiday on Friday) for economic releases. Each of the eleven major economic releases will contribute to the added volatility in markets as very nervous investors attempt to figure out just what the Federal Reserve Board is going to do at the beginning of the week and then at the end of the week trying to figure out if that was the right thing. I do not believe that any of the four major releases due out on Monday, the last day before the Federal Reserve Board's meeting, could provide enough of a surprise to actually influence the Federal Reserve Board's decision; however, they could provide a scare to the markets as traders frantically search for that last piece of evidence and final clue regarding the Federal Open Markets Committee meeting. . . . ***Both the Personal Income and Personal Spending releases should provide strong evidence that the consumer is alive and well.*** These releases are key indicators regarding what is ultimately going to happen to economic growth going forward. Our strong economy has been driven by consumers which actually accounted for ⅔ of Gross Domestic Product. In many respects, the future of consumption is mirrored in these two numbers. Does the consumer have money to spend? (Personal Income) and is the consumer spending the money that they have? (Personal Spending) On Monday I expect the answer to both of these questions to be a resounding YES. . . . In many respects all of the economic releases this week are nothing more than a preview for the markets, killing time until the all important employment reports are released on Thursday. ***I expect the Unemployment Rate to catch the markets off guard by continuing its record fall to 4.7%.*** The labor market continues to display solid strength as it has no problem in continuing to put anyone to work who wants to work. With the economy running on all cylinders, the Unemployment Rate has nowhere to go but down.

ECONOMIC RELEASES				
Economic Indicator	Period	Release Date	Previous Actual	Consensus
Personal Income	May	6/30 - M	+0.1%	+0.4%
Personal Spending	May	6/30 - M	+0.1%	+0.3%
New Home Sales	May	6/30 - M	+0.5%	-7.6%
Chicago Purchasing Mgrs. Index	June	6/30 - M	56.8	57.0

continued

ECONOMIC RELEASES				
Economic Indicator	Period	Release Date	Previous Actual	Consensus
Nat'l Assn. of Purch. Mgrs. Index	June	7/1 - T	57.1	56.1
Leading Indicators	May	7/1 - T	-0.1%	+0.2%
Construction Spending	May	7/1 - T	-0.1%	+0.6%
Factory Orders	May	7/2 - W	+1.2%	+0.6%
Unemployment Rate	June	7/3 - Th	4.8%	4.8%
Change in Non-farm Payrolls	June	7/3 - Th	-0.1%	-0.1%
Housing Completion's	May	7/3 - Th	-0.1%	-0.1%

For the Week of July 7, 1997

It will be a very light week from the economic front as there are only three major economic indicators to be released this week and with the exception of the Producer Price Index, none are closely followed by traders as the bellwether indicators that predict where the economy is headed. . . . *The first release of the week will be Consumer Credit which will weaken this month.* One of the reasons that the Consumer Credit number holds little weight with traders is that at times the number seems to be out of touch with economic reality. Take last month's April Consumer Credit number for example. In April we witnessed a weakening in Retail Consumption. When Retail Consumption weakens, Consumer Credit should follow suit. However, last month, despite weakening Retail Consumption, Consumer Credit actually rose to $7.6 billion which is above trend growth. Much of the weakening this month will be fueled by weaker auto sales. . . . *I look for the Producer Price Index to possibly surprise on the high side, or at the very least meet the consensus forecast.* The consensus forecast of +0.1% may not seem like much to worry about; however, some traders may take this number as a watershed event. You see for the last five months (January 1997 to May 1997) the Producer Price Index declined. Those monthly declines ranged from as little as -0.1% to as large at -0.6%. All of that will change as this month will post the first increase of the year for the Producer Price Index. This turnaround in prices is being driven by two factors. First, energy prices have stopped their dramatic free fall from the first of the year and not only have they stopped falling, but natural gas prices have actually risen. Second, the electronic equipment and computer components of the index have also stopped their steady declines. This one-two punch will push the Producer Price Index into positive territory for the first time this year. While +0.1% increase is certainly not an inflation scare. It may mark a turning point and the psychology of this number could impact our market in a far greater way than we would expect from only a +0.1% increase.

ECONOMIC RELEASES				
Economic Indicator	Period	Release Date	Previous Actual	Consensus
Consumer Credit	May	7/8 - T	7.6B	5.6B
Wholesale Inventories	May	7/9 - W	-0.7%	+0.4%
Producer Price Index	June	7/11 - F	-0.3%	+0.1%

For the Week of July 14, 1997

It will be a very hectic week from the economic front as seven major releases will hit the markets this week. . . . ***Even though there is no inflation to worry about, the Consumer Price Index will still surprise on the high side.*** This month's release on consumer inflation should not be read as a developing long term trend, but rather a unique month driven by some unique circumstances. First, energy prices moved upward for the first time in months this past June, and this development will serve to push the index higher. Second, the wet summer season to date is playing havoc with food prices, especially fruits, and that will also serve as a force to increase the index. Finally, the Airline Industry, in anticipation of getting hit with higher taxes during the Federal Government's balanced budget debate, has already begun pushing fares higher to collect more revenues. Even though I remain very confident in the long run that there is no inflation, in the short run, this number could throw the markets a curve. . . . *I look for Housing Starts to surprise on the high side for the last time this year.* While I believe housing will slow down the second half of the year, this week's release is for the last month in the first half of the year (June) and there is a chance that this number could really catch the markets off guard. The markets are expecting a very weak Housing Starts number because the June employment report that has already been released and digested by the markets, showed that the very wet weather that we had all across the United States had a negative impact on construction employment. Thus, the markets are concluding this will translate into a low Housing Starts number. I think the markets will be wrong because there is more going on with Housing Starts than just the weather. The below average inventory of new homes on the market as well as the strong gains posted the last two months in building permits (remember you have to get a permit before you start a house) should combine to overwhelm the weather factor and deliver the final Housing Starts surprise of the year.

ECONOMIC RELEASES				
Economic Indicator	Period	Release Date	Previous Actual	Consensus
Retail Sales	June	7/15 - T	-0.1%	+0.3%
Consumer Price Index	June	7/16 - W	+0.1%	+0.2%
Business Inventories	May	7/16 - W	+0.3%	+0.3%
Industrial Production	June	7/16 - W	+0.3%	+0.2%
Capacity Utilization	June	7/16 - W	83.7%	83.6%
Housing Starts	June	7/17 - Th	-4.8%	0%
Trading Balance	May	7/18- F	$-8.48B	$-8.5B

For the Week of July 21, 1997

It will be a very quiet week from the economic front as only three major economic indicators are released this week and two of the three are not released until Friday. . . . The first release of the week is the Treasury Budget report for June. *I expect no surprises from this month's Treasury Budget report that will show that our budget surplus continues to widen.* The quarterly estimated tax receipts from both individuals and corporations continue to sizzle higher due to our strong economy. Compared to last year, quarterly estimated tax revenue will be up over 10%, which will be the first double digit increase not due to a tax rate hike in the last decade. This puts us on track to end the fiscal year with an overall budget deficit at below $50 billion. The bond market will certainly cheer this news. . . . *I expect this week's Durable Goods Orders to be relatively flat which is pretty much in line with market expectations.* This number has been very volatile in recent months in so much as every good month was followed by a bad month and vice versa. This trend will not change. In April, Durable Goods were up +1.8% (good); in May, they plunged to -0.6% (bad); now in June, they will be back in positive territory. If there are any surprises in this number, it will most likely be driven by aircraft orders at Boeing or surprisingly continued strength in the computer and electrical equipment components of Durable Goods. . . . If there is a surprise from the economic front this week, it will come from the Existing Home Sales release. *I expect Existing Home Sales to catch the markets off guard with a big surprise on the high side.* This surprise will be driven in part by a measurement "glitch." Over the past few months, New Home Sales have been stronger than Existing Home Sales. The main reason for this divergence is due to how the housing market is measured. When you buy a home, whether it is a new home or an existing home, you follow the same process. First you sign a contract, then several weeks or even months later, you "close" on the purchase. New Home Sales are counted when the contract is signed while Existing Home Sales are not counted until contract closing. Thus, Existing Home Sales tend to lag New Home Sales due to this measurement "glitch." The strength in New Home Sales over the past few months means that sales of existing homes will soon follow. Look out, I feel that June (this week's release) will be the month when Existing Homes Sales catch up.

ECONOMIC RELEASES				
Economic Indicator	Period	Release Date	Previous Actual	Consensus
Budget Statement	June	7/22 - T	-48.5B	+47.3B
Durable Goods	June	7/25 - F	-0.7%	-0.1%
Existing Home Sales	June	7/25 - F	+4.4%	+1.0%

For the Week of July 28, 1997

This will be a very busy week from the economic front as ten major economic indicators are released to the financial markets this week. There are two things that we can be certain of this week. First, *we will receive mixed economic signals regarding the overall strength of the economy.* These mixed signals are due in part to the fact that some of this week's economic releases are measuring economic activity for July, others are measuring economic activity for June, while others are measuring economic activity for the entire second quarter. Given this time frame spectrum, we can almost be assured of mixed economic signals and this economic uncertainty usually leads to market volatility. Second, Friday will be a very scary day from an economic perspective. A majority of this week's economic indicators will all be released on the same day, Friday. Even though this Friday is not Friday the 13th, six major economic indicators in one day is enough to scare anyone. . . . The most significant release of the entire week is the Employment Cost Index. *I think that the Employment Cost Index will rise slightly over last quarter.* This increase will be driven by a combination of a slight increase in wages along with a mild increase in benefits. There is very little risk that this number could surprise on the high side. The "benefits" component of this index continues to be influenced by employer health benefit reductions and the sharing of health benefit costs with employees. In addition, there remains little if any, medical care inflation which continues to be held down by the very pro-active "cost conscious" Health Maintenance Organizations that are dominating the health care scene. Look for the markets to really cheer this number. The Employment Cost Index remains the broadest measure of employment cost as it covers both salaried and hourly employees from both the private and public sectors and it includes the cost of health and insurance benefits. In addition, it covers the widest time frame because it is a quarterly release. Finally, and most importantly, it is one of Alan Greenspan's closest watched releases. . . . *The Consumer Confidence Index could supply the biggest surprise of the week.* While the market consensus calls for this release to decrease, I think this number will catch the markets off guard on the high side. I just don't see any way possible that Consumer Confidence will not continue to march toward new record levels. Unemployment remains at levels that we have not seen since the 1960s. There is no inflation from any front. The wealth creation machine (the stock market) continues to churn out record numbers of new millionaires (at least on paper). And, we have become mesmerized as a nation with the photo's of exploration on Mars. About the only thing to complain about is if you are a Chicago Cubs fan; and even then, the cooler weather has made the ivy covered walls more beautiful than ever. Life is truly good and the Consumer Confidence Index will prove it.

ECONOMIC RELEASES				
Economic Indicator	Period	Release Date	Previous Actual	Consensus
Comsumer Confidence	July	7/29 - T	129.6	129.5
Employment Cost Index	2nd. Quarter	7/29 - T	+0.6%	+0.8%
New Home Sales	June	7/30 - W	+7.1%	-0.7%
Gross Domestic Product	2nd. Quarter	7/31 - Th	+5.9%	+1.7%
Unemployment Rate	July	8/1 - F	+5.0%	5.0%
Change in Non-farm Payrolls	July	8/1 - F	+217K	+199K
Personal Income	June	8/1 - F	+0.3%	+0.4%
Personal Spending	June	8/1 - F	+0.3%	+0.3%

continued

ECONOMIC RELEASES				
Economic Indicator	Period	Release Date	Previous Actual	Consensus
Factory Orders	June	8/1 - F	-0.7%	+1.3%
Nat'l Assn. of Purch. Mgrs. Index	July	8/1 - F	55.7	56.1

For the Week of August 4, 1997

After last week's very hectic economic release calendar, this week will feel like a vacation. All in all, it should be a pretty normal week from the economic front as five major economic indicators are scheduled to be released this week. None of the five, however, are "bell-wether" releases that have the markets holding their collective breath, waiting to see what these indicators show us. Thus, it will take a release dramatically out of the realm of expectations (either higher or lower) to get the markets to take notice. . . . The first release for the week is Construction Spending, and if there is a potential land mine in this week's economic releases, it will most likely come from Construction Spending. *I look for Construction Spending to rebound sharply from last month.* Construction Spending in May registered in at -1.8%. This number, however, had more to do with the weather than it did our economy. Remember, May posted very wet weather conditions all across the United States. These unusually wet weather conditions (even for May) served as the chief reason why construction spending dipped. Well, the weather turned around dramatically in June, and as such, all of the construction spending that was delayed by the wet May weather, will now show up in June. There are two other factors that will serve to force Construction Spending higher. First, we have already been given a good clue with what to expect in June Construction Spending by the already released June Housing Starts. Housing Starts posted a dramatic increase in June. This dramatic reversal, in turn, implies a strong reading in Construction Spending. Second, and maybe even more importantly, with our unbelievably strong economy, the markets have been so focused on the increased tax receipts at the federal government level, that we forgot about the two other levels of government, namely state and local. State and local tax revenues have spiked higher due to the strong economy just like the Federal Government's trend. While the start of summer (June) typically brings with it a "pop" in

Construction Spending as state and local governments begin their infrastructure season, this year that "pop" will be an explosion. With tax coffers brimming over at the state and local level, I look for many more brick and mortar projects to move forward which will provide an unexpected spike to Construction Spending. . . . *I look for Leading Economic Indicators to remain strong again this month.* The Leading Economic Indicator Index is comprised of eleven separate components, and the bulk of this month's uptick will be driven by three of those eleven components. I look for the Durable Goods, Building Permits and Stock Price Components to provide the fuel for this month's Leading Economic Indicators.

ECONOMIC RELEASES				
Economic Indicator	Period	Release Date	Previous Actual	Consensus
Consumer Spending	June	8/4 - M	-1.8%	+2.0%
Leading Economic Indicators	June	8/5 - T	+0.3%	+0.1%
Housing Completions	June	8/5 - T	+0.1%	-0.1%
Wholesale Trade	June	8/7 - Th	+0.2%	+0.2%
Consumer Credit	June	8/7 - Th	$3.0B	$2.7B

For the Week of August 18, 1997

It will be a very slow week from the economic front as only three major economic indicators will be released this week and none of the three should greatly surprise the markets. . . . *I look for Housing Starts to remain flat* for July. While the market consensus is looking for a slight increase due to favorable mortgage rates, a very confident consumer and a low inventory of unsold new homes (a twenty-five year low in fact), I feel home builders will remain cautious. The recent Capital Gains Tax cut will bring a glut of existing homes to the market for sale and builders are not interested in building their inventory in that environment. . . . *The Trade Balance will continue to get worse,* although it will stay within expectations. While much of the market continues to focus on Boeing's overseas shipments as the barometer for our trade deficit, we must remember that even though Boeing shipments are off, exports from other industries across the board will more than make up for this slippage, thus our trade balance will not improve. . . . *The Treasury Budget release will show that the Federal Government is on track to close the fiscal year with a deficit of under $30 billion.* Remember we started this fiscal year with a federal budget deficit of over $100 billion. Our strong economy has made the recent landmark spending and tax compromise legislation irrelevant. We don't have to wait until the year 2002 for the politicians to balance our budget, the economy will balance our budget for us in 1998!

ECONOMIC RELEASES				
Economic Indicator	Period	Release Date	Previous Actual	Consensus
Housing Starts	July	8/19 - T	+1.45K	+1.46K
Trade Balance	June	8/20 - W	-$10.2B	-$10.7B
Treasury Budget Statement	July	8/21 - Th	+$54.5B	-$22.1B

For the Week of August 25, 1997

It will be a very hectic week from the economic front as eight major economic indicators will be released this week and surely at least one of the numbers will catch the market napping. . . . *I expect Existing Home Sales to surprise on the high side,* however, not enough to cause the markets much concern. This release will make the housing market appear stronger than it actually is due to the recent Capital Gains Tax relief. This tax break will flood the existing home sale market as homeowners look to cash in (or more appropriately, cash out) on this windfall real estate tax break that Congress has provided to them. . . . *I look for the Durable Goods number to continue its monthly volatility as this month's number will be even lower than the market's consensus.* The Durable Goods drop should not be read as an overall weakening economy, rather it's the combination of two very strong forces: Boeing and Automobiles. Boeing's weakness in terms of aircraft bookings will drive down the aircraft component of the Durable Goods release, while the typical summer slowdown and re-tooling for next year's new models will crush the automobile component. This one-two punch should push the Durable Goods' number below the already negative market expectations. . . . The most interesting number of the week just might be the Consumer Confidence Index. This number will be pulled at both ends by very powerful and unique events. On the positive side, we have the landmark adoption of the federal budget and tax cut legislation which should serve as a real boom for Consumer Confidence. While on the negative side, the United Parcel Service strike was in full bloom during this survey period. High profile strikes always eat into Consumer Confidence. One positive force plus one negative force equal one negative number. ***Bad news always outweighs good news in the consumer's mind; look for the Consumer Confidence Index to take a big drop.*** . . . The most important number of the week will be the revision to Second Quarter Gross Domestic Product. This revision will push economic growth to near 3.0% for the second quarter. ***This sharp unexpected revision is due to a strong build up in inventory along with much stronger trade numbers.*** This combination of strong trade along with overall inventory accumulation could very well push the economy into the Federal Reserve Board's danger zone.

ECONOMIC RELEASES				
Economic Indicator	Period	Release Date	Previous Actual	Consensus
Existing Home Sales	July	8/25 - M	-2.6%	+1.0%
Durable Goods	July	8/26 - T	+2.4%	-0.1%
Consumer Confidence	Aug	8/26 - T	126.5	125.0
Gross Domestic Product	2nd Qtr-R	8/28 - Th	+2.2%	+2.6%
Personal Income	July	8/29 - F	+0.3%	+0.2%
Personal Spending	July	8/29 - F	+0.3%	+0.7%

continued

ECONOMIC RELEASES				
Economic Indicator	Period	Release Date	Previous Actual	Consensus
New Home Sales	Aug	8/29 - F	820K	809K
Chicago Purch. Mgrs. Index	Aug	8/29 - F	59.8	59.5

For the Week of September 1, 1997

While it will be a somewhat busy week with six major economic releases squeezed into the holiday shortened four day week, all eyes are on Friday's Employment Reports. . . . There are some indicators that are due out before Friday that could certainly add to the volatility in the markets. *I think that the National Association of Purchasing Managers Index could surprise on the high side* and even touch the landmark 60 level. If this happens, the markets will most certainly over-react; however, most of this sharp increase is the result of the United Parcel Service strike. There will be a major spike up in the Suppliers Deliveries Component of the index as manufacturers rushed to move goods in anticipation of the United Parcel Service strike. In addition to the Suppliers Deliveries Component, the Employment Component should also post a strong gain. The reason for this gain is to take care of these increased supply deliveries, again as a result of the United Parcel Service strike. . . . *I also think that Construction Spending will surprise on the high side.* Two things are happening with this release; first, our economy was much stronger than anyone thought in the second quarter. This bodes well for economic momentum heading into the third quarter and (remember this release is for July, the first month of the third quarter), Construction Spending tends to benefit the most from economic momentum. Second, last month's negative number had more to do with our very wet weather than it did our economy. The combination of a stronger economy and a weather related rebound will push Construction Spending above market expectations. . . . The most difficult releases of the week to figure out because of the United Parcel Service strike also happens to be the most important. The strike actually began at the same time as the employment survey. *I think that the Non-farm Payrolls' number will increase higher than market consensus* and could easily go over 100,000. Even though there were approximately

180,000 United Parcel Service workers on strike, a majority of those strikers immediately found temporary employment elsewhere. In addition, the competitors of the United Parcel Service who stepped in to fill the void went on a hiring binge to find additional employees to handle their exploding volume of business. . . . *The biggest surprise of the week just might be in the Unemployment Rate; I think it can drop lower to 4.7%.* Two things are happening, first our overall economy has remained very strong and second, the United Parcel Service strike may not have as big an impact on this number as it has on other indicators. The reason is psychological. People who are on strike do not consider themselves "unemployed," they consider themselves employed and on strike. This psychological twist to the unemployment survey could set our Unemployment Rate to yet another record.

ECONOMIC RELEASES				
Economic Indicator	Period	Release Date	Previous Actual	Consensus
Nat'l Assoc. of Purch. Mgrs. Index	Aug.	9/2 - T	58.6	58.1
Construction Spending	July	9/3 - W	-1.1%	+1.0%
Leading Economic Indicators	July	9/3 - W	0.0%	+0.2%
Factory Orders	July	9/4 - Th	+1.2%	+0.1%
Unemployment Rate	Aug.	9/5 - F	4.8%	+4.8%
Change in Non-farm Payrolls	Aug.	9/5 - F	+316,000	+68,000

For the Week of September 8, 1997

It will be a rather light week for economic releases as only five major economic indicators are scheduled to hit the markets this week. Once again this week, all eyes are on Friday's releases. Last week it was the Employment Reports and this week it is our first peek at August inflation with the Producer Price Index . . . Earlier in the week, *I think that Consumer Credit could surprise the markets on the high side.* Two things will drive the higher Consumer Credit number. First, Consumer Confidence has remained at record levels and a confident consumer is much more willing to use credit. Second, Automobile Sales have spiked dramatically higher which will in turn be reflected in a higher Consumer Credit number . . . Look out, *I think that Retail Sales could also surprise on the high side.* Two components are combining to move Retail Sales higher. First, as with the Consumer Credit release, very strong Automotive Sales will help push Retail Sales higher. Second, I expect a very, very strong back-to-school Retail Sales season. The first sign of this strong back-to-school sale season will show up in the August Retail Sales release . . . The week will end with the much antici-pated Producer Price Index. Once again, *I think the Producer Price Index will also surprise the markets on the high side.* Even though I continue to firmly believe that, in our global economy, we do not need to fear inflation running out of control, this week's release will once again put everyone on red alert. The real damage with this week's release will be more psychological than it will be as a source for future inflation. The psychological damage comes from the fact that every single month this year, without fail, the Producer Price Index has gone down. The markets have almost come to expect no inflation pressure at the wholesale level. That amazing record will come to an end this month as the Producer Price Index will post its first positive number of the year. This increase will be driven by a single factor, the price of oil. The tremendous run up in the price of oil recently means that we will see a sharp increase in gasoline prices. A big swing in this major component will impact the entire index. Once we get past the initial shock of this Inflation release, the markets should settle down, realizing that the fear of inflation is truly overblown.

ECONOMIC RELEASES				
Economic Indicator	Period	Release Date	Previous Actual	Consensus
Consumer Credit	July	9/8 - M	+$5.2B	+$4.5B
Wholesale Inventories	July	9/9 - T	+1.9%	-0.6%
Productivity & Cost	2nd. Qtr	9/9 - T	+0.6%	+2.1%

continued

ECONOMIC RELEASES				
Economic Indicator	Period	Release Date	Previous Actual	Consensus
Retail Sales	Aug.	9/12 - F	+0.6%	+0.5%
Product Price Index	Aug.	9/12 - F	-0.1%	+0.3%

For the Week of September 15, 1997

As the financial markets remain very nervous, the economic releases take on even greater importance this week. Look out for Terrible Tuesday when four of this week's six economic releases will hit the market . . . ***The Consumer Price Index should come in close to market expectations*** unless one of the components throws the Index a curve. The real story in the Index is not the number itself, rather what's going on within the number. I expect a sharp run up in both gasoline prices and the almost traditional annual increases in college tuition to pressure the Index on the high side. While the continued automobile discounts and computer and electronic equipment "mini price wars" should continue to push the Index lower. The wild card within the Index should come from apparel prices. If it has weakened as I suspect, we could be in for a pleasant surprise from the Consumer Price Index . . . ***I expect Business Inventories to come in somewhat below market expectations.*** While I certainly feel that this number will continue last month's buildup trend, the market is failing to account for the very, very robust consumer spending that we witnessed in July that depleted inventories, at least at the retail level . . . ***The biggest surprise of the week may come from the Industrial Production release which I expect to post very strong gains.*** Three unrelated factors could drive this index to the highest level of the year. First, motor vehicle assemblies are in full gear with the new model year change-over completed. Second, the sweeping weather changes across the United States which found it unseasonably hot in some spots and unseasonably cold in others, should mean that the electric utility generation component also posted strong gains with the only question being whether you were turning on the heat or air conditioning. Finally, I look for solid strength to continue from the computer component (which also spills over into office equipment for those computers) as I feel the Computer Industry is preparing to make a strong run the remainder of the year . . . Possibly ***the best news of the week for the market will come from Housing Starts which will surprise*** *on the low side*. Even though the inventories of new homes available for sale remain lower than historical averages, the concern regarding the glut of existing home sales coming to the market as a result of the Capital Gains Tax relief will keep many builders on the sidelines. Also, don't forget the August Employment Reports revealed a slowdown in the hours worked in the Construction Industry. This slowdown will most likely be reflected in a weaker Housing Starts number. I still can't get used to bad news about the economy (weak housing starts) is really good news for the markets (because it reduces the fear of a strong economy causing the FOMC to raise interest rates).

ECONOMIC RELEASES				
Economic Indicator	Period	Release Date	Previous Actual	Consensus
Consumer Price Index	Aug.	9/16 - T	+0.2%	+0.3%
Business Inventories	July	9/16 - T	+0.6%	+0.3%
Industrial Production	Aug.	9/16 - T	+0.2%	+0.5%
Capacity Utilization	Aug.	9/16 - T	83.5%	83.1%
Housing Starts	Aug.	9/17 - W	0%	+0.5%
Trade Balance	July	9/18 - Th	-$8.2B	-$9.6B

For the Week of September 22, 1997

It should be a pretty quiet and slow week from the economic front as there are only four major economic indicators scheduled to hit the markets this week. All of the releases this week should be positives for the markets, the real question remains, how much of this expected economic good news has already been priced into the markets? . . . *The Treasury Budget Report should come in very close to market expectations.* If this report simply hits the market consensus for this month, that will imply that the overall year-end budget deficit will be slightly under $30 billion. Remember, we began this fiscal year with a budget deficit of $107 billion. Here's an interesting perspective that is sometimes lost with all of the hoopla regarding our recently approved landmark budget agreement that will actually balance our budget by the year 2002. If you were to look at total government spending, not just the federal government, we have a surplus today in 1997. The combined balance sheets of state and local governments will close out the year with a $34 billion dollar surplus. If you then subtract the $30 billion federal government deficit, that still leaves you with a $4 billion overall government surplus today. Here is another interesting deficit perspective for you. Every week the saga continues in Europe over which countries will and will not be able to meet the strict European Monetary Union guidelines that mandate a budget deficit of only 3.0% of Gross Domestic Product. With a projected federal budget deficit of slightly under $30 billion, that places our deficit as a percentage of Gross Domestic Product at 0.4% or lower! . . . ***I expect the Durable Goods Orders to come in below market expectations.*** This number is always a very volatile one and I certainly expect it to bounce back into positive territory this month, fueled in part by the strong signals we continue to receive from the manufacturing front. However, I feel that the recent rumblings from Boeing regarding a decline in bookings may drive the aircraft component number lower than market expectations . . . ***Existing Home Sales should surprise on the high side.*** The supply demand fundamentals are very, very positive for the existing home sale market. There is a limited supply of new home construction going on and with the newly enacted Capital Gains Tax breaks, existing homes are coming on the market in record numbers. The high inventory of existing homes is the real key to increased sales this month . . . ***Second Quarter Gross Domestic Product will be revised upward again,*** although, I don't think that there is much of a chance that the final second quarter Gross Domestic Product (GDP) number could reach 4.0%. A revision of 3.8% is not out of the question. The adjustments to this number will once again be fueled by stronger than expected consumption levels in the second quarter. What was originally reported as a very weak second quarter economy based on the initial 2.2% GDP will now end up to be a very strong 3.8% GDP. No wonder the markets are volatile.

ECONOMIC RELEASES				
Economic Indicator	Period	Release Date	Previous Actual	Consensus
Treasury Budget Statement	August	9/22 - T	-$41.8B	-$38.2B
Durable Goods	August	9/25 - Th	-0.3%	+0.6%
Existing Home Sales	August	9/25 - Th	+2.2%	-0.9%
Gross Domestic Product	2nd Quarter (final)	9/26 - F	+3.6%	+3.7%

For the Week of September 29, 1997

It will be a very hectic week from the economic front as the market is bombarded with economic releases every single day of the week. All in all, there will be eleven major economic releases to hit the market this week culminating with the bellwether Employment reports on Friday . . . As the week begins, *all eyes will be on the Personal Spending release which I think will surprise on the high side*. The market consensus is calling for a steep decline in Personal Spending from last month based on the less than exciting retail sales figures we have received to date. In addition, the consensus has concluded that last month's spike was weather related as shoppers across the United States scurried to the malls to get a break from the extreme heat and while at the mall, they did a little shopping. The markets just don't get it; the consumer is not ready to slow down. The consumer accounts for two thirds of our economy. The strong economic growth we have witnessed this year has been on the back of the consumer. I don't know how we can expect the consumer to slow down with unemployment rates at 30-year lows, consumer confidence at 25-year highs and the stock market letting people accumulate more wealth (at least on paper) than they ever dreamed of . . . *I expect New Home Sales to surprise on the low side*. The market impact of the Capital Gains Tax exclusion of the first $500,000 in profit for couples and $250,000 for singles is alive and well. This tax break has created a glut of existing homes on the market as homeowners rush to liquidate the equity from their home. Even though the inventory of unsold new homes is currently at a 25-year low, Housing Starts are simply not going to pick up until we work off the impact that the Capital Gains Tax cut has had on Existing Home Sales . . . ***The Non-farm Payrolls' number will be infected by the United Parcel Service strike.*** The headline will be bad, especially for the bond market as I expect Non-farm Payrolls to come in well over the nervous 300,000 level. If the markets can get past the headline shock of 300,000 new jobs and realize that over 150,000 are UPS employees who were on strike and are now back in the work force, the impact will be short lived. However, don't forget it is Friday and the story of the markets this year seems to be that every Friday behaves like it's Friday the 13th!

ECONOMIC RELEASES				
Economic Indicator	Period	Release Date	Previous Actual	Consensus
Personal Income	Sept.	9/29 - M	+0.1%	+0.5%
Personal Spending	Sept.	9/29 - M	+0.8%	+0.4%
Consumer Confidence	Sept.	9/30 - T	129.1	129.4
New Home Sales	Aug.	9/30 - T	817K	806K
Chicago Purchasing Mgrs. Index	Sept.	9/30 - T	64.3	61.4
Leading Economic Indicators	Aug.	10/1 - W	+0.3%	+0.1%
Nat'l Assn. of Purch. Mgrs. Index	Sept.	10/1 - W	56.8	56.2
Factory Orders	Aug.	10/2 - Th	+0.2%	+0.4%
Housing Completion's	Aug.	10/3 - F	-7.8%	+1.0%
Unemployment Rate	Sept.	10/3 - F	+4.9%	+4.8%
Change in Non-farm Payrolls	Sept.	10/3 - F	49K	336K

For the Week of October 6, 1997

It will be an extremely light week from an economic release perspective. This week's three economic releases will certainly seem like a non-event, especially on the heels of last week's hectic eleven major economic release calendar . . . The major concern in our markets is inflation; thus, whenever we have one of the key inflation indexes on the calendar, that will always be the focus. Such is the case this week as all eyes will be on Friday's Producer Price Index report. *I expect the Producer Price Index to present mixed signals on inflation even though the overall index may surprise on the low side.* The very volatile food and energy component of the index should remain flat which certainly bodes well for future inflation concerns. However, there should be a key price increase in several components to give inflation watchers plenty to worry about. First, there has been a major run-up in tobacco prices in preparation to pay huge financial settlements for any Congressional deal and/or current litigation concerns. Second, the new model year for automobiles is in full swing. With this new model year most dealers drop all of their discount promotions aimed at getting rid of inventory. This lack of any discount pricing is the same as a price increase. Third, the raw material component could also rise, driven in part by an increase in base most metal prices, with the exception of copper. All of these increases should be offset by the continued decline in the computer and electronic component of the index. If these prices do not continue to fall, the markets could be in for a real surprise from the overall Index . . . Lost in all of the focus on inflation this week will be an important number that will measure if the "consumer" can continue to drive the economy, that number in Consumer Credit. *I think that the Consumer Credit number could surprise the market on the low side.* I feel that Consumer Credit is slowing, being driven in part by the recent increases in loan delinquencies and personal bankruptcies which are taking out the marginal consumer and thus, Consumer Credit is falling.

ECONOMIC RELEASES				
Economic Indicator	Period	Release Date	Previous Actual	Consensus
Consumer Credit	Aug.	10/7 - T	+$6.58	+$4.4B
Wholesale Inventories	Aug.	10/8 - W	-0.6%	+0.4%
Producer Price Index	Sept.	10/10 - F	+0.3%	+0.2%

For the Week of October 13, 1997

It will be a rather typical week from the economic front, however, compared to last week's very light calendar of three economic releases, this week's calendar of six releases may make the week seem more hectic than it actually is . . . Economic releases will have to fight for the headlines as most market watchers will be glued on earnings' reports. Potential headline grabbers from the economic front this week start with the Retail Sales release on Wednesday. *I think that Retail Sales could surprise on the high side.* The consumer is simply not ready to slow down. These stronger than expected numbers will begin to put some "meat" around the theory that we did enjoy a strong "back-to-school" retail season. And remember, a strong back-to-school sales season usually is a great indicator for an equally strong retail Christmas season . . . *The Consumer Price Index will surprise on the low side.* The markets just don't get it; there is no inflation despite what Alan Greenspan says. Inflation watchers have convinced themselves that this is the month that consumer inflation will spike up. On the surface, their argument appears compelling. First, the recent rise in gasoline prices will be reflected in this month's release. Second, the Tobacco Industry has pushed cigarette prices higher in anticipation of the need for huge amounts of cash either for a global agreement or individual legislative settlements. Third, even though the increase was not as much as airlines originally hoped for, airfares have also moved up. Finally, automobile prices also moved up as a result of the removal of any discount promotions on last year's models, as the new model year begins. While these individual, isolated high profile cost increases certainly give the appearance of consumer inflation, the fact of the matter is that they are very independent and isolated price events. They will not carry over to the other major components of the index; and as such, when we tally the score, we will once again find out that inflation is still dead . . . Possibly the most controversial number of the week is Housing Starts. *The market consensus is calling for a tremendous rebound in Housing Starts, I think that the consensus is wrong, as Housing Starts should surprise on the low side.* At the foundation of this extreme optimism is the fact that the inventory of new homes for sale is at a 25 year low. This low inventory "almost" always means a spike up in Housing Starts to rebuild the inventory. Not this time, however, the slowdown in Housing Starts isn't about inventory, it's about the impact that Capital Gains Tax relief is having on the housing market by flooding that market with "existing homes" as homeowners want to cash out of the equity they have built up in their homes. It's the tax law changes, not inventory, that will drive Housing Starts, and these changes will drive starts lower.

ECONOMIC RELEASES				
Economic Indicator	Period	Release Date	Previous Actual	Consensus
Retail Sales	Sept.	10/15 - W	+0.4%	+0.1%
Consumer Price Index	Sept.	10/16 - Th	+0.2%	+0.3%
Business Inventories	Aug.	10/16 - Th	+0.2%	+0.3%
Housing Starts	Sept.	10/17- F	-4.8%	+4.2%
Industrial Production	Sept.	10/17 - F	+0.7%	+0.3%
Capacity Utilization	Sept.	10/17 - F	83.9%	83.6%

For the Week of October 20, 1997

It will be an extremely light week from the economic front as there are only two major economic indicators scheduled to be released this week. Both will probably get much more attention than they deserve simply because there is nothing else to focus on or worry about from an economic perspective . . . First up is the Trade Balance Release on

Tuesday and *while the market consensus is calling for the Trade Balance picture to improve, I feel that the consensus is wrong and that our balance of trade will get worse, not better.* There is simply no way that our Trade Balance can improve this month. First of all, imports are booming, especially from Japan where that country's entire economy is being balanced on the back of their exports (our imports) to the United States. Secondly, retail demand has remained very strong, which means that we will have a major increase in the area of consumer goods that are imported. Now thirdly, when you overlay the fact that Boeing continues to have a manufacturing bottleneck and production problems, I look for our exports, especially from the manufacturers' shipment component, to be trending lower as well. With exports moving lower while imports continue to move higher, there is simply no way that the balance of trade picture can improve (at least for this month) . . . The second release of the week comes the next day when the markets receive the Treasury Budget Report. For as bad as the Trade Balance Report will be, the Treasury Budget report will be good. *I fully expect the Federal Government to close out fiscal year 1997 with a deficit under $20 billion.* The currently revised official forecast of the Congressional Budget Office calls for the Federal Government to end the fiscal year with a deficit of $23 billion. Whether it's $23 billion or $20 billion really doesn't matter much to the markets. What really matters is the Federal Government began the fiscal year with a deficit of $107 billion and will end the year (September 30 fiscal year end) with a deficit of under $25 billion. This tremendous improvement has not gone unnoticed by the financial markets. And secondly, while all of Europe continues to struggle with what appears to be strict government spending guidelines by mandating them to join the European Monetary Union, a country deficit must be 3% or less of Gross Domestic Product. Now in order to meet these strict guidelines, countries are trying every budget and accounting trick possible; remember Germany even went so far as to consider re-valuing its gold reserves. Meanwhile, in the United States after this month's release, our deficit as a percent of our economy (Gross Domestic Product) will be less than ½ of one percent with no budget gimmicks. A strong economy can make any politician look good . . . With such an extremely light calendar, the "B" team of economic releases just might get their day in the sun this week. With all of the concern regarding the consumer slowing down, both the Mitsubishi Bank/Schroder Wertheim and LJR Redbook Research "weekly" Retail Sales releases could have an impact on the markets. Also, the initial weekly state unemployment compensation insurance claims on Thursday will also draw some attention because there is simply nothing else to focus on at the end of the week.

ECONOMIC RELEASES				
Economic Indicator	Period	Release Date	Previous Actual	Consensus
Trade Balance	Aug.	10/21 - T	-$10.3B	-$10.1B
Treasury Budget	Sept.	10/22 - W	-$34.6B	-$25.6B

For the Week of October 27, 1997

Look for the economy to keep the markets very nervous this week as there is at least one major economic indicator scheduled to be released every single day this week. I look for these economic indicators to cause extreme volatility in the markets due to the "mixed signals" these releases will send the markets. You can almost be assured of mixed economic signals whenever you have economic releases that are measuring so many different economic reporting periods. Some of the economic releases this week are measuring economic activity in September, others are measuring economic activity in October while still others are measuring economic activity for the entire third quarter . . . *The first surprise of the week will come from Existing Home Sales which will surprise on the high side.* The market consensus which is calling for a negative number is failing to account for the impact of the recent Capital Gains Tax cut legislation. This tax break has flooded the Existing Home Sale market with homeowners looking to cash in on the real estate Capital Gains Tax break that Congress has provided to them. When you then overlay the limited supply of new home construction going on, the overall supply/demand fundamentals in the Existing Home market are extremely strong, which should fuel this month's release into positive territory and catch the markets off guard . . . The most significant release of the week is the Employment Cost Index. *If there is any risk to the Employment Cost Index this quarter, it is that it could surprise on the high side.* Any increase beyond market expectations will be driven by the combination of a mild increase in wages along with a slight increase in benefits. On the wage front, the minimum wage was increased during this quarter's reporting period which will serve as a one-time turbo charge to wages. From the

ECONOMIC RELEASES				
Economic Indicator	Period	Release Date	Previous Actual	Consensus
Personal Income	Sept.	11/3 - M	+0.6%	+0.3%
Personal Spending	Sept.	11/3 - M	+0.3%	+0.2%
Nat'l Assn. of Purch. Mgrs. Index	Oct.	11/3 - M	54.2	54.0
Construction Spending	Sept.	11/3 - M	-0.3%	+0.5%
Leading Economic Indicators	Sept.	11/4 - T	+0.2%	+0.2%
Factory Orders	Sept.	11/5 - W	+1.3%	+0.2%
Housing Completion's	Sept.	11/6 - Th	+0.2%	+0.2%
Unemployment Rate	Oct.	11/7 - F	4.9%	4.8%
Change in Non-farm Payrolls	Oct.	11/7 - F	215,000	203,000
Wholesale Inventories	Sept.	11/7 - F	+1.0%	+0.3%

For the Week of November 10, 1997

It will be an extremely light week from the economic front as there are only three major economic indicators scheduled to be released this week. After last week's hectic economic survey calendar, this week will seem like the lazy Thanksgiving holiday is starting early, at least from an economic perspective . . . There are no economic releases prior to the Federal Open Markets Committee meeting on Wednesday, so the markets will not get any final clues before that meeting. It's a good thing that no clues are necessary; there is no way that the Federal Open Markets Committee will do anything but sit on the sidelines this Tuesday . . . The first economic release of the week is one I will call one of the unknown major releases, namely the Business Productivity Indicator. One of the reasons that this release tends to get lost in the shuffle is the fact that it is a quarterly release and as such, it is easy to fall into the out of sight, out of mind syndrome. This release has recently taken on greater importance as economists debate our New Era which has as its cornerstone, tremendous productivity improvements that in turn, hold down inflation and costs while allowing the economy to grow at above trend levels. *This quarter's Business Productivity release will serve as another reminder that the New Era economy is being driven by productivity.* I feel that the Business Productivity release could even surprise on the high side by approaching a 3.0% increase which would be well above the 2.1% consensus. If the release is over 3.0%, that will make it the fastest growing productivity quarter in the last five years . . . *I look for Retail Sales to surprise on the high side being driven there by the confluence of three factors: autos, malls and fall.* From auto's corner, motor vehicle sales have remained strong being driven in part by consumers snapping up the new 1998-model-year vehicles. From the malls, I expect a real upswing being driven mostly by apparel. And from fall, cool temperatures all across the United States not only drove consumers to the mall, but also served as a chilling reminder to buy some clothes to bundle up in. With employment at twenty five to thirty year lows, the consumer simply has no reason to slow down, and Retail Sales this month will prove it . . . The final release of the week, *the Producer Price Index should be a non-event as I expect it to come in at the market consensus.* With the focus in the markets shifting from inflation less than two months ago to deflation today because of the Southeast Asia currency and economic meltdown, instead of this number being looked at for a leading sign of inflation, it will now be looked at as a leading sign for deflation. From an economic perspective, things simply cannot get much better than they are today.

ECONOMIC RELEASES				
Economic Indicator	Period	Release Date	Previous Actual	Consensus
Business Productivity	3rd. Qtr.	11/13 - Th	+2.7%	+2.1%
Retail Sales	Oct.	11/14 - F	+0.3%	+0.3%
Producer Price Index	Oct.	11/14 - F	+0.5%	-0.1%

For the Week of November 17, 1997

There will be a heavy dose of economic releases this week as six major indicators are scheduled to hit the market. With earnings' season behind us, these economic releases now take on even greater significance as they will hold the clues to where both the bond market and the stock market are heading in the short run . . . One of the biggest surprises of the week could happen on the first day of the week as *I expect Capacity Utilization to surprise on the high side*. I think that the economy will remain stronger than most forecasts for the 4th quarter. The strong 3rd quarter Gross Domestic Product of 3.5% will create momentum for this October Capacity Utilization number. This release is being supported by three factors. First, factory output has remained very strong. Second, automobile production has actually been increasing; and third, electric utility output has also remained strong. These three factors could combine to push Capacity Utilization to the threshold 85.0% level—a reading the markets have not seen in almost 10 years . . . There is no inflation, especially at the consumer level. As such, *I expect the Consumer Price Index to surprise on the low side*. The two most volatile components of the Consumer Price Index, food prices and energy prices, have both remained very tame. Some energy prices have even posted a slight downtick from the prior month's reading. When you add to the fact that automobile dealers are already discounting their new model vehicles in anticipation of lower priced imports due to the Southeast Asian currency and economic crisis, these forces all add up to a very weak showing for consumer prices . . . The final surprise of the week will come on Thursday when *the Trade Balance number shocks the markets by dramatically increasing* beyond market consensus. This number may pose the greatest single risk to the markets for the entire week. Fresh on the heels of the defeat of the Fast Track Trade legislation, this release could fuel the fears of an all-out trade war with China and Japan. The strongest economy in the world today is right here in the United States. And while demand around the globe is slowing, our demand continues to hit on all cylinders. This combination will move our Trade Balance number to levels that not only make politicians nervous, but will make our markets very nervous as well.

| ECONOMIC RELEASES | | | | |
Economic Indicator	Period	Release Date	Previous Actual	Consensus
Industrial Production	Oct.	11/17 - M	+0.7%	+0.6%
Capacity Utilization	Oct.	11/17 - M	84.4%	84.6%
Consumer Price Index	Oct.	11/18 - T	+0.2%	+0.2%
Business Inventories	Sept.	11/18 - T	+0.2%	+0.4%
Housing Starts	Oct.	11/19 - W	+7.9%	-1.7%
Trade Balance	Sept.	11/20 - Th	-$10.3B	-$10.0B

For the Week of November 24, 1997

This will be a rather hectic week from an economic perspective. The week may be short on days due to the Thanksgiving holiday, but it will not be short on economic releases as seven major economic indicators are scheduled to be released on this holiday shortened week . . . *One of the more closely watched numbers this week will be the Consumer Confidence release. I expect this number to drop dramatically and surprise on the low side.* This major swing, however, is not the beginning of a new trend but rather the confluence of three independent events that really knocked Consumer Confidence for a loop. First was Gray Monday; investors forgot that markets can go down as well as up and the recent 554 point one-day drop in the Dow Jones Industrial Average certainly took a bite out of Consumer Confidence. Second, the on-going Southeast Asian currency and economic meltdown is serving as a major source of confusion for consumers regarding just what the ultimate impact will be. A consumer that has questions is usually a consumer that, because of the uncertainty, looses confidence as well. And finally, the crisis in Iraq and the potential of another Gulf War certainly kept the consumers on edge, which certainly ate away at their confidence. While these three events will most certainly combine to post a major drop in consumer confidence, it is important to note that the drop will be short lived. These are one-time events that will go away and when they do, the consumer's confidence will once again shoot up to record levels . . . *I think that Gross Domestic Product for the third quarter could surprise on the high side.* Do not forget that there is a tremendous link between Gross Domestic Product (the growth of the economy) and Corporate Earnings (the growth of profits). We have the luxury of already knowing what the Third Quarter Earnings' Season has been. With 97% of the S&P 500 having already reported third quarter earnings, here is the tale of the tape. 54% of the S&P 500 companies reported Third Quarter "positive" Earnings' surprises exceeding analysts' expectations. Another 20% of the S&P 500 companies reported Third Quarter Earnings right at analysts' expectations. Finally, the remaining 26% of S&P 500 companies reported "negative" earnings' surprises by failing to meet analysts' expectations. You simply cannot have 74% of the S&P 500 meeting or beating analysts' earnings expectations for any given quarter unless that quarter has a strong underlying economy. I think that we will be closer to 4.0% than 3.0%.

ECONOMIC RELEASES				
Economic Indicator	Period	Release Date	Previous Actual	Consensus
Budget Statement	Oct.	11/24 - M	-$39.8B	-$33.4B
Consumer Confidence	Nov.	11/25 - T	123.3	121.9
Existing Home Sales	Oct.	11/25 - T	+0.2%	-0.9%
Gross Domestic Product	3rd Qtr.	11/26 - W	+3.5%	+3.5%
Durable Goods Orders	Oct.	11/26 - W	+0.1%	+0.5%
Personal Income	Oct.	11/28 - F	+0.4%	+0.3%
Personal Spending	Oct.	11/28 - F	+0.2%	+0.3%

For the Week of December 8, 1997

From an economic perspective, it will feel like the holiday season begins this week as the economic calendar is very, very light and traders are given a "holiday" from potential economic scares. While there are only four major releases, three of the four will still be very closely watched and any of the three could quickly become the "grinch" who stole the holiday . . . The first major release is Wholesale Trade on Wednesday. This number has taken on greater significance as a result of the Southeast Asian currency and economic meltdown. The risk from the "Trade" release number going forward will be more political than economic. ***Look for this number to show our trade picture getting worse,*** which will in turn fuel a series of high profile political responses . . . I think the Retail Sales release will really catch the markets off guard and surprise on the high side. November's Retail Sales release will be driven in a large part by an event that happened in late October; namely, Gray Monday. You see, while Alan Greenspan and company were worried about what he called "The Wealth Effect" fueling the consumer and inflation, it was really what I call "The Negative Wealth Effect" that we should have been worried about. Alan Greenspan's "Wealth Effect" theory went like this: As the stock market continues to rise and rise, consumers see how wealthy they are becoming (at least on paper when they receive 401(k) statements, etc., etc.) and because of this wealth accumulation, go out on a buying spree, overextending themselves and cause inflation. I think Alan Greenspan was wrong. What was going on was not a "Wealth Effect" but rather a "Negative Wealth Effect." You see, as the markets continued to go up and up and investors accumulated more wealth instead of fueling spending, it actually slowed it down. Instead of consumers buying that refrigerator or stereo or even a new car, they would simply plow their money back into the market with the thought of "I'll let the market buy this item for me a year from now with the return I'll receive on my investment." The "Negative Wealth Effect" died on October 27th when the market dropped 554 points. Because investors were reminded that markets go down as well as up, they also realized that it may be time for them to buy something instead of expecting the market to buy it for them . . . The final number of the week on Friday, ***the Producer Price Index should send everyone home happy as once again we realize that there simply is no inflation.***

ECONOMIC RELEASES				
Economic Indicator	Period	Release Date	Previous Actual	Consensus
Wholesale Trade	Oct.	12/10 - W	+1.2%	-0.1%
Retail Sales	Nov.	12/11 - Th	-0.2%	+0.3%
Producer Price Index	Nov.	12/12 - F	+0.1%	+0.1%
Business Inventories	Oct.	12/12 - F	+0.7%	+0.2%

For the Week of December 15, 1997

This will be a busy week from an economic perspective as there are six major economic indicators scheduled to be released this week. Two thirds of these releases will hit the markets in the first two days, so you better come to work prepared for some early action . . . *I think that the Capacity Utilization release will surprise on the high side.* Remember that this release is for the month of November and we have already received a great clue from the November employment report regarding just how strong our economy was, especially in the manufacturing area. The manufacturing sector continues to improve. This sector has recovered from the recent inventory overhang which caused manufacturing to level off. These inventories were wiped out by a stronger than expected second half of the year and as such, manufacturing finds itself in the mist of a slight rally. A strong manufacturing base usually means higher capacity utilization. Remember, Capacity Utilization measures the percentage of industrial output currently in use. A change in the rate indicates a change in the direction of the economy. When the percentage rate moves closer to 90%, our industrial output is practically at full capacity which is obviously inflationary. A number closer to 70% is recessionary. When you combine a strong economy with an expanding manufacturing sector, you can only get higher Capacity Utilization . . . *The Consumer Price Index will once again show us that there simply is no inflation.* I actually think that this number could even surprise on the low side and come in below the already below trend forecast of +0.2%. The two most volatile components of this index are both trending down. Food prices across the board continue to head lower. The great hype about El Niño causing food prices to sky-rocket has failed to materialize (say, what has happened to El Niño anyway?). Meanwhile, price drops from the energy front has been even more dramatic. Natural gas prices are down and oil prices continue to fall as supply becomes abundant due to both OPEC raising the production limits to an additional 2.5 million barrels a day and the Iraq food for oil deal with the United Nations that will flood the market with even more oil . . . Maybe the closest watched number of the week will be the October Trade Balance number on Thursday. *I think that the Trade Balance release will catch the markets off guard by quantifying just how bad our balance of trade has become.* Think about it for a minute: our Trade Balance is getting hit from both fronts, so it has to get worse. First, exports are down not only because of weakening demand all throughout Asia, but also because our strong dollar is making our products more expensive as well. Second, imports are surging. Remember our economy has remained strong and two thirds of our economy is driven by the consumer. Well again because of our strong dollar, consumers are able to buy imports at cheaper levels. The double whammy of weaker exports and stronger imports will combine to push the balance of trade over the edge.

ECONOMIC RELEASES				
Economic Indicator	Period	Release Date	Previous Actual	Consensus
Industrial Production	Nov.	12/15 - M	+0.5%	+0.6%
Capacity Utilization	Nov.	12/15 - M	84.3%	84.2%
Consumer Price Index	Nov.	12/16 - T	+0.2%	+0.2%
Housing Starts	Nov.	12/16 - T	+1.4%	-2.1%
Trade Balance	Oct.	12/18 - Th	-$11.1B	-$10.9B
Budget Statement	Nov.	12/19 - F	-$33.8B	-$24.3B

For the Week of December 22, 1997

This will be a very light week from an economic perspective as there are only four economic indicators scheduled to be released this week . . . *I expect the Durable Goods Orders release to surprise on the low side, which will be good for bonds and bad for stocks.* The Durable Goods release has been one of the most volatile economic releases for 1997 with dramatic swings one month after the next. The consensus in the market is calling for that trend to continue as this month the market is looking for major gains in Durable Goods following last month's steep drop in Durable Goods. I think that the market consensus will be wrong and here is why. There will be two keys to a weaker Durable Goods order. First will be Boeing. You see, to figure out what the Durable Goods release will be, just pay close attention to Boeing bookings and production. Boeing is the single greatest company influence on the Durable Goods release. Boeing has stated that aircraft orders slowed down in November, thus so will the Durable Goods release. Second, remember what the Purchasing Managers said. The recent National Association of Purchasing Managers' release for November revealed a slowdown in manufacturing order activity in November. This order activity slowdown will also re-appear in a weaker than expected Durable Goods release . . . It's only fitting that the Personal Spending indicator would be released the day before Christmas. *I expect the Personal Spending release to catch the markets off guard and surprise on the high side.* I simply can't figure out how the consensus of Wall Street economists continue to call for Personal Spending to slow down. First of all, this release is for November; the same November month that created over 400,000 new jobs, sent unemployment to levels not seen in 25 years and posted nice increases in average hourly earnings. Economists just don't get it. These November employment releases are telling us that just about anyone who wants a job can get a job and anyone that has a job is probably making more money. These two factors are very positive forces that will fuel Personal Consumption. Also, don't forget that the stock market has recovered all of its losses and then some from Gray October, so that investors are wealthy once again (at least on paper, according to their 401(k) statements). Finally, Consumer Confidence is a great forecaster for Personal Consumption. A confident consumer spends money. As our Consumer Confidence releases continue to flirt with record territory, I think that these consumers will show us just how confident they are by driving Personal Consumption upward.

ECONOMIC RELEASES				
Economic Indicator	Period	Release Date	Previous Actual	Consensus
Durable Goods	Nov.	12/23 - T	-0.3%	+0.6%
Gross Domestic Product (Revised)	3rd Qtr.	12/23 - T	+3.3%	+3.3%
Personal Income	Nov.	12/24 - W	+0.5%	+0.7%
Personal Spending	Nov.	12/24 - W	+0.5%	+0.4%

3 STOCK MARKET PERSPECTIVE

OVERVIEW

Once again, everyone who thought the stock market could not have another good year in 1997 were wrong again. For an unprecedented third year in a row, the stock market returned over 20%. The Dow Jones Industrial Average (DJIA) actually closed the year at 7908.25 which was an increase of 22.64%. The year was not without its ups and downs. In fact, at various times during the year the stock market, as measured by the DJIA, was at the 6,000 and 7,000 and 8,000 level.

The real story in our great stock market run may be because of a new and unique group of underlying fundamentals and these underlying fundamentals don't have anything to do with price-earnings' ratios, betas or stock capitalization levels. My underlying fundamentals have to do with greed, alternatives and something I refer to as "bear proof" insurance.

First let me address greed. Specifically the greed factor—Investors do not want to be out of the market for any period of time. The two most recent corrections show why investors have become greedy. After the corrections of April and October of 1997, the market actually recouped all its losses in a matter of weeks and marched on to new highs. It wasn't the people who were in the market that lost money, it was people who got out of the market and missed the rebound that lost money. When the greed factor takes hold, it can overwhelm market indicators, and fuel strong demand.

My second underlying fundamental is alternatives, specifically alternative investments. In theory, different asset classes compete for our investment dollars. Until other investment alternatives can provide the return of stocks, I see no alternative—especially for longer term investment horizons like pension fund assets—but to continue to allocate a majority of their assets to stocks.

Finally, I would never be so bold as to say that we will never have a bear market again; however, I will tell you that I think we may be developing Bear-Proof Insurance. Think about it; something is going on here. In the summer of 1996, the market sells off 10% and then snaps right back and marches on to new levels. Last year the market corrects 9.8% in March and April and it once again snaps back and marches on to new highs and the 554 point drop in October of 1997 only took 26 days to recoup. I'm convinced that the reason that these potential bear markets never materialize is because of Bear-Proof Insurance.

At the foundation of Bear-Proof Insurance lies the Mutual Fund Industry. At the beginning of this year, the trillions of dollars in stock mutual funds could almost be divided into equal thirds. One third owned by individual retail investors, one third by institutional investors and one third by retirement type accounts.

Well, my Bear-Proof Insurance comes from the combination of the last two thirds—institutional investors and retirement type accounts. Combined they provide a great base of ongoing support for when the market does correct. Think about both institutional investors and retirement type accounts in mutual funds.

First the institutional investors are businesses, corporations, financial institutions, unions, not-for-profit groups and the like. Overall, they invest for the long-term and do not trade actively in response to market fluctuations. In addition, most invest through a professional financial advisor who would counsel them to ride out the correction.

Now think of the retirement type accounts. I'm basically talking about Individual Retirement Accounts, 401(k) and the like. Again, most investors view this as a long-term investment. And you cannot completely withdraw your money out of these plans without a big financial penalty. In addition, some programs make it very difficult to move your money by requiring signature guarantees, notarized authorization letters, and it's rumored that some even require a note from your mother!

This powerful combination of the long term investment horizon of institutional and retirement investors just may be creating the newest investment insurance product. . . . Bear Proof Insurance.

Hold on as we recap the wild ride on which the stock market took us, week by week from Tax Day (April 15th) through the end of 1997.

For the Week of April 14, 1997

The stock market will get back to doing what it does best this week and that is focusing on earnings reports as earnings season is in full swing. Even though earnings will dominate the scene on the stock market front, one eye will still be kept on the economy and interest rate hike fears. *The big industry mover in the stock market this week could come from the over all technology sector* as high profile names (Intel, LSI, Sun Micro Systems, Apple, Compaq and Digital) dominate the earnings report season. With technology stocks overall taking a beating recently, they are now at very attractive levels and a solid earnings season should begin to move this industry back up to its lofty levels. . . . There is one change from my industry weighting this week as *the Banking Industry moves from Overweight to Neutral.* With the very real near term prospects of another interest rate hike by the middle of the year, this industry will stay extremely volatile with some major downside risk. Earnings for the overall industry remain strong; thus, a rotation out of this industry should be able to be accomplished with leaving very little money on the table. Also, with the continued focus on major banking reform and the ever present merger mania there should be plenty of short-term good news to assist in any industry rotation. . . . Even though I am not making an allocation switch at this time, I am *putting the Health Care Industry on special watch.* Although I think it is way too early to be worried about Health Care Reform II, the signals from the Clinton Administration show that if the administration moves to balance the budget with the Republican Congress, Clinton would like to have it balanced on the "backs" of the Health Care Industry. . . . This week earnings releases are expected from the following companies: AT&T, Bank America, Caterpillar Inc., Eastman Kodak Co., IBM, Kroger, McDonnell Douglas Corp., Office Depot, Pfizer Inc., PPG, Sears Roebuck & Co. and Travelers.

INDUSTRY ALLOCATIONS		
Underweight	*Neutral*	*Overweight*
Paper	*BANKS*	Foods
Construction	Drugs	Investment Banking
Railroad	Airlines	Telephone
Chemicals	Household Furn.	Beverages

continued

INDUSTRY ALLOCATIONS		
Underweight	*Neutral*	*Overweight*
Automobiles	Oil	***HEALTH CARE***
Trucking	***TECH-COMP. SOFTWR.***	***TECH-COMMUN. EQUIP.***
Steel	Tobacco	Gas
Home-building	***TECH-COMPUTER SYS.***	Household Products
Textiles	Lodging	***TECH-SEMI CONDUCTORS***
Machinery		Entertainment
Retail		Insurance
		Electric Utilities
		Aerospace & Defense

For the Week of April 21, 1997

This should be another good week for the stock market as ***the continued parade of solid earnings reports should move the stock market higher.*** I look for the rally to broaden out this week as strong demand in the overall market is expected to have a positive impact across the board. . . . There is no change to my industry weightings this week; however, don't be fooled by the recent strong earnings reports, ***the Automotive Industry is still an underweight.*** Even though most automotive stocks are cheap from a price/earnings relationship, the worst is still ahead for the industry. The strength of the dollar over the last year has not yet been fully reflected in the earnings of this industry. Earnings should weaken as the strong dollar will hurt exports and help Japanese imports. And more importantly, we are in a rising interest rate environment. There is a major lag between the time interest rates move and the impact that move has on auto sales, either positive or negative. But the relationship is there and it is very strong. The Automotive Industry will feel a negative economic impact as a result of the most recent rate hike. If there are more rate hikes on the horizon, that, combined with the strong dollar, should continue to spell trouble for the Automotive Industry (in addition, labor conflicts are rising in this industry and slowdown/shut-downs seem to be the order of the day). . . . Despite the global slowdown in defense spending ***the***

Aerospace/Defense Industry remains an industry overweight. . . . Two fundamental issues should continue to drive the aerospace component of the Aerospace/Defense Industry. The first is global air traffic demand. Global air traffic is being driven by both the business travelers as everyone now has a global focus and leisure travelers who have stepped up their travel pace as air safety/terrorist issues now seem to have been removed from most global travelers' minds. Second, safety as well as noise and air pollution regulation will continue to drive demand to replace older aircraft. It is interesting to note that this safety and noise focus is not just in the United States, but Europe as well.

INDUSTRY ALLOCATIONS		
Underweight	*Neutral*	*Overweight*
Paper	Banks	Foods
Construction	Drugs	Investment Banking
Railroad	Airlines	Telephone
Chemicals	Household Furn.	Beverages
AUTOMOBILES	Oil	Health Care
Trucking	Tech-Comp. Softwr.	Tech-Commun. Equip.
Steel	Tobacco	Gas
Home-building	Tech-Computer Sys.	Household Products
Textiles	Lodging	Tech-Semi Conductors
Machinery		Entertainment
Retail		Insurance
		Electric Utilities
		AEROSPACE & DEFENSE

For the Week of April 28, 1997

This should be another good week for the final stage of earnings reports season. *The overall direction of the stock market this week, however, will be determined by economic releases not earnings releases.* If there are no major surprises on the economic front, I expect the trend of strong earnings reports to continue to push the market toward 7,000 and beyond. If we do get any major surprises on the economic front, expect the stock market to overreact on the downside to interest rate hike fears. . . . There is no change to my industry weightings this week; however, with all of the focus on interest rates, expect the interest sensitive industries and subsectors like Biotechnology to have an especially volatile week. When the stock market becomes concerned about interest rates, industry fundamentals no longer matter. Despite the improving pipeline of biotechnology products—along with the ongoing great news from the Public Policy front—comprehensive health care reform appears dead while the ongoing reform at the Food and Drug Administration to streamline the process of new technology approvals is moving ahead at breakneck speed. *Look for Biotechnology stocks to lead the stock market sell-off if nervous investors free the market due to interest rate fears.* The industry is driven in part by the perceived illiquidity of this narrow market.

INDUSTRY ALLOCATIONS		
Underweight	*Neutral*	*Overweight*
Paper	Banks	Foods
Construction	Drugs	Investment Banking
Railroad	Airlines	Telephone
Chemicals	Household Furn.	Beverages
Automobiles	Oil	Health Care
Trucking	Tech-Comp. Softwr.	Tech-Commun. Equip.
Steel	Tobacco	Gas
Home-building	Tech-Computer Sys.	Household Products
Textiles	Lodging	Tech-Semi Conductors
Machinery		Entertainment
Retail		Insurance
		Electric Utilities
		Aerospace & Defense

For the Week of May 5, 1997

I expect the stock market to stay on economic red alert. ***Wherever the economic releases and bond market lead, expect the stock market to follow closely behind.*** It's the economy, stupid, (remember President Clinton's battle cry) not earnings that will once again this week determine the direction of the stock market. Even though earnings releases will continue to trickle in this week, they will be dominated by the focus on the economic calendar. While earnings releases will move individual stocks, industries and the overall market will be moved by interest rate fears or the lack thereof. . . . While the overall market worries about rates, I expect the real activities to be in industry rotation. ***There are two changes to my industry allocations as I move both Gas and Electric Utilities from Overweight to Neutral.*** With the economy running strong (despite last week's weaker than expected employment number) and interest rates on the rise, this defensive industry play is unwinding. I have stayed with these industries longer than most in this strong economic environment. My unwavering support for these industries was due to the combination of attractive valuations and stable fundamentals. In addition, the landscape of these industries provide tremendous opportunities. I am strongly convinced that the consolidation in both the Gas and Electric Utility Industries will continue. This consolidation means great merger and acquisition activity which should equate into greater growth potential for the new formed entity. . . . The Tobacco Industry goes global as the talks regarding a potential settlement in the U.S. now open the question to what are the international risks that will follow any U.S. settlement. I believe the answer is none, and ***I continue to hold Tobacco as Neutral in my industry allocations.*** The reason for my confidence in no international impact as a follow-up to any U.S. settlement is housed in the uniqueness of our legal system. Two overwhelming issues will play down the global risk. First, there is no such thing as punitive damages outside of the United States. This legal penalty is a United States phenomenon. Outside of the United States, the courts cannot punish (with punitive damages) a manufacturer. Without big punitive damages, the real economic benefits of litigation disappear. Second, the structure of class-action suits does not exist outside the United States either. Without the potential for big class action suits again the potential economic benefits are greatly reduced. The worst will be over for the Tobacco Industry once they get through the mine fields in the United States legal system.

INDUSTRY ALLOCATIONS		
Underweight	*Neutral*	*Overweight*
Paper	Banks	Foods
Construction	Drugs	Investment Banking
Railroad	Airlines	Telephone
Chemicals	Household Furn.	Beverages
Automobiles	Oil	Health Care
Trucking	Tech-Comp. Softwr.	Tech-Commun. Equip.
Steel	*TOBACCO*	Household Products
Home-building	Tech-Computer Sys.	Tech-Semi Conductors
Textiles	Lodging	Entertainment
Machinery	*GAS*	Insurance
Retail	*ELECTRIC UTILITIES*	Aerospace & Defense

For the Week of May 12, 1997

Look for a wild ride from the stock market again this week. Even though earnings reports will continue to trickle in (does earnings season ever really end), it's the economy that will drive the market once again this week. Each economic release will be interpreted by the stock market as either the final reason to be bullish or bearish on interest rates. ***Expect the interest rate sensitive industries, especially the financial services area, to have an extremely volatile week.*** . . . Also the announcement of the Capital Gains Tax cut effective date of May 7, 1997 by Senator Roth and Congressman Archer could add some volatility to the market this week as well. I would caution anyone not to make a decision on selling stocks based on this May 7th effective date. Until the actual legislation is written and adopted, no one knows when the effective date will be! Remember, it has already changed once, what makes you think that it won't change again. It was the exact same Senator Roth and Congressman Archer who earlier in the year said any Capital Gains Tax legislation will have an effective date of January 1, 1997. We moved from January 1, 1997 to May 7, 1997, in the blink of an eye. When the other eye blinks, the effective date just may be October 1, 1997 (which by the way would coincide with the start of the fiscal year for the Federal Government). . . . There is only one change to my industry allocation this week as I *move Health Care from Overweight to Neutral*. With the details of the recent balanced budget agreement coming to light, it has become very clear that the Health Care Industry will feel the most pain in balancing the budget. I think that Health Care Reform "Lite" is here. As the legislation drafting process begins, I look for all aspects of the Health Care Industry to be fair game. First on the list are Health Maintenance Organizations, followed by hospitals, physicians and physician groups, medical equipment providers and even long-term care facilities. It is way too early to speculate on what will finally be "in" or "out" of any final legislation. The only thing that we know for sure is that health care has been targeted. As the process evolves, I expect this sector to become extremely volatile with most of the risk being on the down side.

INDUSTRY ALLOCATIONS		
Underweight	*Neutral*	*Overweight*
Automobiles	Airlines	Aerospace & Defense
Chemicals	Banks	Beverages
Construction	Drugs	Entertainment
Home-building	Electric Utilities	Foods
Machinery	Gas	Household Products
Paper	*HEALTH CARE*	Insurance
Railroad	Household Furn.	Investment Banking
Retail	Lodging	Telephone
Steel	Oil	Tech-Commun. Equip.
Trucking	Tech-Comp. Softwr.	Tech-Semi Conductors
	Tobacco	
	Tech-Computer Sys.	

For the Week of May 19, 1997

I do not expect the stock market to begin another 10% correction (actually 9.8%) after the FOMC raises interest rates. The last stock market mini correction from March 11 to April 11 was fueled by more than just the FOMC's 25 basis point interest rate hike. In addition to the interest rate hike, there was growing pessimism that first quarter earnings would be weaker than expected and that the continued strong rise in the dollar would eat future profits, especially from the "blue chip" multinationals. We simply don't have those same fears today. First quarter earnings not only hit expectations, they actually exceeded them. Secondly, the recent fall of the dollar has removed the concern regarding currency deterioration of future profits as well. Thus, *I expect only a one to two percent correction at most following this rate increase*. Then the market will reclaim its loses immediately. The direction of the market after that will be determined by second quarter earnings, which by the way will be solid. . . . There is no change in my industry allocations this week; however, *I am putting the Airline Industry on special watch*. My renewed concern with the Airline Industry centers around the proposed balanced budget. Currently, the major air carriers and the discount air carriers are fighting over the airline ticket tax that is part of the balanced budget deal. At issue is the fact that most of the major carriers do not feel that the discount carriers pay their "fair" share of airport operations. This is due to the fact that the airline tax is based on ticket prices and because of their low ticket prices, they pay a lower tax. The discount carriers counter with their argument that their low fares enable more people to fly which brings more people to the airport to use parking, buy concessions, etc., etc. The longer this battle continues, the longer Congress will be required to focus on it. Given the opportunity to focus long enough, my fear is that Congress may eventually realize that the airline tax pays for only 64% of the Federal Aviation Administration (FAA) operations. The rest is paid by Congress (actually the Federal Government). The old $64,000 question may become the new 64% question when some Congressman demands 100%, not just 64%, from the Airline Industry to fund the FAA. When two components within the same industry take their battles to Washington, they usually both come back losers.

INDUSTRY ALLOCATIONS		
Underweight	*Neutral*	*Overweight*
Automobiles	*AIRLINES*	Aerospace & Defense
Chemicals	Banks	Beverages
Construction	Drugs	Entertainment
Home-building	Electric Utilities	Foods
Machinery	Gas	Household Products
Paper	Health Care	Insurance
Railroad	Household Furn.	Investment Banking
Retail	Lodging	Telephone
Steel	Oil	Tech-Commun. Equip.
Trucking	Tech-Comp. Softwr.	Tech-Semi Conductors
	Tobacco	
	Tech-Computer Sys.	

For the Week of May 26, 1997

The stock market will make its moves based on the economy this week as there are very few earnings releases and none with the potential to have industry-wide ramifications, let alone market-wide impacts. Like everyone else, the focus of the stock market for the next few weeks will be trying to anticipate the next FOMC move. *Unless there are major economic surprises, it should be a rather quiet week in the stock market and I would expect the market to trade in a rather narrow range. . . .* There is no change in my industry allocations this week; however, *I look for the Banking Industry to outperform the overall market over the next few weeks.* With the consensus of the market not expecting the FOMC to raise interest rates anytime soon, bank stocks will begin to appear on everyone's radar screen again. In addition, I expect a great deal of momentum to build up in the entire financial services area—especially banks— regarding reform and further deregulation. There is no doubt in my mind that the removal of Glass-Steagall's banking securities "Chinese Wall," as well as allowing banks into the Insurance Industry, are both a done deal. However, this is the beginning and not the end. The landscape of the Financial Services Industry will continue its dramatic evolution. The lines will become so blurred, it will be difficult to tell a commercial bank from an investment bank, from an insurance company, from a savings and loan, from a credit union, from a mutual fund company, etc., etc. When the dust finally settles, look for the Banking Industry to be the big winner.

INDUSTRY ALLOCATIONS		
Underweight	*Neutral*	*Overweight*
Automobiles	Airlines	Aerospace & Defense
Chemicals	**BANKS**	Beverages
Construction	Drugs	Entertainment
Home-building	Electric Utilities	Foods
Machinery	Gas	Household Products
Paper	Health Care	Insurance
Railroad	Household Furnishings	Investment Banking
Retail	Lodging	Telephone
Steel	Oil	Tech-Commun. Equip.
Trucking	Tech-Comp. Softwr.	Tech-Semi Conductors
	Tobacco	
	Tech-Computer Sys.	

For the Week of June 2, 1997

The story in the stock market once again this week is the economy and what the Federal Open Markets Committee (FOMC) will do in July. As we head into June, expect some very choppy trading days in the market. Don't forget, June is the time for second quarter earnings disappointments to be pre-announced, so no news is good news. *The one-two combination of economic releases showing the FOMC needs to raise interest rates along with a few pre-earnings disappointment announcements (we always have at least a few), should cause the market to be more volatile than usual. . . .* There is one change from my industry allocation this week as I move Drugs from Neutral to Overweight. Last week's Roche Holding/Boehringer Mannheim mega-Drug Industry merger will set the wheels in motion for further industry consolidation. *Even though I am still somewhat concerned about the Clinton Administration going after the Drug Industry for Health Care Reform II, it's impossible to deny the strong fundamentals in this industry.* There is improved pricing. There have been important breakthroughs on the new drug front which will also help the bottom line. Meanwhile, the Food and Drug Administration has improved the turnaround time for new drug review and approval which will help companies get new products to the market sooner. And finally, most companies are operating under more efficient cost structures as a result of the scare the original Health Care Reform program put into the industry. When you combine all of these factors with the additional lift that continued mergers will give the group, I feel that the Drug Industry will outperform the overall market the remainder of the year.

INDUSTRY ALLOCATIONS		
Underweight	*Neutral*	*Overweight*
Automobiles	Airlines	Aerospace & Defense
Chemicals	Banks	Beverages
Construction	Electric Utilities	**DRUGS**
Home-building	Gas	Entertainment
Machinery	Health Care	Foods
Paper	Household Furnishings	Household Products
Railroad	Lodging	Insurance
Retail	Oil	Investment Banking
Steel	Tech-Comp. Software	Telephone
Trucking	Tobacco	Tech-Commun. Equip.
	Tech-Computer Systems	Tech-Semi Conductors

For the Week of June 9, 1997

The stock market will find itself once again driven by the fear of a Federal Open Markets Committee (FOMC) rate hike and the fear of weaker corporate earnings. The FOMC rate hike fear will not be made clear to the markets until the end of the week when the three major economic releases are issued. ***The bigger problem to the markets again this week will be the pre-earnings disappointment announcements***. The problem with this new season (I remember when there were just two seasons: earnings season and not earnings season. Now we have three seasons: earnings season, pre-earnings disappointment announcement season and not earnings season) is that it only presents one side of the story and that story is bad. You see, the only pre-earnings announcements that have any impact on the markets before earnings are actually released are the disappointments. With no earnings reports or bellwether economic releases to offset this focus, the driving force in the stock market this week just may be the unscheduled, unplanned wild card called pre-earnings disappointment announcements. . . . ***I expect the Small Cap market to continue to show signs of strength and we can thank Congress for that***. The Small Cap recovery actually began in early May when the Balanced Budget Agreement (including a Capital Gains Tax cut) was announced. Remember, you don't buy a small cap stock for the dividends, you buy it for the capital gains; and if the Capital Gains Tax rate goes down, the overall return on small cap stocks will go up . . . There are no changes from my industry allocations this week; however, don't forget as small cap stocks go so goes the Technology Industry. Remember the small cap market is dominated by the Technology Industry, thus any movement in that Small Cap market should bode well for the overall Technology Industries.

INDUSTRY ALLOCATIONS		
Underweight	*Neutral*	*Overweight*
Automobiles	Airlines	Aerospace & Defense
Chemicals	Banks	Beverages
Construction	Electric Utilities	Drugs
Home-building	Gas	Entertainment
Machinery	Health Care	Foods

continued

INDUSTRY ALLOCATIONS		
Underweight	*Neutral*	*Overweight*
Paper	Household Furnishings	Household Products
Railroad	Lodging	Insurance
Retail	Oil	Investment Banking
Steel	*TECH-COMP. SOFTWARE*	Telephone
Trucking	Tobacco	*TECH-COMMUN. EQUIP.*
	TECH-COMPUTER SYSTEMS	*TECH-SEMI CONDUCTORS*

For the Week of June 30, 1997

The focus of the stock market this week will once again be driven by the fear of a FOMC rate hike and how that rate hike could weaken corporate earnings and profits. There is also substantial risk that we will be hit with another round of pre-earnings disappointment announcements as the second quarter draws to a close and the earnings releases for that quarter are set to hit the markets shortly. . . . *I expect the Drug Industry to have a strong second half of the year by outperforming overall markets.* As the details of the balanced budget agreement blue print continue to circulate, it appears that this plan is not going to look to the Drug Industry in the same negative financial way that President Clinton's ill-advised Health Care Reform Plan did a few years ago. This was a major bullet that the Drug Industry just dodged. Secondly, we sometimes forget the strong fundamentals in this industry that are being driven by our country's aging baby boomers. Children age five and under, on average, receive eight prescription drugs per year. After age five and continuing for the next forty years, that usage of prescription drugs trends downward. Then at age forty-five, the trend reverses itself and prescription drug usage continues back upward to a point that at age seventy-six the average person takes eighteen prescription drugs annually. The graying of America presents strong demand fundamental not just for this year, but for many years to come!

INDUSTRY ALLOCATIONS		
Underweight	*Neutral*	*Overweight*
Automobiles	Airlines	Aerospace & Defense
Chemicals	Banks	Beverages
Construction	Electric Utilities	*DRUGS*
Home-building	Gas	Entertainment
Machinery	Health Care	Foods
Paper	Household Furnishings	Household Products
Railroad	Lodging	Insurance
Retail	Oil	Investment Banking
Steel	Tech-Comp. Software	Telephone
Trucking	Tobacco	Tech-Commun. Equip.
	Tech-Computer Systems	Tech-Semi Conductors

For the Week of July 7, 1997

This should be a very quiet week for the stock market. *Earnings season has not yet begun for the second quarter and a very light economic calendar should combine to keep the market trading in a very narrow range this week.* . . . I expect that the story in the stock market this week will be one of rotation, aligning investments with the industries that should out-perform the overall market. *Don't be fooled by our rather strong economy; the Paper Industry should continue to under perform the overall market.* This industry has not been able to implement any substantial rate hikes. In addition, the wood component of this industry is very closely tied to the housing market. As housing begins to slow down, this home building contraction will put a big hit on the Paper Industry. . . . Look for the Tobacco Industry to take a one-two punch this week from Washington. *I expect downward movement in the Tobacco Industry stocks this week as all of the news will be bad.* First of all, the highly influential Koop-Kessler Commission will step up their political attack on numerous provisions in the proposed tobacco settlement. Top on the list is making sure that the

Food and Drug Administration's authority over nicotine remains in tack. When the Koop-Kessler Commission gets done taking shots at the proposed settlement, no one in the market will think the settlement will ever win Congressional approval (which by the way it won't). As if this is not bad enough, look for the Conference Committee on the tax bill to look to the Tobacco Industry as the first source to hit with higher taxes if more revenue is needed to balance the proposed tax cuts.

INDUSTRY ALLOCATIONS		
Underweight	*Neutral*	*Overweight*
Automobiles	Airlines	Aerospace & Defense
Chemicals	Banks	Beverages
Construction	Electric Utilities	Drugs
Home-building	Gas	Entertainment
Machinery	Household Furnishings	Foods
PAPER	Houschold Products	Health Care
Railroad	Lodging	Insurance
Retail	Oil	Investment Banking
Steel	Tech-Comp. Software	Telephone
Trucking	*TOBACCO*	Tech-Commun. Equip.
	Tech-Computer Systems	Tech-Semi Conductors

For the Week of July 14, 1997

The second quarter earnings' season is in full swing and the stock market will focus all of its attention on earnings and not have to worry about the economy, at least for a while. *I expect the Second Quarter Earnings' reports to exceed analysts' forecasts.* The story of the market is not whether you are in or not in. The story continues to be where are you in? In other words, industry rotation will be the key this earnings season. I am making two changes to my industry allocations this week based on what I feel will be the industries that surprise on the upside and the downside. First, I'm moving Health Care from Neutral to Overweight. *The Health Care Industry should lead the market with higher than expected earnings.* With an economy that slowed down in the second quarter, the demand variable in this industry remained very strong. Next, I'm moving Household Products from Overweight to Neutral. *The Household Products Industry should lag the markets as this industry will even have trouble just meeting analysts' expectations.* With no pricing flexibility, margins have slipped on the Household Products front. When pricing and margins slip, so do earnings.

INDUSTRY ALLOCATIONS		
Underweight	*Neutral*	*Overweight*
Automobiles	Airlines	Aerospace & Defense
Chemicals	Banks	Beverages
Construction	Electric Utilities	Drugs
Home-building	Gas	Entertainment
Machinery	Household Furnishings	Foods
Paper	*HOUSEHOLD PRODUCTS*	*HEALTH CARE*
Railroad	Lodging	Insurance
Retail	Oil	Investment Banking
Steel	Tech-Comp. Software	Telephone
Trucking	Tobacco	Tech-Commun. Equip.
	Tech-Computer Systems	Tech-Semi Conductors

For the Week of July 21, 1997

As earnings' season continues, *I look for most industries to post better than expected earnings.* This continued string of strong earnings should continue to move the market higher. The foreign flow of capital into our stock market will continue to serve as a turbo-charge that continues to push our markets higher. The story behind our sudden surge over 8,000 on the Dow Jones Industrial Average last week is not because of something happening in the United States, but rather, it was because of something happening in Europe. *Our stock market has served as magnet, attracting capital from European markets due to the political clouds of uncertainty.* The entire issue of whether the

European Monetary Union will happen or not has become very clouded after the elections in France. In fact, the entire political landscape in Europe has taken a dramatic shift to the "left" leaving investors with a lot of unanswered questions. Even Germany, the most stable of all European countries, continues to play accounting games in an attempt to meet the financial criteria necessary for the Common Currency Union. Every time there is another headline about high unemployment and rising government deficits throughout Europe, foreign investors look across the ocean where our unemployment hovers at almost 25 year lows and our budget deficit is almost nonexistent. If we measure our deficit as a percent of Gross Domestic Product (GDP), it is less than 1%. Europe just can't compete with the report card that the United States has put together. The story behind 8,000 is not just earnings, it's earnings plus EMU. That one-two combination put the market over 8,000 faster than anyone expected. With no end in sight (in the short run) for the problems in Europe, I look for foreign capital to continue to turbo-charge our markets. Forget 9,000; the next stop is 10,000 by the end of 1998.

INDUSTRY ALLOCATIONS		
Underweight	**Neutral**	**Overweight**
Automobiles	Airlines	Aerospace & Defense
Chemicals	Banks	Beverages
Construction	Electric Utilities	Drugs
Home-building	Gas	Entertainment
Machinery	Household Furnishings	Foods
Paper	Household Products	Health Care
Railroad	Lodging	Insurance
Retail	Oil	Investment Banking
Steel	Tech-Comp. Software	Telephone
Trucking	Tobacco	Tech-Commun. Equip.
	Tech-Computer Systems	Tech-Semi Conductors

For the Week of July 28, 1997

Earnings' season continues this week, and once again, I expect more positive earnings' surprises. Although with almost everyone expecting companies to beat their earnings' estimates, is it really a "surprise" when they actually do it? . . . . I think that the markets may have underestimated the significance of the Dow Jones Industrial Average busting through 8,000. Breaking two milestones in the same year (we crossed 7,000 on February 13th) will cause some investors to take some profits off the table. Thus, I think that the stock market may hover around 8,000 for the near term. *In fact, we may break 8,000 then fall back and then break it again several times before we are ready to move on to the next plateau.* This narrow market range would be no different from what happened when we crossed 7,000 earlier in the year. . . . There is no change in my industry allocations this week; however, I am highlighting the Electric Utility Industry. Investing in Electric Utilities can be simplified by focusing on two risks: interest rate risk and deregulation risk. While the regulatory landscape of the Electric Utility Industry continues to change, the interest rate risk may be disappearing for at least the remainder of the year. In a falling or flat interest rate environment (like the one we are currently in), electric utilities should perform quite nicely. Even though the regulatory concern remains, remember the focus is really deregulation, which means increased competition which tends to drive even more mergers and acquisitions or at the very least, strategic alliances. This activity tends to lift the entire industry as it really doesn't matter if you are the "buyer" or the "buyee": the combined firm will be better and stronger and thus, more profitable. In addition, with all of the concern about the high valuation of stocks today, the Electric Utility Industry is a welcome relief. As an industry the Electric Utilities have some of the lowest industry wide price/earnings' ratios anywhere in the stock market today.

INDUSTRY ALLOCATIONS		
Underweight	*Neutral*	*Overweight*
Automobiles	Airlines	Aerospace & Defense
Chemicals	Banks	Beverages
Construction	*ELECTRIC UTILITIES*	Drugs
Home-building	Gas	Entertainment

continued

INDUSTRY ALLOCATIONS		
Underweight	*Neutral*	*Overweight*
Machinery	Household Furnishings	Foods
Paper	Household Products	Health Care
Railroad	Lodging	Insurance
Retail	Oil	Investment Banking
Steel	Tech-Comp. Software	Telephone
Trucking	Tobacco	Tech-Commun. Equip.
	Tech-Computer Systems	Tech-Semi Conductors

For the Week of August 4, 1997

As earnings season continues to wind down, earnings reports continue to trickle in. Does it ever stop?. . . . ***The stock market will become very sensitive to economic releases and bond market movements in the weeks ahead.*** With precious few earnings reports left to worry about, the stock market has to worry about the economy. The stock market is typically flat or experiences minor corrections when all it has to focus on is the economy because no matter what the economic indicators show us regarding the economy, the stock market interprets it as bad news. You see, if the economy stays strong, that increases the risk of the Federal Reserve Board raising rates which means the cost of doing business goes up and earnings will go down, thus the market goes down. If on the other hand, the economy slows, that increases the risk that demand will weaken and weaker demand usually means a decrease in earnings and as we know, when earnings go down, the market goes down. I can't wait for the next quarter's earning's season to begin. . . . There is one change in my industry allocations this week as I move Retail from Underweight to Neutral. Even though I remain very concerned about the tight pricing and intense competition in this industry, there are other short-term factors that warrant moving it from an underweight. First, consumer spending appears to be rebounding nicely in the third quarter. I feel that this rebound from the second quarter should stay in place the entire second half of 1997. In times of a low interest rate environment and low unemployment levels (record lows) we typically see high consumer confidence. That is exactly the environment that we find ourselves in today. And remember, a confident consumer spends money. And when a consumer spends money, their first stop is usually retail. Secondly, let's not forget what's happening to the overall stock market. There is a strong correlation between rapid swings in the stock market as measured by the Dow Jones Industrial Average and Retail Sales. *The record run up in the stock market implies that we can expect a run up in Retail Sales.* Don't forget that when a consumer finds out that they are richer (at least on paper anyway) as a result of the stock market move, they will spend the money without liquidating the stock.

INDUSTRY ALLOCATIONS		
Underweight	*Neutral*	*Overweight*
Automobiles	Airlines	Aerospace & Defense
Chemicals	Banks	Beverages
Construction	Electric Utilities	Drugs
Home-building	Gas	Entertainment
Machinery	Household Furnishings	Foods
Paper	Household Products	Health Care
Railroad	Lodging	Insurance
Steel	Oil	Investment Banking
Trucking	*RETAIL*	Telephone
	Tech-Comp. Software	Tech-Commun. Equip.
	Tobacco	Tech-Semi Conductors
	Tech-Computer Systems	

For the Week of August 18, 1997

We are entering into a volatile time for the stock market. With second quarter earnings season now behind us, the market will have to wait a while until third quarter earnings are released to determine which direction the market will take for the remainder of the year. Until earnings' season begins again, the stock market will be taking its cue from three different fronts and two of the three are bad. From the first front we have pre-earnings' releases. This should more appropriately be labeled pre-earnings "disappointment" releases as the clear majority of pre-releases are intended to let the markets know ahead of time that bad news is coming. The second front is from unexpected events. These events run the full spectrum of issues such as labor problems (UPS strike), litigation news (Tobacco Industry lawsuits), terrorist acts, natural disasters, etc., etc. Once again, a majority of these events tend to be negative for the market. The third and final front is from the bond market. Frantically searching for something to trade off of, if there is nothing from the other two fronts, stocks will follow the lead of the bond market which will follow the economy. Mixed economic signals will mean a volatile bond market which in turn will mean a volatile stock market.

INDUSTRY ALLOCATIONS		
Underweight	*Neutral*	*Overweight*
Automobiles	Airlines	Aerospace & Defense
Chemicals	Banks	Beverages
Construction	Electric Utilities	Drugs
Home-building	Gas	Entertainment
Machinery	Household Furnishings	Foods
Paper	Household Products	Health Care
Railroad	Lodging	Insurance
Steel	Oil	Investment Banking
Trucking	Retail	Telephone
	Tech-Comp. Software	Tech-Commun. Equip.
	Tobacco	Tech-Semi Conductors
	Tech-Computer Systems	

For the Week of August 25, 1997

I expect the stock market to remain extremely volatile as it continues to guess where the economy is going, and what does that mean for earnings and interest rates? I would suggest keeping one eye on the dollar and the other on the bond markets. The recent gyrations in the market began when the dollar weakened which raised concern that foreigners may become sellers of U.S. Treasury Bonds which then caused the bond market to weaken. The weak dollar and bond market served as a noose around the neck of the stock market. I expect this volatile relationship to stay on track until Third Quarter Earnings' Season begins. . . . Although I am not changing any of my industry allocations, I am highlighting two developments. First, even though the Retail Industry remains very, very competitive, *I think we are going to have a "blow-out" back-to-school sale season which will be very positive for retailers* across the board. All of the economic and financial stars are aligned when you compare where we are beginning this back-to-school season as opposed to where we were last year at this time. Consumer Confidence is higher, the unemployment rate is lower, the Dow Jones Industrial Average is higher, the Consumer Price Index is lower, the Yield on the 30-year Treasury Bond is lower and the price of oil is even lower. You simply could not ask for anything more to set this up as one of the best back-to-school seasons yet. . . . The Defense Industry should benefit from the new Chairman of the Joint Chiefs of Staff, General Shelton. General Shelton is the first chairman with direct experience in counter-terrorism. I expect him to push the United States to become the world leader in counter-terrorism technology. Becoming the world's leader in counter-terrorism will find great support in Congress as well as tremendous appeal on Main Street. When both the politicians and their voters get behind an issue, you can expect the money flow to soon follow. Under General Shelton's direction, *I expect huge increases in Department of Defense funding for terrorism which could be an unexpected boost to the Defense Industry.*

INDUSTRY ALLOCATIONS		
Underweight	*Neutral*	*Overweight*
Automobiles	Airlines	***AEROSPACE & DEFENSE***
Chemicals	Banks	Beverages
Construction	Electric Utilities	Drugs
Home-building	Gas	Entertainment
Machinery	Household Furnishings	Foods
Paper	Household Products	Health Care

continued

INDUSTRY ALLOCATIONS		
Underweight	*Neutral*	*Overweight*
Railroad	Lodging	Insurance
Steel	Oil	Investment Banking
Trucking	*RETAIL*	Telephone
	Tech-Comp. Software	Tech-Commun. Equip.
	Tobacco	Tech-Semi Conductors
	Tech-Computer Systems	

For the Week of September 1, 1997

Summer may be officially over; however, the dog-days of the summer stock market are not. *I expect the market to remain extremely vulnerable this week to news from the economic front.* Last week's stronger than expected revision to the Second Quarter Gross Domestic Product release has thrown the stock market an unexpected one-two punch. First, with the economy growing at a blistering 3.6% pace, the consensus of the market is quickly shifting to one that expects the Federal Reserve Board to raise interest rates, if not at their next meeting on September 30th, certainly sometime between now and the end of the year. A rise in interest rates, bringing with it the fear of the cost of doing business, has now risen which means that profits will fall. Second, Wall Street economists are now frantically revising their third quarter Gross Domestic Product economic forecast downward. The consensus is quickly becoming that if we had a strong second quarter of almost 4% growth, that means the third quarter will be much weaker. A slower economy in the third quarter means less economic activity, which again means lower corporate profits. . . . *I expect the rotation in the market to continue away from the "Blue Chips" and into the Small Capitalization stocks* at least until third quarter earnings' season begins. Two forces are driving this shift. First is the continued effect that the reduction of the Capital Gains Tax from 28% to 20% is having on investors' preferences. Investors see this tax cut as a turbo-charge to their total returns for investment in the dividend poor, capital gains rich, small cap stock universe. Second, the Blue Chip stocks have received a very serious psychological blow that can not be turned around until earnings come out. When the bluest of the Blue Chips,

Coca-Cola and Gillette talk about earnings' disappointments, the psychological impact is much greater than the actual one. Investors had deemed these companies immune from any earnings' downturn. The real impact is that now investors fear that if it can happen to Coke or Gillette, it can happen to any Blue Chip stock.

INDUSTRY ALLOCATIONS		
Underweight	*Neutral*	*Overweight*
Automobiles	Airlines	Aerospace & Defense
Chemicals	Banks	Beverages
Construction	Electric Utilities	Drugs
Home-building	Gas	Entertainment
Machinery	Household Furnishings	Foods
Paper	Household Products	Health Care
Railroad	Lodging	Insurance
Steel	Oil	Investment Banking
Trucking	Retail	Telephone
	Tech-Comp. Software	Tech-Commun. Equip.
	Tobacco	Tech-Semi Conductors
	Tech-Computer Systems	

For the Week of September 8, 1997

I think that the story in the market will continue to be one of rotation. Rotation both between industries as well as capitalization levels. The Capital Gains Tax correction is over. The most recent sell-off in the stock market started as a result of the Capital Gains Tax cut enacted by Congress. Once this minor correction began, it was made worse by some nervous investors who were afraid that their capital gains were disappearing, so they too rushed to the market and made the correction much worse than it should have been. *We can now close the book on the short term impact of the Capital Gains Tax cut on the stock market.* Our focus now needs to be on the long-term impact. I firmly believe that the long-term impact of the Capital Gains Tax cut will continue to be a rotation into smaller capitalized stocks. I think that these stocks could be clearly poised to outperform the market in the fourth quarter.

INDUSTRY ALLOCATIONS		
Underweight	*Neutral*	*Overweight*
Automobiles	Airlines	Aerospace & Defense
Chemicals	Banks	Beverages
Construction	Electric Utilities	Drugs
Home-building	Gas	Entertainment
Machinery	Household Furnishings	Foods
Paper	Household Products	Health Care
Railroad	Lodging	Insurance
Steel	Oil	Investment Banking
Trucking	Retail	Telephone
	Tech-Comp. Software	Tech-Commun. Equip.
	Tobacco	Tech-Semi Conductors
	Tech-Computer Systems	

For the Week of September 15, 1997

The combination of a strong economy and cheap prices should combine to lift cyclical stocks the remainder of the year. The robust economic growth in the second quarter of our economy does not appear to be slowing down substantially in the third quarter. If anything, consumers appear even stronger in the third quarter than they did in the second. This strong economy should bode well for earnings on the wide range of cyclical industries such as Automotive, Home Building, Airlines and Retail. Their strong performance for the remainder of the year, however, may have more to do with price than the economy. Most of these cyclical industries are considerably cheaper than the high priced blue chip consumer multinationals. If you are looking for a bargain, this just might be it . . . The recent volatility in the stock market shows that the market is clearly nervous as it awaits the beginning of earnings' season. The greatest risk to the stock market this week will not come from pre-earnings' releases but rather the rubber-chicken circuit. Three Federal Reserve Bank Presidents (Guynn of Atlanta, Jordan of Cleveland and Stern of Minneapolis) are all giving a public speech on Monday. With Alan Greenspan's stock market valuation model the talk of Wall Street, I am sure each of these Federal Reserve officials will be asked to tell us if the stock market is too rich. Hold on, I'm not sure how they will answer that question, but I can almost assure you that the answers will not be the same.

INDUSTRY ALLOCATIONS		
Underweight	*Neutral*	*Overweight*
AUTOMOBILES	*AIRLINES*	Aerospace & Defense
Chemicals	Banks	Beverages
Construction	Electric Utilities	Drugs
HOME-BUILDING	Gas	Entertainment
Machinery	Household Furnishings	Foods
Paper	Household Products	Health Care
Railroad	Lodging	Insurance
Steel	Oil	Investment Banking
Trucking	*RETAIL*	Telephone
	Tech-Comp. Software	Tech-Commun. Equip.
	Tobacco	Tech-Semi Conductors
	Tech-Computer Systems	

For the Week of September 22, 1997

The greatest risk to the stock market this week will not be from the economic front, but rather who will be issuing the next pre-earnings report disappointment announcement. If the markets are not hit with any unexpected pre-earnings "shockers" *it could be a rather lackluster week for the stock market* . . . I continue to think that we had or are still having a strong back-to-school retail season and with what appears to be an almost perfect economy, I expect a great Christmas selling season as well, especially with consumer confidence at all time highs. *All of these facts should help the Retail Industry the remainder of the year.* And don't forget how the Taxpayers Relief Act of 1997 helped the Retail Industry. While most market observers overlook the indirect impact the tax act will have because they are too busy worrying about the direct impact on other industries such as Airlines and Tobacco, I feel that the Retail Industry will prosper, not because of anything that specifically happened to it as a result of the tax act, but rather what happened to its consumers. The "Kiddie Tax Credit," the "Education Hope Tax Credit" as well as the education interest deduction together should combine to put more money in the pockets of consumers. When consumers have more disposal income (money in their pockets), their first stop is usually at the retail level.

INDUSTRY ALLOCATIONS		
Underweight	*Neutral*	*Overweight*
Automobiles	Airlines	Aerospace & Defense
Chemicals	Banks	Beverages
Construction	Electric Utilities	Drugs
Home-building	Gas	Entertainment
Machinery	Household Furnishings	Foods
Paper	Household Products	Health Care
Railroad	Lodging	Insurance
Steel	Oil	Investment Banking
Trucking	*RETAIL*	Telephone
	Tech-Comp. Software	Tech-Commun. Equip.
	Tobacco	Tech-Semi Conductors
	Tech-Computer Systems	

For the Week of September 29, 1997

The stock market will be taking its cue from the bond market and the blizzard of economic releases due out this week. Most investors will be on the sidelines fearful of placing any "big bets" until the first signs of this quarter's earnings season start to come in. While most pre-earnings' disappointments have already been announced, there is still the risk that the market could get hit with a few more just before earnings' season begins in full swing. *It could be a very volatile week for the stock market as it usually is when it is left to follow the paranoid bond market* . . . While I am not changing any of my industry allocations, I am putting the Airline Industry "on alert." *I expect a great deal of volatility in the Airline Industry over the next few weeks*, primarily driven by two factors. First, the labor conflict at Continental Airlines is likely to get very ugly this week. I fully expect the union not to settle by October 1, and instead, send out strike authorization ballots to its union membership. This will simply draw a deeper line in the sand. It is this union negotiating ploy of threatening to strike that is the true impact of the UPS settlement. I hope someone informs the union before they strike; comparing United Parcel Service's role in the Parcel Delivery Industry to Continental Airlines role in the Airline Industry would be like comparing a Lexus to a Yugo. The second factor that will fuel volatility into this industry is the reality of just how much this industry got hurt by the recent balanced budget agreement. While much of the focus was on the battle within the industry between regional discount carriers versus major carriers, now that the dust has settled and we have chalked up the score, we realize the entire industry lost. The overall ticket tax and fee structure for the entire industry has been revamped. Over the next five years, this industry will be hit with an additional $3 billion tax bill. In this very cyclical industry, any slowdown in the economy combined with this increased tax liability will pressure both growth and earnings.

INDUSTRY ALLOCATIONS		
Underweight	*Neutral*	*Overweight*
Automobiles	*AIRLINES*	Aerospace & Defense
Chemicals	Banks	Beverages
Construction	Electric Utilities	Drugs
Home-building	Gas	Entertainment

continued

INDUSTRY ALLOCATIONS		
Underweight	*Neutral*	*Overweight*
Machinery	Household Products	Foods
Paper	Household Products Lodging	Health Care
Railroad	Lodging	Insurance
Steel	Oil	Investment Banking
Trucking	Retail	Telephone
	Tech-Comp. Software	Tech-Commun. Equip.
	Tobacco	Tech-Semi Conductors
	Tech-Computer Systems	

For the Week of October 6, 1997

The stock market has made it to the beginning of earnings season for the third quarter as earnings will begin to trickle into the market toward the end of the week. It is always a positive for the stock market when it takes its cues from earnings rather than the economy or the bond market . . . As earnings season is about to begin, *I am moving Banks from Neutral to Overweight as I expect Bank earnings to be very strong.* The combination of the recent decline in interest rates along with the continual consolidation, merger and strategic alliances should all add up to a pretty bullish quarter for bank earnings . . . Looking further ahead into the fourth quarter, *I think that Large Capitalization stocks will begin to make up some ground that they lost recently to the Smaller Capitalization and Mid-capitalization stocks.* Two forces should combine to drive the Large Capitalization stocks back into favor. First, as our economy continues to slow down in the fourth quarter, the psychology of equity investors should begin to shift. When the economy slows, investors look for steady earnings and profit margin stability. Investors seeking steady earnings and profit margin stability will flock to Large Capitalization stocks, not Small or Mid-capitalization stocks. Second, with the current global landscape, I expect foreign investors to continue to be major buyers of United States equities. Foreign investors tend to invest in company names that they recognize and most of the names that they recognize tend to fall in the Large Capitalization asset class.

INDUSTRY ALLOCATIONS		
Underweight	*Neutral*	*Overweight*
Automobiles	Airlines	Aerospace & Defense
Chemicals	Electric Utilities	*BANKS*
Construction	Gas	Beverages
Home-building	Household Furnishings	Drugs
Machinery	Household Products	Entertainment
Paper	Lodging	Foods
Railroad	Oil	Health Care
Steel	Retail	Insurance
Trucking	Tech-Comp. Software	Investment Banking
	Tobacco	Telephone
	Tech-Computer Systems	Tech-Commun. Equip.
		Tech-Semi Conductors

For the Week of October 13, 1997

Earnings' season for the third quarter steps into high gear this week as earnings' reports will flood the markets. *I think that we will have more Earnings' reports that surprise on the high side than we will have disappointments on the low side*. Our economy has remained so much stronger than any economist thought possible in the third quarter. That very strong economy will serve as a great foundation for solid earnings' growth and earnings' season. As earnings reports continue to surprise on the high side across most industries, this market is going to make its end of the year bull run. I think that once earnings' season is behind us, we will have seen the last of the 7,000's on the Dow Jones Industrial Average. This strong earnings' season should send the Dow Jones Industrial Average above the 8,000 level for good and well above 8,250 by the end of the year. In the short run, rhetoric from Alan Greenspan may make the markets go down, however, in the long run, *it doesn't matter what Alan Greenspan says, it matters what the Earnings' reports say and these Earnings' reports once again say the "bull market" is alive and well. Next stop could be 10,000 by the end of 1998.*

INDUSTRY ALLOCATIONS		
Underweight	*Neutral*	*Overweight*
Automobiles	Airlines	Aerospace & Defense
Chemicals	Electric Utilities	Banks
Construction	Gas	Beverages
Home-building	Household Furnishings	Drugs
Machinery	Household Products	Entertainment
Paper	Lodging	Foods
Railroad	Oil	Health Care
Steel	Retail	Insurance
Trucking	Tech-Comp. Software	Investment Banking
	Tobacco	Telephone
	Tech-Computer Systems	Tech-Commun. Equip.
		Tech-Semi Conductors

For the Week of October 20, 1997

Earnings season continues in full swing this week and while I continue to expect a very strong earnings season with more surprises on the high side than disappointments on the downside, it is apparent from last week that no matter how big you are (Merck and Intel), any disappointment will be both swiftly and harshly punished by the markets. One of the reasons for this harsh reaction has been the evolution of a new season called "pre-earnings' report disappointment season," during which companies admit before the quarter ends that they will not be able to meet expectations. The market has now grown to expect everyone to be "in tune" with this new season. The only surprises that the market wants are surprises on the high side. Reflecting on their recent plunge, I'm sure that both Intel and Merck would explore a different market reporting strategy if they were given a second

107

chance . . . *I look for the Electric Utility Industry to post strong gains this earnings' season.* While every industry has their own set of complex issues that will determine overall industry performance, sometimes we tend to make things more complicated than they really need to be. Take the Electric Utility Industry for example. One could get caught up in so many terms and technical issues to worry about that you would have to be an engineer before you could decide to invest in this industry. While there may be times when all of this "noise" is important to focus upon, I suggest focusing on two things or two risks: interest rate risk and deregulation risk. First from the interest rate risk front; remember during the third quarter, we were in a falling interest rate environment; electric utilities perform best in a falling interest rate environment. Second, even though deregulation remains a concern, it is a short-term concern; in the long term, deregulation simply "turbo charges" more strategic alliances and merger and acquisition activity. And don't forget, as a final treat to investors, as an industry, the Electric Utilities have some of the lowest industry wide price/earnings' ratios anywhere in the stock market. These factors should all add up to a great earnings' season for Electric Utilities.

INDUSTRY ALLOCATIONS		
Underweight	*Neutral*	*Overweight*
Automobiles	Airlines	Aerospace & Defense
Chemicals	Electric Utilities	Banks
Construction	Gas	Beverages
Home-building	Household Furnishings	Drugs
Machinery	Household Products	Entertainment
Paper	Lodging	Foods
Railroad	Oil	Health Care
Steel	Retail	Insurance
Trucking	Tech-Comp. Software	Investment Banking
	Tobacco	Telephone
	Tech-Computer Systems	Tech-Commun. Equip.
		Tech-Semi Conductors

108

For the Week of October 27, 1997

This has been a very strong earnings' season with most companies meeting or exceeding analysts' expectations. The market, however, has been caught up in the concern with the Southeast Asia currency and economic meltdown. The concern is more psychological than factual. In other words, the psychology of this meltdown will have a greater influence on the markets than any earnings deterioration as a result of the crisis. While I continue to expect that the markets will have a great deal of concern with our multinational companies, the facts are that the Southeast Asian crisis will have little, if any impact on their profits. The reason is that these economies have simply not matured to the point where they are major consumers globally. In fact, if you combined the entire economies of Thailand, Indonesia, Malaysia, Singapore and the Philippines, they would equal less than 6% of the United States economy. *The impact of a major slowdown in these Asian "Tiger" economies will not have great impact on our multinational companies.* Any potential negative impact is most likely to come from Japan, not Thailand, Indonesia, Malaysia, Singapore or the Philippines. When the economies of these Southeast Asian "Tigers" slow down, that means that they will purchase less exports from Japan. (Remember, Japanese exports to these five countries has more than doubled over the last ten years. In 1987, exports to these five countries accounted for less than 20% of Japan's total exports. Today, they account for more than 40%.) This in turn will slow down the Japanese economy, which means Japan will purchase less exports from the United States. It is this potential slowdown from Japan that could impact our multinational companies; however, this impact is a ripple effect that probably will not be seen for at least a year. In the meantime, as the price of these multinational stocks are driven down due to individual investor nervousness, that could present some excellent discount buying opportunities.

INDUSTRY ALLOCATIONS		
Underweight	*Neutral*	*Overweight*
Automobiles	Airlines	Aerospace & Defense
Chemicals	Electric Utilities	Banks
Construction	Gas	Beverages
Home-building	Household Furnishings	Drugs

continued

INDUSTRY ALLOCATIONS		
Underweight	*Neutral*	*Overweight*
Machinery	Household Products	Entertainment
Paper	Lodging	Foods
Railroad	Oil	Health Care
Steel	Retail	Insurance
Trucking	Tech-Comp. Software	Investment Banking
	Tobacco	Telephone
	Tech-Computer Systems	Tech-Commun. Equip.
		Tech-Semi Conductors

For the Week of November 3, 1997

Once the headlines slow down regarding the currency and economic meltdown in Southeast Asia and now some parts of Latin America, investors will once again focus on earnings. The stock market has had another exceptional earnings' season. The problem is no one is focusing on these great results because of all of the concern with the global meltdowns. As we begin the week, here is the scorecard for third quarter earnings through October 31, 1997. Eighty-seven percent of the companies that comprise the S&P 500 (433 companies) have reported third quarter earnings. Of that total, 54% or 234 companies have exceeded analysts' expectations with their earnings reports. Another 19% or 83 companies met analyst targets. Finally, 116 companies or 27% failed to meet analysts' expectations. *This is a very bullish earnings' season. When 73% of the companies that have reported earnings have met or exceeded analysts' expectations it sets the foundation for a strong profit picture going forward* . . . While I expect companies with heavy exposure to Southeast Asia to come under heavy investor scrutiny, I do not feel that this crisis is going to drag down the entire stock market. Remember, the entire Asia Pacific Rim only accounts for 5% to 6% of all corporate profits. Additionally, less than 10% of our exports as a nation go to the Southeast Asian Tiger economies. In addition, *even the companies that have tremendous direct exposure to Southeast Asia may not be in as bad a shape as it would first appear.* You see, many companies that have significant exposure to

110

Southeast Asia for their revenue and earnings have a limited currency risk because most of their products are actually priced in United States dollars. Second, we need to understand how many American companies do business in Southeast Asia. Many companies ship a large percentage of their products to Southeast Asia in varying stages. Thus, many products are assembled, re-assembled, enhanced, etc., etc., while in Asia and from there are sent to other parts of the world for ultimate consumption of the product. Earnings' deterioration from the Southeast Asia currency and economic crisis may not be as great as the markets first feared.

INDUSTRY ALLOCATIONS		
Underweight	*Neutral*	*Overweight*
Automobiles	Airlines	Aerospace & Defense
Chemicals	Electric Utilities	Banks
Construction	Gas	Beverages
Home-building	Household Furnishings	Drugs
Machinery	Household Products	Entertainment
Paper	Lodging	Foods
Railroad	Oil	Health Care
Steel	Retail	Insurance
Trucking	Tech-Comp. Software	Investment Banking
	Tobacco	Telephone
	Tech-Computer Systems	Tech-Commun. Equip.
		Tech-Semi Conductors

For the Week of November 10, 1997

With earnings season just about over; the stock market will be driven the remainder of the year from two fronts; economic and international. I fully expect the stock market to begin to pay much more attention and react to the major economic releases going forward. These major economic releases will be viewed as a barometer for future rate hikes. And

111

future rate hikes are used as the barometer for future earnings' forecasts. *While I expect the stock market to continue its march to 8,000 by the end of the year, we must remember a stock market with one eye on economic releases tends to be more volatile than a stock market focused on earnings.* We can add to that volatility when we realize that the other eye is on the international markets. The equity markets are not just global; they are global and interrelated. If the meltdown in Southeast Asia proved one thing very clearly it was how all of the equity markets around the globe both relate to and react to one another. The struggle for the past two weeks has been who or, more appropriately, which markets are leading and which are following. As the equity market problems in Hong Kong spilled over into Europe and then the United States, the struggle began to determine who is reacting to who? Will the United States equity market be strong if the Hong Kong market is strong? And in turn, if the European market is strong, does that equate to a stronger Hong Kong market which then leads to the question; who is really leading who? When you throw Latin and South America equity markets into the mix, it is easy to see why the global markets were volatile and nervous. While I expect the markets to remain volatile going forward, one clear difference will be the United States equity market emerging as the global leader and benchmark upon which all other markets will react to (after all, the U.S. equity market accounts for 50% of the total global equity market). Our market will remain very focused and nervous about international news and markets, however, I don't expect the reaction to be as volatile as Gray Monday's market reaction . . . *I am putting the Machinery and Steel Industry on special alert.* Even though I currently have both industries as an Underweight, I expect those industries to feel the brunt of the global economic slowdown in Southeast Asia. In addition, if the crisis in Southeast Asia spills over into Latin and South America, this would simply serve as a one-two punch against the Machinery and Steel Industries.

INDUSTRY ALLOCATIONS		
Underweight	*Neutral*	*Overweight*
Automobiles	Airlines	Aerospace & Defense
Chemicals	Electric Utilities	Banks
Construction	Gas	Beverages
Home-building	Household Furnishings	Drugs

continued

INDUSTRY ALLOCATIONS		
Underweight	*Neutral*	*Overweight*
MACHINERY	Household Products	Entertainment
Paper	Lodging	Foods
Railroad	Oil	Health Care
STEEL	Retail	Insurance
Trucking	Tech-Comp. Software	Investment Banking
	Tobacco	Telephone
	Tech-Computer Systems	Tech-Commun. Equip.
		Tech-Semi Conductors

For the Week of November 17, 1997

It is extremely difficult to keep a perspective of the strong fundamentals in our stock market with all of the external events grabbing the
headlines. First, the situation in Iraq remains very volatile and many
market watchers predict if we do ever have a true "bear" market, it will
be fueled by an event such as this. Second, with the failure of Fast Track
Trade legislation comes the new concern that this will be negative for
multinational companies and will also slow growth to companies that
do business with South and Latin America. And finally, the Bank of
England raises interest rates, which in turn throws the global markets a
curve regarding global rates trending lower or higher. While these
events are important, they are not the story of our stock market. *The
story of our stock market is the search for leadership*. The recent run-up
in our stock market was fueled by the leadership provided by capital
goods' stock and technology stocks. About the only real consensus
emerging out of the crisis in Southeast Asia is that our capital goods
and technology sectors should get hit first and maybe the hardest. With
the wind clearly taken out of the sail of the leadership sectors in our
market, the search begins for new market leadership to emerge. When
the market finds itself searching for leadership between earnings'
seasons, it can tend to produce a more volatile market as any industry's
new leadership can be quickly challenged with a sell-off because that
leadership was not established by earnings, but rather expectation of
future earnings . . . Who knows, maybe retail can lead the way. Most

economists and strategists fear that the recent correction in the stock market that wiped out some of the consumer's wealth will dampen consumer spending, which will in turn dampen the Retail Industry. I do not. I think just the opposite will happen. I felt all along that the high level in the stock market was actually causing a reverse wealth effect. In other words, *instead of people spending because the value of their stocks was increasing, people actually held back spending and invested even more in the stock market* because they were convinced it could only go up. Gray Monday was a wake-up call to remind us that the markets go up and down. No longer do we have to worry about the negative wealth effect. I think that investors will be satisfied with what they have made in the stock market this year and the biggest beneficiary of these satisfied investors could be the Retail Industry.

INDUSTRY ALLOCATIONS		
Underweight	*Neutral*	*Overweight*
Automobiles	Airlines	Aerospace & Defense
Chemicals	Electric Utilities	Banks
Construction	Gas	Beverages
Home-building	Household Furnishings	Drugs
Machinery	Household Products	Entertainment
Paper	Lodging	Foods
Railroad	Oil	Health Care
Steel	*RETAIL*	Insurance
Trucking	Tech-Comp. Software	Investment Banking
	Tobacco	Telephone
	Tech-Computer Systems	Tech-Commun. Equip.
		Tech-Semi Conductors

For the Week of November 24, 1997

I expect the stock market to continue its march toward 8,000 by the end of the year. Last week was a very important one for the psychology of the stock market. On Wednesday, November 19, the Dow Jones Industrial Average had climbed back to where it was before Gray Monday, October 27, 1997. Thus, it took only 26 days to recoup the entire 554 point loss and then some. Contrast that with the 463 days needed to recoup from Black Monday. The market did not recover from its 22.6% October 19, 1987 market correction until January 24, 1989! *In other words, today's market recovered 18 times faster from our Gray Monday correction than it did from Black Monday.* Eighteen times faster, just as a frame of reference for you, is the difference between driving a car 55 miles an hour and 990 miles an hour! As you all know, this was not the first 500 point drop nor will it be the last 500 point drop in the market. This one, however, will serve as a very valuable history lesson for investors. You see, history will show us that the investors who really were hurt by Gray Monday are the ones that thought they could time the market and get out, not the ones who stayed in. Investors with a longer term time horizon have once again been rewarded for their investment discipline. Only this time the reward came 18 times faster. See ya at 8,000! . . . Several events will serve as confidence points for our markets and push it forward. First, the hint of rumors that Japan is considering some sort of government bail-out for its troubled financial system is good news for our stock market. While I don't expect Japan to put into place some massive rescue plan as we did for our failed savings & loan companies, just the mere fact that the government clearly understands the magnitude of the problem and knows that they must do something about it is a positive. Second, Sadam Hussein blinked and the threat of war and skyrocketing oil prices are now greatly diminished. And finally, the latest round of mega mergers means that the market may not be over valued after all. You see when a market is truly over valued, merger and acquisition activity tends to come to a grinding halt. That is certainly not the case in our markets today. With First Union's bid to acquire CoreStates followed by Merrill Lynch's bid to acquire Mercury Asset Management, maybe valuations are not as extended as we thought. I look for this latest round of major mergers to snowball and trigger even more merger and acquisition activity.

INDUSTRY ALLOCATIONS		
Underweight	*Neutral*	*Overweight*
Automobiles	Airlines	Aerospace & Defense
Chemicals	Electric Utilities	Banks
Construction	Gas	Beverages
Home-building	Household Furnishings	Drugs
Machinery	Household Products	Entertainment
Paper	Lodging	Foods
Railroad	Oil	Health Care
Steel	Retail	Insurance
Trucking	Tech-Comp. Software	Investment Banking
	Tobacco	Telephone
	Tech-Computer Systems	Tech-Commun. Equip.
		Tech-Semi Conductors

For the Week of December 8, 1997

While I expect the market to trade in a rather narrow trading range the remainder of the year, *the story in our markets will be one of "rotation" as we continue our search for leadership* to take the markets to the next level . . . I am moving the Oil Industry from a "Neutral" allocation to an "Underweight." Over the next six months *I clearly expect the price of oil to continue its downward trend which will really begin to put the pinch on the Oil Industries' earnings' picture*. The fact that OPEC recently decided to lift the production of oil by 2.5 million barrels a day will simply flood the market with even more oil; which in turn, will push prices even lower. And while the situation in Iraq will always remain volatile, the current somewhat state of calm means that the United Nations "food for oil" deal with Iraq is also back on track. This deal will also flood the market with a new supply of oil . . . *While I am not changing my allocation for Electric Utilities, I am putting that industry on alert*. The industry had had a nice run over the past several months, however, I fear next year could be a different story. My concern is nothing that the industry did, but rather something that President Clinton and Congress did a few months back. The recent Taxpayer Relief Act of 1997 in which the Capital Gains Tax Rate was cut, could have an adverse impact on all high dividend paying stocks of which the Electric Utility Industry is the leader. You see, prior to the Capital Gains Tax cut, investors didn't really care if they were rewarded with a dividend (which was taxed at the top rate of 39.6%) or a capital gains (which was taxed at a top rate of 28%). In most investors' minds, these rates were so close together, it didn't really matter. Well, that is certainly not the case anymore. Investors that receive dividends will still be taxed at the highest rate of 39.6%; however, if you were to receive capital gains instead, you would only be taxed at 20%. The further the spread between the highest Capital Gains Tax rate and the highest "ordinary income tax rate" (which is where dividends fall) the less investors want dividend producing industries. Also, the year after a Capital Gains Tax cut has always been a difficult one for the Electric Utility Industry.

INDUSTRY ALLOCATIONS		
Underweight	*Neutral*	*Overweight*
Automobiles	Airlines	Aerospace & Defense
Chemicals	*ELECTRIC UTILITIES*	Banks
Construction	Gas	Beverages
Home-building	Household Furnishings	Drugs
Machinery	Household Products	Entertainment
OIL	Lodging	Foods
Paper	Retail	Health Care
Railroad	Tech-Comp. Software	Insurance
Steel	Tobacco	Investment Banking
Trucking	Tech-Computer Systems	Telephone
		Tech-Commun. Equip.
		Tech-Semi Conductors

For the Week of December 15, 1997

As we head into the most volatile season for the stock market, the pre-earnings disappointments announcement season, *you better hold on as a couple hundred point swings either way may now be the order of the day for the remainder of the year.* The problem with this new season (I remember when there were just two seasons; earnings season and "not" earnings season—now we have three seasons in the stock market; earnings season, pre-earnings disappointment announcement season and "not" earnings season) is that it only presents one side of the story and that story is bad. You see, the only pre-earnings announcements that have any impact on the markets before earnings are actually released are the disappointments. With no Earnings' reports until mid-January and economic releases taking a back seat to the Asian crisis, there is nothing to offset the focus that the markets will place on these earnings' disappointments. The real driving force in the stock market this week and maybe for the remainder of the year just may be the unscheduled, unplanned wild card called pre-earnings' disappointment announcements. And while these announcements always move the markets, this time they will turbo-charge it. And the reason is because of the uncertainty caused by the economic and currency meltdown in Southeast Asia. The markets continue to search for evidence regarding just how bad this meltdown will be and what impact it will have on corporate profits. *No stocks are immune from a sell-off the remainder of the year as I expect the market to overreact to every event.* These pre-earnings disappointment announcements will not only have tremendous ramifications for the individual company that issues the announcement; the announcements will have industry-wide, market-wide and even global market ramifications.

INDUSTRY ALLOCATIONS		
Underweight	*Neutral*	*Overweight*
Automobiles	Airlines	Aerospace & Defense
Chemicals	Electric Utilities	Banks
Construction	Gas	Beverages
Home-building	Household Furnishings	Drugs
Machinery	Household Products	Entertainment
Oil	Lodging	Foods

continued

INDUSTRY ALLOCATIONS		
Underweight	*Neutral*	*Overweight*
Paper	Retail	Health Care
Railroad	Tech-Comp. Software	Insurance
Steel	Tobacco	Investment Banking
Trucking	Tech-Computer Systems	Telephone
		Tech-Commun. Equip.
		Tech-Semi Conductors

For the Week of December 22, 1997

As the stock market continues its search for leadership, a new industry is emerging to drive the markets the first part of the year and that industry is Airlines. ***I am moving Airlines from Neutral to Overweight.*** There are two fundamental factors converging to drive the Airline Industry higher. The first is the market's shift from inflationary concerns to now deflationary concerns. The global meltdown in Southeast Asia will keep a lid on prices everywhere—especially, commodity prices are continuing to plunge, driven by our two benchmarks of gold and oil. And remember, as I've talked about before, there are some other fundamental issues that are also driving the price of oil lower. First, OPEC has increased the production ceiling by 2.5 million barrels a day. This additional supply will drop the price of oil. Second, as the off-again, on-again crisis in Iraq is off again, that means that the food for oil deal is on-again. This deal will also flood the market with more oil which will drive prices lower as well. While everyone is concerned with the deflationary impact of oil, let's not overlook the biggest industry winner, Airlines. In the simplest sense, there are two cost keys for Airlines—labor cost and fuel cost (after the meal I had two weeks ago, I'm betting that airline food doesn't even make the top 20). This global deflationary shift along with the fundamental issues driving oil prices down, should drive the Airline Industry up. The second factor is, I expect that airline usage will be at record levels this holiday season. With record levels in our stock market, no inflation, low unemployment, soaring consumer confidence and an economy that just will not quit, all signs are telling the consumer to "go ahead" and take that holiday trip. This combination of increased airline traffic along with the

119

lower cost structure because of the price of oil, should combine to make a strong case for the Airline Industry to be one of the early industry leaders for 1998 earnings.

INDUSTRY ALLOCATIONS		
Underweight	*Neutral*	*Overweight*
Automobiles		Aerospace & Defense
Chemicals	Electric Utilities	***AIRLINES***
Construction	Gas	Banks
Home-building	Household Furnishings	Beverages
Machinery	Household Products Lodging	Drugs
Oil	Lodging	Entertainment
Paper	Retail	Foods
Railroad	Tech-Comp. Software	Health Care
Steel	Tobacco	Insurance
Trucking	Tech-Computer Systems	Investment Banking
		Telephone
		Tech-Commun. Equip.
		Tech-Semi Conductors

4 BOND MARKET PERSPECTIVE

OVERVIEW

The combination of little or no inflation, a decreasing federal deficit and a strong dollar all combined to send interest rates lower. In fact, the yield on the benchmark 30-year bond ended at 5.92%; certainly within striking distance of the all time low record for the 30-year bond which was 5.78% (achieved in October of 1993).

Trying to figure out where the bond market is going in reality is trying to guess where interest rates are going.

John Kenneth Galbraith summed it up best when he said 'we have two types of interest rate forecasters; those who don't know . . . and those who don't know they don't know.'

Let me start by saying that I don't believe that any economist truly knows where interest rates are going, remember economists aren't prophets and most aren't even rich.

Let's take a recent look at history for a clue. In 1994 we began the year with the Long Bond at 6.35%; the consensus of economists called for the Long Bond to move up to 6.39%. The Long Bond ended the year up at 7.88%.

In 1995, we then began the year with the Long Bond at 7.88%; the consensus of economists called for the Long Bond to move down to 7.75%. The Long Bond ended the year down at 5.95%.

In 1996, we then began the year with the Long Bond at 5.95%; the consensus of economists called for the Long Bond to move up to 6.08%. The Long Bond ended the year up at 6.63%.

In 1997 we started the year at 6.63%; the consensus of economists call for the Long Bond to move down to 6.57%. The Long Bond ended the year down at 5.92%.

I think that we can learn a lesson from the history of the past few years. First of all we are always convinced that things are not going to change. In 1994 we said the Long Bond would only move from 6.35% to 6.39% in 1995 from 7.88% to 7.75% in 1996 from 5.95% to 6.08% in 1997 from 6.63% to 6.59%. Economists have been consistently wrong with the magnitude of the interest rate move.

The story of the bond market in 1997 was not just inflation, but wage inflation. Everyone was focusing on it. With low unemployment, a strong economy and the adoption of a new minimum wage law it is easy to see why most experts were expecting wage inflation. Even though this concern over wage inflation hurt the bond market in the short run, however, in the long run it had no impact because the market became convinced that we do not have wage inflation. Here's why.

Wage inflation is when you get paid more money to do the same job. That is not what is happening. We are getting paid more money to do better jobs; they are simply called the same job. Just think of the case of the stock room clerk.

It is the stock room clerk's job to take boxes from the loading dock and put them on the shelves in the warehouse. That clerk used to make $6.50 an hour. Now they make $8.50 an hour and everyone screams wage inflation. It's not wage inflation, in fact it's wage deflation.

Here's what that same stock room clerk does today. They are still responsible for taking boxes from the loading dock and putting them on the shelves of the warehouse. However, now after they do that, they take a hand held computer that is clipped to their belt and they scan the bar code on the boxes to take inventory. Later in the day they down load the inventory data in their hand held computer and then they set the shipping schedules for the next day. Finally, shipping schedules are crossed checked against inventory lists and new orders are processed at the end of the shift.

Where's the wage inflation?—We give this person an extra $2.00 an hour and not only are they the stock room clerk, but they are also the inventory clerk, the shipping clerk and the order clerk. An additional $2.00 an hour to do the job of four people—That is not wage inflation, that's wage disinflation.

Here we go, enjoy the ride as I recap with you how the issues and events that drive my bond market outlook evolved on a week by week basis from Tax Day (April 15th) through the end of 1997.

For the Week of April 14, 1997

With one interest rate hike now behind us, the new focus of the bond market becomes when the next rate hike will occur. The risk to the bond market this week will be on the high side. If the economy continues to show solid strength (which I think it will) *expect the bond market to continue to deteriorate*. While the market will be closely watching and reacting to every piece of economic news, it will also be keeping one eye on the value of the U.S. Dollar. Any weakening in the dollar would spell bad news for the bond market. Strong demand from foreign investors has served as a tremendous stabilizing force for the bond market. If the dollar weakens and foreign investors no longer get the positive currency exchange rate as well as the yield, the bond market would have to rely on domestic buyers for support. Don't count on it, even with rates above 7%. Crossing the 7% threshold is important for demand only if you think that rates aren't going higher. But with the expectation of still higher rates, I don't look for the 7% handle to be a strong boost for demand.

For the Week of April 21, 1997

While all eyes will be on the stock market as it digests a full plate of earnings reports, *the bond market should rally this week*, possibly for the last time until the summer. No news is good news for the bond market. The light economic calendar presents the bond market with what may be its last chance to rally for quite some time. As long as the Existing Home Sale number doesn't surprise too much on the high side, this should be a good week for bonds. It is, however, the calm before the storm. Next week the bond market will be faced with both the Quarterly Employment Cost Index report and the April Employment reports. Recent economic releases over the past few weeks suggest that both of these numbers could be very strong. . . . *I also look for renewed interest in municipal bonds.* With the ink still not dry on the check to the Internal Revenue Service, most Americans will be more apt than ever to explore tax exempt investing strategies. Especially now that the short-term fear of any major tax reform (flat tax) appears dead.

For the Week of April 28, 1997

It's back to interest rate hike fears as the bond market braces itself for a very volatile week as it is bombarded every single day of the week with major economic releases. *I expect the bond market will sell off this week as the key economic releases should surprise on the high side and thus, fuel another round of interest rate hike fears.* . . . Look for a heavy calendar of corporate debt issues to attempt to come to the market this week prior to the all important bellwether Employment reports on Friday. *Corporate debt yields may have to rise to unload this heavy calendar.* Corporate America views this as possibly the last window of opportunity to issue any corporate debt prior to the market beginning to build in another 50 basis point rate hike.

For the Week of May 5, 1997

Forget the fundamentals. The thing that really matters to the bond market is what is going to happen at the Federal Open Markets Committee (FOMC) meeting on May 20th. Having sliced and diced just about every piece of economic data available, maybe the markets will now look to history for a clue. Look out, because history has not been kind to the bond market. Over the past twenty five years the FOMC has increased (tightened) rates during eighteen separate periods. Fourteen of the eighteen periods contained more than one rate hike. In other words, the FOMC usually doesn't stop after just one move. Each of the four occasions when the FOMC only moved once, inflation was above 4%. In other words, it certainly was not a pre-emptive strike. On the other hand, *every single time in the past quarter of a century when the Fed raised rates "preemptively" when inflation was below 4%, (like it is today) the FOMC, without fail, has always tightened more than once.* History is telling us this is not an isolated move. There is a reason Greenspan continues to use the term "preemptively." *In his own round-about way, Greenspan is telling us once is not enough* according to history and Alan Greenspan is certainly a student of history.

For the Week of May 12, 1997

This should be a very difficult week for the bond market as the risks are clearly on yields going higher. If we have relatively weak to moderate economic releases, I do not expect to see much of a rally in bond yields as the market continues to stare into the face of a potential interest rate increase on May 20th. If, however, there are any economic releases that surprise on the high side, we could easily see the Long Bond test the 7% level prior to the FOMC meeting. *I don't expect any major economic shocks this week so I look for the Long Bond to trade in a rather narrow range*. Anyone looking for those 7% yields will have to wait an additional week. The Long Bond will not go through 7% until after the FOMC raises interest rates at their May 20th meeting.

For the Week of May 19, 1997

This could shape up to be a very interesting and very volatile week for the bond market. The only thing that really matters to the bond market is what happens at the FOMC meeting. *I expect the bond market to drop dramatically after the FOMC raises rates*. After the bond market finishes its customary overreaction, I think it will actually rally toward the end of the week. I think that this end of the week rally will be fueled by a chain of events. After the FOMC raises rates, I think that you will see a rebound in the dollar as foreign investors look to move money back into the United States fixed income markets. *I look for a strong pick-up in foreign demand by the end of the week that could actually set off a pre-Memorial Day bond market rally*.

For the Week of May 26, 1997

I look for some potential big swings in the bond market this week as it tries to interpret the latest economic releases, in light of the next FOMC meeting in July. The bond market's volatility in part is being driven by the psychology of the market. *The bond market is not trying to determine if the FOMC will raise rates, but rather when they will raise rates*. The bond market does not believe that Greenspan will stop after a single 25 basis point move on March 25th. There remain enough mixed signals on the economic front to justify whatever action the FOMC deems appropriate. In addition, the dramatic fall of the U.S. Dollar over the past few weeks has started to take its toll on the bond market through both selling by Japanese investors and weak new demand by these same Japanese investors. The underlying strength in the bond market has been a solid foundation by foreign investors, especially Japanese investors. *When you combine the weakening dollar*

125

along with the growing consensus (which I think is wrong!) that the Bank of Japan is ready to raise interest rates, that one-two punch could prove a knock-out to our bond market. Japanese investors have flocked to our markets because of low rates in Japan and the strong dollar. If rates in Japan do rise and the dollar remains weak, the bond market may be the biggest loser.

For the Week of June 2, 1997

With the very heavy calendar of economic releases, I expect the bond market to be very active this week. Good news from the economic front will not be enough to keep the market below the key 7% threshold, while bad news (releases that show strong economic growth) will continue to move bond yields higher. *With a string of strong economic releases, the Long Bond could easily find itself over the critical 7.25% level by week's end.* . . . The currency market brings on a whole other set of concerns for the bond market. The weakened dollar has greatly slowed down foreign demand for our bond market. And this foreign demand and foreign buyers have dominated our fixed income markets for the entire year. There is no one on the horizon to step in to take the place of the Japanese investors. *If rates do back up to 7.25%, Japanese investors will take notice and I expect them to come rushing back to our markets in a big way.* I'm afraid things are going to get worse (rates going up) before they get better (rates going down) in the bond market.

For the Week of June 9, 1997

After last week, this should be a very quiet week for the bond market. *Only a major surprise on the economic front (bad news) could break the Long Bond out of an expected narrow trading range this week.* With so few economic releases, the bond market will have to worry about something else to give it its clue regarding what the FOMC will do at its next meeting July 1st and 2nd. I expect the bond market to worry about the stock market and the dollar. The bond market does not want to see the stock market moving much higher. Continued strength in the stock market increases the risk of FOMC raising rates to slow the economy down fearing that the "wealth effect," as the result of rising stock prices, will encourage consumption which in turn could fuel inflation. On the other hand, the bond market is hoping that the dollar continues to rally. A strong dollar does two things for the bond market. First, it actually helps keep down inflation by lowering the cost of imports to consumers thus forcing U.S. producers to keep prices low in order to compete with the cheaper imports. Second, the strong dollar serves as a magnet for foreign capital, the same foreign capital that usually makes its way to the bond market. A falling (or flat) stock market and a rising dollar will make the bond market very happy (at least until the July FOMC meeting).

For the Week of June 30, 1997

The bond market continues to show a great deal of strength and confidence. This is a very very critical week for the bond market. *If the market survives this week, it could stay under the threshold 7% level for the remainder of the year.* The real strength in the market was evidenced last week when Japanese Prime Minister Hashimoto's threat barely moved the bond market while it sent the stock market crashing. In theory, just the opposite should have happened; the stock market should have shrugged off these comments and the bond market should have crashed. These are indeed strange times. I expect the bond market to display a little more volatility this week as the holiday shortened schedule leaves the second tier "B Team" traders at the helm to pull the trigger. The "B Team" always tends to overreact to any news.

For the Week of July 7, 1997

Now that the bond market has dodged another bullet with no rate hike at last week's FOMC meeting, *the bond market should be in for a rather quiet time for the next several weeks* or at least until the weeks leading up to the next meeting which is scheduled for August 19th. The bond market will be watching two things very closely over the weeks ahead. The first thing it will watch for is the results of the stock market's second quarter earnings season. A stronger than expected showing with earnings will push the stock market even higher. If Alan Greenspan was worried about "irrational exuberance" with the Dow Jones Industrial Average (DJIA) at 6,200, what's he going to think about a DJIA at 8,200? The "wealth effect" of the stock market continues to be a great concern to the FOMC. The FOMC feels that future inflation will not be fueled by a shortage of labor or commodities but rather an over confident and wealthy (at least on paper) consumer.

One sure fire way to make a consumer over confident and wealthy is by having the stock market soar through 8,000. The second item that the Bond Market will be watching is the consumer. What the consumer does or more importantly does not do during the first month of the third quarter will be a key indicator to just what the FOMC will do next. I continue to have a hard time trying to come up with reasons why the consumer is going to slow down. Income growth remains strong. Consumer confidence continues to remain at all-time highs. The labor markets remain very tight. And the Federal deficit is under control. When you add it all up and throw in a healthy earnings season, you will quickly realize that last week's FOMC meeting didn't resolve anything for the bond market. The only thing that changed was the timetable. Stay tuned, August 19th is right around the corner.

For the Week of July 14, 1997

The great summer bond rally has officially begun. *I expect the bond market to post strong gains the remainder of the year.* All of the ingredients necessary for a bond rally are falling into place. First, we have slower, but steady economic growth combined with low if not no inflation. Second, the Federal Government's deficit just gets lower and lower. Some of the current forecasts call for the deficit to fall to as low as $35 billion dollars when the fiscal year ends in September (we started the fiscal year with a deficit of $107 billion dollars). Don't forget the technical market significance of a lower Federal Government deficit. The lower the deficit, the smaller the amount of bonds that the Federal Government will have to issue. Tighter supply serves to increase demand that will drive prices up. The bond market also has two "wild cards" going for it that should help continue the rally through the summer. The first wild card was dealt by Japanese Prime Minister Ryutaco Hashimoto. His ill-advised threat did not hurt our bond market, it actually helped it. The financial world was outraged that Japan would consider manipulating the financial markets in order to negotiate another political agenda. The eyes of the financial world are on Japan. They have backed themselves into a corner where they can't sell their U.S. bonds even if they wanted to because it would give the appearance that they are making good on their ill-advised threat. The second wild card is being dealt by the stock market. As the stock market has continued its record climb toward 8,000 these great gains in the stock market are causing "asset allocators" to re-balance their portfolios. For an investor that wants 60% to be invested in stock and 40%

in bonds, the great bull market of the first half of this year means that your once 60% may now be over 70% and it's time to buy bonds to re-balance your asset allocation. As more investors re-balance their assets in the second half of the year, I expect more bonds to purchased.

For the Week of July 21, 1997

With the very light economic calendar, the bond market will be focused on Alan Greenspan's Humphrey-Hawkins testimony. The two greatest risks in the bond market this week both lie in Washington from two different fronts. The first bullet to dodge is Alan Greenspan's Humphrey-Hawkins testimony. I certainly wouldn't rule out Alan Greenspan giving the bond market something to worry about. The second risk in Washington comes from the political lines that are being drawn in the balanced budget process. It was one thing when all that you had to worry about was Democrats versus Republicans, but now you have Republican fighting Republican, highlighted by the attempt to overthrow House Speaker Newt Gingrich, while Democrats are fighting among themselves over their position on the proposed Tobacco Industry settlement. These problems could easily spill over into the balanced budget debate. As tempers flare and headlines get ugly, *the bond market will have the most to lose if it looks like the balanced budget accord is in trouble*. Maybe we should issue ear plugs to bond traders this week.

For the Week of July 28, 1997

Things simply could not get much better for the fixed income market. The Federal Open Markets Committee (FOMC) appears to be on hold for the short run and maybe even through the remainder of the year. There is no inflation anywhere in sight to "eat into" the returns of fixed income products. Both the European market and the emerging markets remain in chaos for different reasons. On the European front, continued questions about the European Monetary Union and the political shift to the "left," which historically has meant more government spending and higher deficits, has served as a reason for investors to flock to the United States fixed income market until Europe resolves its crisis. Secondly, on the emerging market front, the new currency concern that began with just Thailand's Baht, has now spread to other currencies in other emerging market countries. As these currencies weaken, foreign investors will move some of their fixed income assets from these emerging markets to the United States. ***For our bond market to move on the next level, breaking 6%, it will have to be fueled by the final balanced budget and tax cut plans***. Once the final details are worked out and approved by congress and signed by the President, the long awaited elimination of our federal budget deficit will happen. When this plan is signed, sealed and delivered, the bond market will rally on to the next level. Remember, the lower the Federal deficit, the less need the government has to issue debt. This potential lack of future supply will also serve as a catalyst to the markets. One final note, it will now be much more difficult to forecast when the bond market will sell-off. Life was much simpler when "public enemy number one" was the FOMC. Figure out the FOMC and you could figure out the bond market. Now that the FOMC appears to be on the same side as the bond market, traders have to look for a new enemy. The new market movers will be much more difficult to figure out than the FOMC ever was. At least with the FOMC, after you ran to the dictionary to look up "quiescent inflation," only to realize that was a "good" thing, the market would move forward. There is no dictionary to look up Indonesia-gate, Newt-coup-gate and Asia's currency-gate, as these issues now vie to replace the FOMC as the bond market's public enemy number one.

For the Week of August 4, 1997

Solid bond market fundamentals remain in place for the market to stay strong the remainder of the year. ***There may be temporary economic shocks that back the market up along the way, however, the direction has been set for the bond market for the remainder of the year, and that direction is lower rates***. First of all, there is no inflation. Whether you measure it by the Producer Price Index or the Consumer Price Index, it doesn't matter; there is still no inflation. Remember, the Producer Price Index has declined for a record setting unprecedented six consecutive months this year. Meanwhile, over that same time period, the Consumer Price Index (the core rate) is at its lowest level in over thirty years. Secondly, the balanced budget deal is finally a reality. There is no industrialized country on the face of the earth that has a stronger debt to Gross Domestic Product ratio than we do. This great news is not lost on the bond market and will remain the major fuel that keeps this rally going. ***If I had to focus on one red flag for the bond market, it would be the unemployment rate***. As our economy rebounds, the second half of the year, the combination of a stronger economy and tight labor markets could move the unemployment rate even lower. The psychological impact of an unemployment level that approaches 4.5% is unprecedented, and if anything could cause the Federal Reserve Board to overreact and raise interest rates, this would be it. . . . This week is also a heavy supply week for treasury securities as the Treasury Department plans to sell $38 billion in its quarterly refunding. There will be $16 billion of three-year notes on Tuesday, $12 billion of ten-year notes on Wednesday and $10 billion of thirty-year bonds on Thursday.

For the Week of August 18, 1997

The bond market has survived its major setback over the past few weeks and should have a good week as the inflation fears of last week are now behind us. The ***Federal Reserve Board will not raise interest rates on August 19***. And even though this had been priced into the market, the recent back-up in the market now gives it room to rally after the Federal Reserve Board decides to leave rates alone. ***The fundamentals for the bond market remain very strong.*** No inflation at the producer or consumer level continues to present proof every single month that our economy is different this time; we can grow above economic trend growth and still not have inflation. Also, the market sometimes forgets the very basic concept of supply and demand. As the Federal Government deficit continues to decline at a record setting pace, there will be less federal debt that needs to be financed. Even with no more demand for bonds, the decreased supply alone will create a bullish technical market for bonds. One caution for the market remains the strength of the dollar. Our bond market remains very nervous about foreign capital flowing out of the bond market. As a result, any weakening of the dollar will tend to serve as a leading indicator that foreign investors may now be more inclined to sell their U.S. securities.

For the Week of August 25, 1997

This could be a volatile week in the bond market depending upon what the heavy supply of economic releases tell us. ***Even though the market may be faced with some short term volatility due to inflation and interest rate fears, longer term, the market is fundamentally sound.*** Even though we can never abolish the concern for inflation, there are two tremendous forces that bode well for a low/no inflation environment. First, global capacity is growing faster than global growth. Which means that there are more things to buy than there are people to buy them. This is not inflationary, in fact, it is actually deflationary. Second, our technology revolution will continue to improve productivity which will keep inflation in check. We have not even seen the tip of the iceberg of the internet and how it will continue to change the way we live and work. The more we use the internet, the more productive we become and productivity enhancements will also keep inflation in check. . . . *Possibly the greatest risk that the bond market faces this week will be from the speakers' circuit.* On Tuesday, Federal Reserve Bank of Chicago President, Michael Moskow speaks. Then on Friday, when most people are taking off to start a long Labor Day weekend, Federal Reserve Chairman, Alan Greenspan is speaking in Jackson Hole, Wyoming at the Kansas City Federal Reserve Bank's Annual Symposium. If the GDP release hits the markets unexpectedly on Thursday, Alan Greenspan could deliver the knockout punch on Friday when he tells us all what it means.

For the Week of September 1, 1997

While the focus of the bond market will be this week's bellwether employment releases on Friday, *the risk to the market remains the dollar, not the economy.* The bond market has begun de-coupling itself from the stock market. As the stock market moves wildly, trying to anticipate the direction of the economy, the bond market has remained rather calm, at least in comparison to our stock market. I think that there are two reasons for the bond markets' strength. First, the market is still celebrating the landmark balance budget and tax cut deal. Second, and even more importantly, as our federal deficit continues to trend lower and lower, the reality that the Federal Government will have less federal debt to finance in the future is serving as a price support for holders of U.S. Treasury debt today. . . . Watch the dollar closely. The greatest risk in the bond market is if foreign investors begin to liquidate their holding of United States Treasury Bonds. Any weakening of the dollar will tend to make foreign investors nervous about when they should pull the trigger on their United States investments. The dollar will have a lot more to say about where the bond market is heading than this month's UPS infected employment reports.

For the Week of September 8, 1997

I expect the bond market to begin to show increased volatility leading up to the Federal Open Markets Committee meeting at the end of the month. The basis of this volatility continues to be the mixed signals we are receiving. The bond market still can't figure out if it wants to go through 6% or 7%. On the bullish front, pushing the 30-year Treasury Bond yield closer to 6% is the confluence of three key developments. First, the budget and federal deficit news just keeps getting better and better from Washington. Don't underestimate the positive influence that this has on our bond market. Second, even though our bond yields have fallen, they remain very, very attractive and competitive from a global perspective. Our bond market will continue to serve as a magnet for foreign capital. Third, we continue to see a lot of asset allocation re-balancing the second half of the year. This re-balancing means taking some profits out of the equity market and placing it in the bond market. Even with these tremendous positive forces, our bond market remains very, very nervous. The source of this nervousness can be found in two factors. First is the strong economy. Now that second quarter Gross Domestic Product numbers have been revised up to almost 4%, the market realizes that we have somehow strung together three straight quarters of not just above trend growth, but three straight quarters of explosive growth. The bond market can take one quarter and sometimes even two, but from the bond market's perspective, it's three strikes and you're out. The second factor is the expectation of wage inflation as a result of the United Parcel Service strike. Remember the bond market moves more on expectation than it does on facts. We are clearly in for a couple of volatile weeks; however, *I still firmly believe that the yield on the benchmark 30-year Treasury Bond will be lower at the end of the year than it is now.*

For the Week of September 15, 1997

The current global investment landscape continues to be a positive for the United States bond market. The currency devaluations all across the Pacific Rim simply serves as one more reason why fixed income investors should allocate a major portion of their global assets to the United States. Also it's important to remember that when you look at the overall global landscape, bond yields in the United States remain very attractive. Japanese ten-year government bonds are currently yielding just 2%. This is a 50-year low for any country in the world that issues debt. There is just no way that Japan can compete for global capital at those levels . . . The bond market will continue to worry about inflation; as such, some news in the coming weeks may increase volatility in the bond markets. Energy prices are staying high, which is a negative for inflation. Tobacco is up (specifically cigarettes) in order to pay the bill for litigation and settlement issues. Airfares are rising both because of the strong economy and because Congress stuck it to the Airline Industry in the landmark balanced budget deal. *All of these factors, once combined, could cause a temporary spike in inflation at the consumer level which would certainly throw the bond market a curve.*

For the Week of September 22, 1997

A strong dollar, no inflation and Warren Buffett buying bonds, I'm not sure if it's possible for things to get much better for the bond market. *I expect the rally in the bond market to continue the remainder of the year*, however, at a somewhat slower pace. There are two key fundamentals driving this rally. First, with our federal budget deficit disappearing before our eyes, so will the supply of Treasury Bonds. The lower the deficit, the slower the amount of new Treasury financings. This projected slowdown in future supply will increase the value of the current treasury debt. If we don't pay close attention, Warren Buffett could very well finance the entire federal deficit by himself; then we wouldn't have to worry about Japanese or Chinese selling, all eyes instead, would be on Omaha. The second fundamental issue is that the bond market finally seems to be excepting the notion that higher economic growth doesn't mean higher inflation. The bond market is always looking over its shoulder for inflation. It seems as if every time that we have a strong economic number, the immediate concern is that will mean higher inflation which is bad for the bond market. This new vision will be put to the test this week when the final second quarter Gross Domestic Product number is released. If the bond market can withstand any sell-off as a result of this upward revision of economic growth then it could clearly be setting the stage for a nice rally the remainder of the year. Keep one eye on the dollar, however, as the greatest risk to the bond market until we can get all the debt transferred to Omaha remains the dollar.

For the Week of September 29, 1997

This will be an extremely volatile week for the bond market. ***The recent rally in the market has made bond traders nervous and, as such, they are looking for any reason to take some money off the table***. The nervousness in the bond market appears to center around three somewhat independent economic issues. First, the Durable Goods surprise of last week truly caught the bond market off guard. The fear is that if companies are still making "big ticket" purchases (which are captured in the durable goods release) then this economy might be much stronger than anyone thinks. Second, consumer confidence remains at record highs. The consumers are not only the wild card to our economy; they are our economy. If the Federal Open Market's Committee is pushed to eventually raise interest rates, it will be because the consumer has stayed strong. And the best measure of how strong the consumer will be is consumer confidence. Third is refinancing activity. Our economy has been void of any economic pick-up due to refinancing. Now however, with the recent drop in interest rates, we are seeing a dramatic pick-up in refinancing activity which could very well serve to add a little more strength to our overall economy and will give the bond market something new to worry about.

For the Week of October 6, 1997

Warren Buffet once again proves why he just might be the world's saviest investor. I'm not sure if he saw this recent "bull" run in the bond market coming or if he caused the rally by buying bonds. Regardless of which came first, the chicken or the egg, the fact remains, things could not be much better for the bond market. With the back drop of low or no inflation in a global marketplace, it appears that the bond market has now bought into the argument that inflation is dead. Secondly, don't underestimate the impact that the major deficit reduction and balanced budget agreement has had on the bond market. The fundamentals are pretty simple, the lower the deficit, the smaller the amount of debt that needs to be issued to fund the deficit. This contraction in supply of new debt is very bullish for bonds . . . When it appears that things are just too good to be true, maybe they are. My major concern with the bond market is that maybe it actually got in front of itself. I'm not sure that our current economic fundamentals can support a bond market on the verge to break through 6%. If it's not the economic fundamentals that are driving the bond market, then what is? I think the recent rally in the bond market is more a story of the global fixed income landscape than it is our economy. The combination of the Asian currency crisis and economic meltdown in the Pacific Rim along with high unemployment and flat economic growth throughout most of western Europe have made our markets the only option for many foreign investors. Combine these forces with the fact that many investors in the U.S. stock market, satisfied with the tremendous gains that they have already made this year, are taking some money off the equity table and parking it in fixed income. *The real story of the recent rally in the bond market may have little to do with our economy. It may have to do with investors here and abroad looking for the safest place to park their money.* With our current federal deficit at less than ½ of 1% can you think of a better place? Stay on alert. Easy come; easy go.

For the Week of October 13, 1997

The fundamentals in our bond market remain very strong despite the recent back-up as a result of Alan Greenspan's comments regarding inflation and future interest rate increases. If we remove the noise (Alan Greenspan's Congressional testimony) and look instead at the facts, fundamentally nothing has changed in the bond market to turn it from a bull to a bear. First, inflation remains nowhere in sight either at the producer or the consumer level. Second, there will continue to be less and less treasury financing necessary (less supply) because of the great job we have done fighting our deficit. The Congressional Budget Office has revised their estimate downward once again and it is now projected that we will end fiscal year 1997 with a federal deficit of less than $23 billion dollars. That sounds like a lot until you realize that we started the fiscal year with a federal deficit of $107 billion. This will mark the smallest end-of-year fiscal deficit since 1974. Third, we continue to see very, very strong demand from foreign investors. In the second quarter alone, they purchased over $50 billion of treasury debt. Until there are other attractive options, foreign capital will continue to flow to the U.S. bond market. *The only part of the fundamental equation that has changed has been the weakening of the dollar. That change, however, is a short term impact not a long term trend.* A country's currency value is no more than a reflection of that country's economy. Our strong economy will serve as an unwavering foundation for a strong dollar.

For the Week of October 20, 1997

The "boom" or "bust" bond market should be heading toward another boom in the next few weeks. The market has been whip-sawed the past few weeks. First, we have a great boom because of the weak linchpin employment number, but before anyone could even celebrate, the market went bust. Raining on the parade was the spike up in oil and fear that it could be the start of inflation fears turning into reality. The steep quick climb in oil prices, however, didn't have anything to do with inflation; it had everything to do with what the bond market does best and that is overreact to everything. This time the bond market overreacted and sold out as a result of the deployment of a United States warship to the Persian Gulf to monitor events more closely in the region. Both employment and oil will remain important to the bond market because both serve as a tool to measure types of inflation. Employment reports will measure wage inflation while the oil price reflects commodity inflation. There is simply no inflation present from either of those fronts, at least for the next few weeks; that should cause a nice rally (boom) in the bond market. Also, don't forget about the Japanese investor. Rates continue to hover at all-time lows in Japan. More and more Japanese investors will continue to look to the United States for the superior return it will provide them with their fixed income investments. I do not expect the spread between U.S. bond rates and Japanese bond rates to narrow anytime soon; and as such, our bond market will continue to be the beneficiary of strong foreign investment flow from Japan.

For the Week of October 27, 1997

Just when you thought things could not get better for the bond market, they just did. First, our Federal Government deficit is in the best shape in the past 30 years. Remember, with our federal deficit getting smaller, so will the supply of Treasury Bonds. The lower the deficit, the lower the amount of new Treasury financings. This slowdown in future supply of treasury debt increases the current value of Treasury debt which is very bullish for bonds. Second, is the Warren Buffett impact. This guy has to be the saviest investor of all time. Remember, this latest bond market rally began when Warren Buffett decided to buy bonds. Warren Buffett buying bonds is certainly bullish for bonds. Now thirdly, **along comes the Southeast Asia currency and economic crisis which is extremely good news, not bad news for bonds.**

Think about it; the bond market is really worried about inflation and Alan Greenspan raising interest rates. The Southeast Asian currency and economic crisis has killed both of those concerns. The tremendous devaluation of the Southeast Asian currencies will flood the global market with cheaper products (due to the currency devaluation) which in turn will force countries whose currency did not devalue (like the United States) to keep a lid on prices in order to compete in this global marketplace. It's deflation not inflation that now has a greater chance of turning the markets on end. Second, as far as Alan Greenspan raising rates anytime soon, forget about it. The Federal Reserve Board will not raise rates this year and it is unlikely that rates will be raised in the first half of 1998 regardless of what the economic releases show. If the Federal Reserve Board were to raise interest rates, it would serve to expand the Asian crisis and chaos to the United States which could trigger a global financial asset meltdown. Alan Greenspan realizes this and so does the bond market. The Southeast Asian currency crisis has tied Alan Greenspan's hands. He can talk all he wants, but the bond market knows he can't risk raising rates anytime soon.

For the Week of November 3, 1997

I expect the bond market to be very volatile the next few weeks as it will be whip-sawed from two fronts; the stock market and economic news. As the stock market continues to strengthen, I expect to see some weakness in the bond market. Secondly, even though all eyes are on international events, the bond market will still worry about and overreact to economic releases. *Even though I see short-term volatility in the bond market, longer term the market will continue its strong run by pushing yields on the benchmark 30-year Treasury Bond under 6%.* The fundamentals in the bond market are simply too strong not to carry the Long Bond through 6%. Think about it for a minute, world wide growth is slowing. While it will be hotly debated how much it will slow; the consensus is that it will slow down due to the crisis in Southeast Asia. A slowdown in the global economy will have a ripple effect by slowing down the U.S. economy. And again, while it will be hotly debated how much of a slowdown the consensus is, our economy will slow down. If the economy slows down on its own, that means that there is not a need for a rate hike which is bullish for bonds. Second, there is no inflation. The major currency devaluation's in Southeast Asia means that cheaper goods and services will flood the global markets. This will pressure all companies to keep their prices in line in order to compete with Southeast Asia's lower prices. Again, no inflation is very bullish for bonds. Third, this week the Quarterly Treasury Auction will entail $35 billion of new debt. This is down $3 billion from last quarter. As we continue to solve our government spending and deficit problems, there will eventually be less government debt issued to finance this deficit. These new supply/demand fundamentals are very bullish for bonds. And finally, I expect the dollar to remain strong the remainder of the year. A strong dollar will continue to attract foreign investors to perhaps the safest investment in the world, U.S. Treasury debt. See ya at 6%.

For the Week of November 10, 1997

With every crisis there are winners and losers. With the Southeast Asia currency and economic crisis, one of the clear winners is the United States bond market. First, Asian investors as well as fixed income investors around the globe looking for a safe haven jumped into our bond market with both feet. Second, the immediate consensus from around the globe regarding the impact of this crisis was that it would shift the global focus from an inflationary bias to a deflationary bias. When everyone around the world declares that inflation is dead that is certainly a bullish sign for bonds. *One can get really bullish on bonds when you consider the lift that both a stronger dollar and reduced treasury financing going forward will do to the technical supply demand fundamentals. A yield on the benchmark 30-year Treasury Bond under 6% by year end is still not out of the question . . .* While I am firmly in the "camp" that inflation is dead, the bond market remains very, very nervous, looking around every corner for the next sign of inflation. Three things from the inflation watch front have appeared to have captured the attention of the bond market and any fall from my rosy scenario will most likely be driven from a spill-over from one of these three fronts. First, the wage component of the quarterly Employment Cost Index was up 3.4% on an annualized basis. The U.P.S. wage inflation fears are still alive and well. Second, the price component of the National Association of Purchasing Managers Index came in at 55.9 and remember, anything over 50 is strong and anything over 55 gets the traders' attention. Finally, Capacity Utilization was high at 84.4%. While I don't believe that any of these issues will keep the Long Bond from going through 6%, they certainly can make the ride getting there very rough and volatile.

For the Week of November 17, 1997

I expect the Long Bond to continue its march through 6%. With the November Federal Open Markets Committee meeting now behind us, all eyes are now on the December 16th meeting. *The exact same issues that drove the Federal Reserve Board to keep interest rates unchanged last week will force them to keep rates steady at the December 16th meeting as well.* Our economy will be slowing down as a result of the Southeast Asia currency and economic meltdown. While the magnitude of the slowdown will continue to be debated, the significance is, you don't raise interest rates on top of an economy that's already slowing down. Second, inflation will remain dead. As the products from Southeast Asia continue to make their way into our marketplace, they will keep inflation in check because one, their prices are lower due to currency devaluation, and two, their lower prices will keep American producers from raising prices in order to remain competitive. When you factor in the reduced supply of Treasury Bonds going forward due to our federal deficit reduction program along with the continued demand from foreign investors for a safe haven, things just could not get much better for fixed-income investors. Bond investors finally have something to cheer about that is not going away any time soon. I expect the Long Bond to break 6% prior to December 25 as an early gift from Santa for all of the pain fixed-income investors have felt over the past two years.

For the Week of November 24, 1997

The biggest event for the bond market this week will be the release of the monthly budget statement on Monday. The yield on the benchmark 30-year Treasury Bond is not going to break through the landmark 6% level just because of a flight to quality. It can only do it based on strong underlying fundamentals. The cornerstone foundation to these strong fundamentals is our shrinking deficit and reduced supply of debt financing going forward. This week's release of the Budget Statement is the first one for the new fiscal year which began October 1st and it is very important that we pick up right where we left off last year. *I expect the Long Bond to continue its rally through the 6% level after it receives the good news that we are continuing to win the budget deficit battle.* The second strong fundamental that the bond market has going for it is the fact that the Southeast Asian currency and economic meltdown will slow our economy down which means that the Federal Reserve Board will not have to raise rates anytime soon to slow economic growth. Whenever you can take the constant fear of the Federal Reserve Board raising interest rates out of the picture, it is certainly a positive for the bond market.

For the Week of December 8, 1997

The outlook for bonds continues to remain very positive. ***We will be below 6% on the Long Treasury Bond by the end of the year.*** Three fundamental factors will continue to converge to push the bond yield lower. First, our economy will be slowing down from its break-neck pace set in the first half of this year. And while the economists will continue to argue just how much it will slow down, the consensus that it will slow down is very bullish for bonds. Second, there is not and will not be any inflation for the bond market to worry about. And while the consensus appears to be no inflation from the commodity market as the price of gold and oil continue to plunge, it's wage inflation that everyone still worries about. Don't worry about wage inflation; it's not going to accelerate. If you want to know why, you don't have to look at the economic release, just open your eyes and look what's happening in our "Services" industries over the past couple of weeks. The public accounting firm of Coopers & Lybrand agree to merge with Price Waterhouse. First Union Bank agrees to buy CoreStates Bank. Ernst & Young, another public accounting firm agrees to merge with Peat Marwick. And finally Merrill Lynch agrees to acquire Mercury Asset Management. What our economic releases fail to tell us is that there is not one person in any of those eight firms worrying about how much their wages will increase next year. They are all worried about whether they will have a job next year. It's job insecurity, fueled by mergers and acquisitions that will keep wage inflation in check. Third, because of our strong economy, our deficit will continue to shrink. A shrinking deficit not only is bullish for bonds because of what it does for the supply/demand fundamentals going forward (less supply), it also helps attract foreign capital. A country that has its fiscal house in order has a magnet for foreign capital.

For the Week of December 15, 1997

The fundamentals for our bond market remain very strong: Slowing economic growth due to the Southeast Asian currency and economic meltdown, little or no inflation—which is actually being helped by the Southeast Asian crisis—and finally, a federal budget deficit that is the envy of the entire industrialized world. With these strong fundamentals, *the market will continue to rally and finally break the 6.0% mark on the 30-year Treasury Bond by year end*. My extreme optimism in the bond market is because, in addition to these strong underlying fundamentals, two additional factors will serve as even more strength in the bond market. First is the pre-earnings disappointments that will be announced in the stock market. These earnings disappointments will cause many United States investors to search for safety and quality. There is nothing stronger or safer than debt backed by the United States. In addition to United States investors, we will continue to see foreign investors pour money into our bond market as well, as they search for a safe haven from the Asian crisis and will become leery of placing money in the United States equity market as well—so the new global strategy is . . . buy bonds. The second additional factor that should help drive the yield below 6% is the tremendous demand for bonds that will be created as investors re-balance their portfolios. You see, because of the tremendous bull run that we have had in the stock market, investors that began the year with an asset allocation strategy of 60% stocks and 40% bonds, may find themselves with 70% in stocks and 30% in bonds because of the tremendous price appreciation in stocks. Thus, as investors re-balance their portfolios, there will be an even greater demand for bonds. 5.5% by the end of 1998 is not out of the question.

For the Week of December 22, 1997

There is nothing from an economic release perspective that could cause the yield on the benchmark 30-year Treasury Bond to go back above 6%. It will take some major external events to spook the market back above 6%. While we are never without a long list of potential issues to scare our markets: Iraq, Japan, South Korea, etc., etc., *I feel that the Long Bond will end the year below 6% and will be poised to continue its strong rally into the first half of 1998*. The combination of no inflation and steady (yet slowing) economic growth should combine to keep the Goldilocks' economy alive and well. And remember, it's this Goldilocks' economy of no inflation and steady (yet slowing) economic growth that is the real story behind our Long Bond breaking the 6% level.

5 CURRENCY MARKET PERSPECTIVE

OVERVIEW

The problems around the globe quickly translated into problems for the currency markets. Two currencies dominated the scene in 1997. The U.S. Dollar had another great year. The U.S. Dollar ended 1997 at 130.57 and the Japanese Yen at 1.7980. The German Mark compared to 115.85 Yen and 1.5400 Marks to begin the year. The strong U.S. Dollar was merely a reflection of the strong underlying fundamentals of the U.S. economy.

Meanwhile the story with the Hong Kong Dollar was really a focus on whether that currency would be protected or if it would fall like the other Southeast Asian currencies.

The Hong Kong Dollar remained protected and here is why. Hong Kong's foreign exchange policy links the Hong Kong Dollar to the U.S. Dollar. What's important to note is that the Hong Kong Monetary Authority is a currency board and not a central bank, with the distinction that a currency board's main mandate is the maintenance of the currency value. A central bank typically has other mandates in addition to the currency, including growth, employment and inflation. As a result, Hong Kong's economic policy is conducted mainly through fiscal policy.

And remember, three banks have the authority to issue currency in Hong Kong. To issue Hong Kong Dollars, these banks are required to submit U.S. Dollars to the Exchange Fund. The U.S. Dollar foreign exchange reserves at the exchange fund now stands at about $65 billion, which is equivalent to about five times the currency currently in circulation. In addition, Hong Kong has $88 billion in foreign exchange reserves and when you add in China's $122 billion, that's an additional $210 billion in reserves. Make no mistake about it; the Hong Kong Dollar will be protected.

Sit back now and enjoy the ride as I recap with you the issues and events that drive my currency market outlook as they evolved on a week by week basis from Tax Day (April 15th) through the end of 1997.

For the Week of April 14, 1997

The near term direction of the U.S. Dollar may have more to do with trade talks than economic fundamentals. With Japanese Prime Minister Hashimoto's visit to the United States right around the corner, I expect the "dollar bashers" (lead by the Automotive Industry) to be lobbying in full force for a weaker dollar between now and the Prime Minister's visit. Any signs of support for a weakening dollar from key administration officials (which I expect to happen. . . . remember the Automobile Industry = Labor Unions = Democratic party = Clinton Administration) could *cause a short term slide in the value of the dollar.* . . . Look for Japan to begin exploring options to strengthen the Japanese Yen against the U.S. Dollar. While it is quite obvious that the only solution is intervention, Japan would be very reluctant to intervene unless it was joint intervention with the United States. I don't think that is going to happen anytime soon. Thus, with intervention not really an option, expect a high profile verbal attack on the dollar from Japan which means *rumors will abound the next few weeks regarding Japanese intervention* in hopes that those rumors alone will weaken the dollar. . . . *Look for the Bank of Canada to increase interest rates in order to support the Canadian Dollar.* The underlying strength in the Canadian Dollar was based on the fundamentals of a strong current account surplus and continued government spending cuts. Both of these trends have slowed; however, and when you combine that with the expectation of another rate hike in the U.S. on May 20, the Bank of Canada must move quickly to support the Canadian Dollar.

For the Week of April 21, 1997

With Japanese Prime Minister Hashimoto meeting with President Clinton this week, it could be a very volatile week for the currency markets. I expect Japan to step up their threats to intervene in the currency markets to support the yen/dollar relationship. Those continued threats combined with Treasury Secretary Robert Rubin's apparent softening of his strong dollar position could combine to *send the dollar lower in the immediate short term.* The real key to the dollar/yen relationship will be the response of the other members of the Group of Seven leading industrial nations regarding backing up Japan's intervention threat. . . . I *look for the Italian Lira to continue its fall* as concerns abound regarding Italy's chances to join the

European Economic and Monetary Union. Italy's deficit problem is real and there is no end in sight fueled by a slowdown in government tax receipts at the same time that government expenditures are continuing to rise. Lower receipts plus higher expenditures equal a major budget deficit problem.

For the Week of April 28, 1997

I expect continued weakness in the Australian Dollar driven by the interest rate relationships in the United States and Australia. Australia's inflation rate is trending lower especially on the consumer front. This trend has all but removed the possibility of the Central Bank of Australia raising interest rates. Meanwhile, interest rates in the United States are expected to rise. Higher interest rates make deposits in a country's currency more attractive. Thus with higher interest rates expected in the U.S. and lower interest rates expected in Australia, I expect global investors to move out of the Australian currency and into the United States Dollar. . . . *I also expect the German Deutsche Mark to continue its slide* as the prospects for the European Monetary Union (EMU) gain ground. To understand the Deutsche Mark's weakness, you have to look to France not Germany for the answer. You see, French President Chirac called an election one year early with the sole purpose of gaining political support for budget cutting measures to enable France to meet the standards for the single currency. There is no way that the EMU would start on time without France. When things look bleak for EMU, investors flock to German assets; however, when things look rosy, all the currencies in Europe rise at the expense of the German Deutsche Mark.

For the Week of May 5, 1997

While the markets continue to be very concerned about a possible coordinated effort among G-7 countries to weaken the United States Dollar, some of the benefits of a strong dollar are becoming clearer and clearer. First, a rising dollar tends to restrain inflation (lowers the price of imports because of the currency exchange which, in turn, keeps domestic prices low so they can compete against cheaper imports). Second, a strong dollar means that our major trading partners, Japan and Germany, will have weaker currencies. *A weaker German Mark and Japanese Yen will actually help those economies recover, fueled by strong exports.* Both the German and Japanese economy are looking for signs of strength for different reasons. In Germany, it's to reach the Maastricht Treaty for the European Monetary Union; while in Japan, it's to offset the recent increase on their Value Added Tax. . . . The currency market may even have a voice in the next FOMC meeting. Neither Germany nor Japan are in a position of economic strength which means neither country can raise interest rates anytime soon. These central bankers, though, may exert political pressure on the U.S. Central Bank (Federal Reserve Board) not to aggressively raise interest rates. *An aggressive increase in U.S. interest rates should only serve to make the dollar even stronger* as foreign investors will "buy" dollars in order to invest in our higher yielding markets. We are truly operating in a global marketplace where even the most micro decisions can have international ramifications.

For the Week of May 12, 1997

Look for the dollar to continue to slide against the yen this week. Two separate events should continue the downward pressure. First, United States auto sales for April lost market share to the Japanese imports which were driven by the weak yen. All eyes continue to watch for any major trade imbalances that the strong dollar is causing. The U.S. Automotive Industry is the most politically sensitive to this trade issue and if any industry can get the Clinton Administration to weaken its support for the strong dollar, it is the labor union intensive Automobile Industry. Second, the Bank of Japan is sending a very clear message to the currency markets that it does not need the support of the other members of the G-7 to intervene against the dollar. Intervention seemed very unlikely if it were to be a coordinated event among G-7 nations. However, *isolated intervention solely by Japan appears to now be a real possibility.* . . . The currency markets better watch out for the speakers circuit this week as Treasury Secretary Robert Rubin (Mr. Strong Dollar) speaks at the Investment Company Institute in Washington, D.C. Any comments about the need to strengthen the yen could certainly rattle the dollar.

For the Week of May 19, 1997

The overall strong fundamentals of the United States economy will eventually turn the dollar around. *I expect the dollar to stay weak but it will begin to show some strength after the FOMC rate hike.* What a difference a few weeks make. The G-7 intervention that we were so worried about may now come to actually support the dollar not to weaken it. While the G-7 officials wanted a weaker dollar, they certainly didn't want to see it get massacred the way it has. Most of the weakness in the dollar can be traced to Japanese Trust Banks acting on behalf of their corporate pension funds. One reason that the dollar will remain weak is that I fully expect Japanese life insurance companies and major exporters to also trim their positions regardless of where rates head. . . . A trader remarked to me that what the dollar really needs is "divine intervention not G-7 intervention." Well, we just may have an angel on the horizon to provide such divine intervention. This angel, however, is spelled Angell. On Wednesday, former Federal Reserve Board Governor Wayne Angell gives a speech in Tokyo on U.S. interest rate trends. It's no secret that Angell is one of the biggest interest rate "hawks" around. By the time he is finished speaking, Tokyo will be convinced that the Long Bond will be above 10% by the end of the year. One sure-fire way to accelerate the strength of the dollar is to increase the foreign investors expectation of rising U.S. interest rates.

For the Week of May 26, 1997

The overall currency market will continue to be dominated by the dollar/yen focus. The dramatic movement of the dollar in recent weeks has the entire currency market on edge. While there certainly was consensus, especially among G-7 Finance Ministers, that the dollar was getting too strong, no one wanted it to fall so quickly. As little as two weeks ago, the market consensus called for U.S. interest rates to move higher and Japanese interest rates to stay flat, or even go lower if that's possible. This interest rate forecast was one of the key reasons why the dollar was strong and the yen was weak. Higher interest rates attract foreign investment and foreign investments first have to become denominated in the currency of the investment. These changing interest rate expectations, no rate increase in the U.S. but maybe a rate increase in Japan, has been the real story behind the story in this dramatic currency market swing. Expectations changed once, why not again. *When investors re-focus on the underlying economic fundamentals, they will soon realize that Japan can't raise interest rates anytime soon and that the U.S. will raise interest rates again, and that will fuel the dollar's rebound.* Although I do not expect the dollar to make up all the ground it lost, a dollar trading at 120 yen is not out of the question by late June.

For the Week of June 2, 1997

Finally the focus of the currency markets has shifted from Japan to Europe, where the concern is dominated by the changing political landscapes in Britain, France and maybe even Germany. All of this change calls into question the timely implementation of the European Monetary Union (EMU). During this time of extreme volatility regarding the EMU, *I expect the German Mark to continue to post strong gains this week against all other European currencies*. In the past, the German currency has become the safe harbor for European currency "plays" if problems appear on the horizon regarding EMU. Things just couldn't look worse for EMU or better for the German Mark, at least in the short run.

For the Week of June 9, 1997

This could be a very important and volatile week for the dollar/yen exchange rate. *The fundamentals of the United States and Japanese economies do not support the recent rise in the yen*. Japanese officials, however, will go to great lengths to see that the yen is supported at this level, while United States officials will become very concerned if it increases any further. Thus look for "High Profile" currency debates from both governments this week. The reason for the renewed focus this week is that next week at the June 20th summit of G-7 officials, both Japanese and United States officials know that they will be taking a back seat to the Maastricht Treaty discussion and the concern for currency stability in Europe. As a result, we could have a very ugly war of words which could very quickly evolve into a very volatile week for the dollar/yen rate. Don't bet against the dollar. When all is said and done, you simply can't hide the fact that the Japanese banking crisis is nowhere near over. The magnitude of the non-performing loans will continue to deteriorate the Banking Industry in Japan. I fully expect there to be some outright bank failures in Japan. You can talk all you want about the currencies, but when you look at the economic fundamentals, the dollar is a clear winner, you can "Bank" on it.

For the Week of June 30, 1997

As the fallout from Japanese Prime Minister Ryutaco Hashimoto continues this week, *I expect both the dollar and the yen to display extreme volatility* as currency traders attempt to figure out exactly what these ill advised comments from the Prime Minister actually mean. It's hard to misinterpret what someone is saying when they say it so clearly "I hope the U.S. will engage in efforts and cooperation to maintain exchange stability, so that we would not succumb to the temptation to sell off treasury bills and switch our foreign reserves to gold." Such a move would have grave ramifications on the currencies of both Japan and the United States. Currency traders are now left on their own trying to figure out if there is any cooperation among the two countries regarding a certain band or range within where they would like to see their currencies trade. Once the markets perceive the lack of any such band of support, it tends to heighten volatility in the market. Prime Minister Hashimoto's threat has all but assured a very volatile currency market over the next few weeks.

For the Week of July 7, 1997

This week will be a very volatile one for the Mexican Peso. The currency markets will be forced to quickly evaluate just what impact Sunday's Mexican election will have on the economy and the currency. I do not see much risk of Mexico changing direction from their economic reform strategy regardless of the outcome of the election. *Even though the peso will be very volatile this week, I expect it to post strong gains from now through the end of the year.* The greatest risks to the peso is if the election does not produce any clear majority in Congress. Remember, the only thing that the currency markets hate more than change is uncertainty. Lack of a clear majority in Congress will create a great deal of uncertainty which will add to an already volatile currency market. That point aside, this election is a watershed event that continues Mexico's march toward democracy. Longer term, the foundation is being set that will attract increased foreign investment flow into Mexico which will certainly serve to keep the peso strong.

For the Week of July 14, 1997

The German Mark should continue its strong showing this week. *I look for the German Mark to strengthen relative to the U.S. Dollar.* The foundation of a stronger German Mark is not a strong German economy but rather, a strong German Central Bank. Bundesbank President Hans Tietmeyer has made it clear that the Central Bank of Germany wants a stronger German Mark. The weak German Mark, however, has not been all bad news for the German economy. The weaker German Mark has served as a nice boost to exports by making German products cheaper in the United States due to the currency exchange rates. It has been these strong exports that have helped the weak German economy. The concern of the Bundesbank Bank right now, however, is not the economy, it's inflation. The source of the concern is that a weak currency causes the price of imports to Germany to cost more due to the currency exchange. The increased price of imports in turn gives German companies the flexibility to raise their prices to keep them in line with the higher prices of imports. It is this deadly one-two punch of inflation that has pushed the Bundesbank to make sure the German Mark rallies.

For the Week of July 21, 1997

I expect the dollar to weaken against the yen in the upcoming weeks. While I remain very bullish on the dollar in the long run, I do not expect it to surge to the record levels that it held against the yen in recent months. Instead of focusing on how high the dollar can go against the yen, it may be more important to focus on how low the dollar can fall. *I feel that the dollar could drop to 110 yen but not below that critical level.* There are three key reasons why the dollar will not drop below 110. First, the United States economy is just too strong. Remember the strength of a country's currency is no more than a reflection of their underlying economy. Second, Japan's economy and especially Japan's Banking Industry is not out of the woods yet. As long as there are major question marks regarding the Japanese banking crisis and their economic recovery, there is just no way the dollar can fall below 110. Third, and finally, Japanese officials won't let the yen rally that far. Japan's economic recovery is centered on the back of their export markets. A strong dollar makes Japanese imports cheaper to U.S. consumers. If the yen strengthens, the cost of Japanese imports to

U.S. consumers rises and the entire economic recovery of Japan would be called into question.

For the Week of July 28, 1997

In case you were wondering why the Finance Minister of Thailand went to Japan to discuss stabilizing Thailand's currency, the Baht, it's because Japan has more to lose than Thailand itself. As a result, *I fully expect Japan to intervene to support Thailand's currency from going into a free-fall.* Two factors will combine to force Japan to intervene. First, Japan has tremendous financial and commercial interests in Thailand. These investments would be severely damaged if the currency continues to weaken. The Japanese Banking Industry is already on the edge. It cannot afford to show huge losses on their investments in Thailand. Second, if Thailand's Baht continues to fall, it will serve as a noose around the currency of Malaysia and other Asian currencies causing them to be devalued as well. Remember, Japan's economic recovery is being driven by their global exports. Think of what happens to that market if all of a sudden the entire Asian region has a weaker currency. That, in essence, means that "their" exports will cost less. Japan can ill afford the risk of letting a whole new level of export market competitors emerge. While there is no doubt that Japan will attempt to arrange broad international support for Thailand, if that support is not forthcoming, Japan will step up to the plate on its own. After all, this isn't about the Thailand Baht, it's about Japanese exports.

For the Week of August 4, 1997

With the prospects of another round of interest rate hikes just around the corner, *I expect the British Pound Sterling to have a great rally the early part of this week* leading up to the Bank of England's next meeting to discuss monetary policy, which is currently set for Thursday and Friday. Whether the rally continues or not, depends on what the Bank of England does at that meeting. Currency markets swing dramatically as they attempt to determine future interest rate moves. The British currency has nowhere to swing but up as all signs point to the likelihood of an interest rate hike sooner rather than later. Consider the recent comments by Britain's Chancellor of the Exchequer Gordon Brown when he made it perfectly clear that he will not raise taxes as a way to slow down the British Consumer. The way that he would slow down the British consumer is to raise interest rates. The Bank of England has already raised interest rates three times in the past three months, and four for four is not out of the realm of possibility. The pure speculation that the Bank of England may raise interest rates is enough to insure a great rally in the British currency as least for the first half of the week.

For the Week of August 18, 1997

Last week's $16 billion bail-out for Thailand will not stop the weakness in Asian currencies for the remainder of the year. There are tremendous downside risks still to be faced in the short run in Thailand as it attempts to implement the necessary spending and tax policy changes to turn its economy around. Any setback for any reason will immediately be felt by the currencies of Hong Kong, Singapore, Malaysia, Indonesia and Japan. The currency markets are already volatile enough but now we have added another level of volatility to these Asian markets. Not only will their currencies move dramatically to reflect changes in the underlying economy, but they will move even more dramatically to reflect what's happening or, more appropriately, not happening in Thailand. There is clearly more downside risk than upside potential in the Asian currency market.

For the Week of August 25, 1997

I expect the landscape of world trade to change rather dramatically over the next few months as the recent currency moves begin to have an impact. The United States should see a weakening of their trade with the so-called "Asian Tigers" of Thailand, Malaysia, Indonesia, Singapore and the like. This shift is being driven by the tremendous drop of these Asian Tiger's currencies against the dollar. The especially strong dollar now makes the cost of United States goods and services even more expensive to the Asian Tigers' consumers. The shift will also be felt within the Asian Tigers' circle. The lone currency to withstand the Asian onslaught has been Hong Kong. Even though Hong Kong has been able to protect the value of the Hong Kong dollar, the Hong Kong economy may now suffer. Because of the tremendous devaluation of other currencies in the region, their products will be cheaper and much more competitive in the region. Hong Kong's economy will not be able to withstand the tremendous new source of export competition from its fellow Asian Tigers. *The real loser in the Asian currency crisis just might be the Hong Kong economy, at least in the short run.*

For the Week of September 1, 1997

If we can step back from the daily volatility in the currency markets and remember that a country's currency is merely a reflection of that country's economy, then *the dollar should continue to strengthen against the Japanese Yen*. The economies of Japan and the United States are heading in the opposite direction. The recovery of the Japanese economy is just not happening. In addition, the recent increase in Japan's Value Added Tax (VAT) is really hindering their economic recovery. Meanwhile, in the United States, our economy just continues to get stronger and stronger. With the second quarter Gross Domestic Product number closer to 4% than 3%, the United States economy continues to hit on all cylinders. In addition, the Japanese economy is also hindered by the Asian currency crisis, especially in Thailand. Japanese financial institutions have tremendous exposure in Thailand; in fact, it is Japanese investments that have really fueled Thailand's rapid economic growth. If the troubles in Thailand persist, they most certainly will spill over into Japan's banking system first and then Japan's economy. In the short term, things just could not look better for the United States nor worse for Japan and these fundamentals should be reflected in a stronger dollar.

For the Week of September 8, 1997

Much of the focus in the currency markets from the United States perspective has been the dramatic movements of the dollar against our benchmark currencies; the Japanese Yen and the German Mark. Much of the recent volatility was fueled regarding potential interest rate hikes in Germany and Japan. Even though the rumors continue to mount, the Bundesbank has held firm and has yet to raise rates in Germany. Meanwhile, Japan is in no position to raise interest rates even if they wanted to move them. Their economy continues to sit on the brink of disaster, especially with the meltdown of the other Pacific Rim Asian economies. Maybe the most interesting development in the currency market is not between the dollar and its two benchmarks, the Japanese Yen and the German Mark, but rather the interplay between the two benchmark currencies, namely the yen and the mark. *I think that the German Mark will continue to weaken versus the Japanese Yen*.

For the Week of September 15, 1997

I look for extreme volatility in the currency markets in the coming weeks, especially the dollar. The major source of this volatility will be political "jawboning" that will attempt to move the currency markets so that public policies do not have to be changed. Look for both President Clinton as well as Treasury Secretary, Bob Rubin, to start talking "down" the United States Dollar as a way to offset the current concerns with our trade deficit with Japan. The markets do quite well when they are asked to trade off of the underlying economic fundamentals. The markets don't do nearly as well when they are expected to trade off of political hot air. Everyone seems to interpret the political motives a little bit differently and as a result, the volatility in the markets increases dramatically. And don't expect the political jawboning to be limited to the United States. Both Germany and Japan will continue their high profile rhetoric in hopes of supporting their currency. Their jawboning will be about the likelihood of raising interest rates in Germany and Japan (which by the way in turn strengthens their currency). There are a lot of uncertainties in the markets ahead, however, I am certain of two things: neither Japan or Germany can raise interest rates in the very near future. When your unemployment rate is pushing double digits as it is in Germany, rising interest rates to slow the economy will make an already politically sensitive unemployment crisis even worse. And in Japan, where their economy last week reported the largest quarterly drop in 23 years, any attempt to move interest rates higher will only serve to further depress an already depressing economy.

For the Week of September 22, 1997

I expect extreme volatility in the weeks and maybe even months ahead in the European Currency Markets. This extreme volatility will not be fueled by changes in the underlying economies of the various European countries, but rather speculation of currency revaluation prior to the official setting of the European Monetary Unions conversion rates next May. Such a move would immediately make some of the European currencies more valuable while making other less valuable. This speculation will cause extreme volatility in the markets. I firmly believe that there will not be any currency revaluation's because of tremendous opposition due to both economic as well as political reasons. Regardless of what finally does or does not happen, the mere discussion of currency revaluation's will move the markets. Remember Health Care Reform was never adopted; however, the mere discussion turned pharmaceutical stocks upside down. Sometimes the fear of something happening moves the markets more than anything happening.

For the Week of September 29, 1997

I think that we can safely sum up the currency markets in Japan and the United States with the simple phrase "all talk and no action." Although the phrase is simple, the consequences most likely will lead to increased volatility in the dollar/yen currency trade. While Japanese officials, especially Finance Minister Sakakibara, will talk down the dollar, *there will be no Japanese intervention to support the yen versus the dollar.* The name of the game is, if you can move the currency market with words, you may never have to use money. I think that the continued threat of potential Japanese intervention will keep the currency markets on edge. However, all the talk in the world cannot change the fact that the economies of Japan and the United States are heading in opposite directions. Remember, a country's currency is really a reflection of the country's underlying economy. Even though we have witnessed a recent rise in Japanese department store sales, the overall economy in Japan remains on the edge and the economic impact of the Asian Tiger meltdown which started in Thailand, hasn't even begun to show up in the Japanese economy. Things are going to get much worse before they get better. Meanwhile in the United States, we are experiencing above trend economic growth with little or no inflation. These strong economic fundamentals mean that all the talk in the world can't stop the dollar's continued rise against the Japanese Yen.

For the Week of October 6, 1997

The Canadian Dollar should remain strong and I expect it to continue to rally in the fourth quarter. Last week the Bank of Canada's decision to raise rates by 25 basis points after the tremendous July Gross Domestic Product increase of 0.8% in Canada means that the

Bank of Canada is going to be a very pro-active inflation fighter. What is of the utmost importance of this recent hike is that it is being regarded as a necessary modest credit tightening move now to avoid any drastic reactionary measures in the future. I do not expect the Canadian economy to slow down in the foreseeable future. Thus, I fully expect that there will be at least one more rate hike from the Bank of Canada between now and the end of the year. Also the next rate hike could be 50 basis points instead of 25. This higher interest rate environment will be extremely bullish for the Canadian Dollar for the remainder of the year. I look for the next rate hike to come sooner rather than later in the fourth quarter; in fact, I would not rule out another rate hike in October. These short-term rate hike expectations should bring speculators to the Canadian currency which will cause the Canadian Dollar to rise even higher.

For the Week of October 13, 1997

It is going to be an extremely volatile currency market for the remainder of the year as currency traders take big bets on who will raise interest rates before the end of the year, which in turn will serve as a major base of support for their currency. Now that Germany has raised its repurchase rate for the first time in five years, and France, Austria, Belgium, Denmark and the Netherlands, quickly followed, all eyes are on England for the next move. *England will not sit still for long as I expect them to jump in and raise rates* as well because they too need to boost the value of their currency which in turn will increase the return on investments denominated in their currency. Don't forget about the United States, or should I more appropriately say Alan Greenspan. Mr. Greenspan is sending the market a clear message that he is looking to raise interest rates and if he needed a trigger, maybe higher rates in Europe are it. And it doesn't stop here. Any movement in rates in the U.S. will force Canada to raise rates to support its currency. Which brings us back to Germany with the question, who said that they were done with just one rate increase? *An uncertain interest rate environment on a global basis can create a very, very volatile currency market*. Things could not be much more uncertain regarding interest rates globally and remember this is like a domino effect once someone moves, everyone moves. This will be the most volatile quarter of the entire year for currency markets.

For the Week of October 20, 1997

Now that the crisis in Italy has been resolved due to the 180° flip-flop by Communist Re-foundation leader Fausto Bertinotti, *I expect the Italian Lira to have a strong run the remainder of the year.* Remember, it was Bertinotti that had forced Prime Minister Romano Prodi's resignation when he rejected the government's 1998 budget. Bertinotti caved into criticism from all fronts about the long-term ramifications of toppling Italy's government. Now Bertinotti is supporting the 1998 budget that is exactly the same deal he rejected two weeks ago. Prime Minister Prodi has, in fact, not given Bertinotti any more than he had already offered in his last ditch attempt to keep the budget deal alive, namely an eventual shift to a 35 hour workweek, and a commitment regarding pension benefits for blue-collar workers. This is a clear victory for one of the real "good-guys" in Europe, Prime Minister Romano Prodi. Investors around the world will cast their vote of support for Prodi by running up the value of the Italian Lira.

For the Week of October 27, 1997

All eyes in the currency markets are on the dollar to determine if this Asian meltdown will come to the United States. It will not. *The dollar will continue to strengthen versus the Japanese Yen.* The Japanese Yen simply cannot strengthen versus the dollar until the Japanese economy strengthens and that does not look as if it is going to occur anytime soon. Real estate continues to depreciate in Japan. Real estate prices have fallen every month this year in Japan. Weak real estate prices tend to have a ripple effect. When real estate is very weak, it tends to slow down the Banking Industry. When the Banking Industry slows down, capital for economic growth and expansion is harder (or more expensive) to come by, which in turn, means that the economy will slow down. Add to this the fact that the Southeast Asian crisis will hit Japan before it does the United States and you will see why there is no end in sight to the bullish run of the dollar against the Japanese Yen . . . *I also look for the dollar to strengthen against our other major benchmark, the German Mark.* The recent strength in the mark versus the dollar was really a reflection of a major sell-off and meltdown in the United States stock market. When investors step back and look at the strong earnings' season in the United States stock market, the knee-jerk reaction of running up the value of the German Mark versus the dollar will not only stop, it will reverse itself. I

For the Week of December 8, 1997

I expect the dollar to remain very strong the remainder of the year.
The United States clearly has the most vibrant and dynamic economy in
the world. It's the fundamentals of a country's underlying economy
that will ultimately drive the value of its currency and our underlying
fundamentals can drive our currencies' value nowhere but up. In
addition to our strength, the major currency benchmarks continue to
have dark clouds over their heads. In Japan, the fact that the
government is being very pro-active in dealing with their Banking
Industry crisis is a positive; but because of the uncertainty that this issue
causes, it will remain a very negative issue for its currency. Meanwhile,
our other major currency benchmark, Germany, continues to struggle
with high unemployment and the ongoing saga regarding whether or
not there will be a European Monetary Union and will it be launched
on time. This combination of good news in the United States and
uncertain news with our major benchmarks all adds up to good news
for a strong dollar.

For the Week of December 15, 1997

Even though South Korea has secured its bailout package from the
International Monetary Fund, the worst is far from over. ***I expect the
South Korean Won to continue its free-fall the remainder of this year.***
I think that there are three important issues that will drive the Won
lower. First, keep in mind the actual bailout amount started at $20
billion and quickly ballooned to where it stands today at $57 billion.
With each couple of billion dollars comes the need for even greater
austerity and fiscal constraint. I'm not convinced that South Korea fully
comprehends what it agreed to. Second, the crisis in South Korea transcends sovereign debt. It's a major mistake to compare South Korea to
Mexico. In Mexico the problem was confined to sovereign debt. In
South Korea, it's not just the sovereign debt that's in trouble, but weak
private loans as well. Oh, and by the way, many of these private loans
are actually guaranteed by the South Korean government. Can you say
tip of the iceberg? Third, and finally, there is a major political wild card
in South Korea. The politically naive International Monetary Funds
expects the global markets to be relieved because they obtained pledges
from all the leading presidential candidates that they wouldn't renege
on the current government's agreement with the International
Monetary Fund. What did you expect them to say? Here in the United

States we clearly understand how politics work . . . What you say to get elected may have little or no bearing on what you do after you are elected. The International Monetary Fund better look close; I wouldn't be surprised if the agreements from the Presidential candidates were signed with disappearing ink.

6 COMMODITY MARKET PERSPECTIVE

OVERVIEW

What a volatile year for the commodities market. Depending on what particular commodity in which you were invested, you either had a terrible year or a great one.

If you invested in gold, you had a terrible year. Gold ended 1997 at $289.90 an ounce which was a decline of over 20% for the year. A good deal of this decline came from the ongoing threats that Central Banks from around the globe were going to flood the markets by liquidating major gold holdings.

If on the other hand you were invested in coffee, you had a great year. At one point in the year coffee surged to over $3.00 a pound which represented the highest level in over 20 years as well as a three-fold increase from where we began the year.

Hold on and enjoy the trip as I recap with you how the issues and events that drive my commodity market outlook evolved on a week by week basis from Tax Day (April 15th) through the end of 1997.

For the Week of April 14, 1997

A cross section of commodity prices (lumber, wheat and coffee) should all continue to rise, each for fundamentally different reasons. . . . The lumber market is being fueled by the mild winter across the United States which allowed builders to get a jump start on the spring building season. That early start has depleted lumber inventories right as we head into the peak of spring building season which *will fuel lumber prices even higher* . . . Weather meanwhile should continue to play havoc with wheat prices as recent cold spells could damage the winter wheat crop, while the melting of snow and flooding will damage the spring crop. All of the supply problems become even bigger as I look for stronger global wheat demand fueled mainly by India. *Look for wheat prices to continue to move upward. . . . Coffee will continue its climb* due to a weaker crop in Columbia and export concerns in Brazil. This price pressure is very short term and I expect the run-up in coffee prices to be very short lived.

For the Week of April 21, 1997

Labor disputes and the weather man should have the greatest impact on the commodity markets. *Look for copper and crude Oil prices to rise amid separate labor conflicts*. In Venezuela tanker pilots are inching closer to a strike that would impact the daily export of almost 2 million barrels of oil. Meanwhile in Chile, almost a quarter of the workforce at the world's largest copper mine are protesting for higher wages. Both of these conflicts should be resolved quickly. Weather is continuing to dominate the wheat market as frigid temperatures have destroyed a quarter of the winter wheat crop in the United States. Weather forecasters are calling for more frigid weather in the wheat-belt areas of the United States which will send wheat prices even higher.

For the Week of April 28, 1997

All eyes in the Commodities market will be on Russia as that country clearly has the world's attention from a precious metals standpoint. Russia has not exported any precious metals at all this entire year. And I don't foresee a policy reversal anytime soon. *Thus, I expect platinum and palladium prices to continue to climb higher.* When Russia stopped exporting precious metals, the worldwide supply of platinum and palladium felt the pinch first. Russia is the world's largest producer of palladium and is the world's number two producer of platinum. This strain on supply comes at a time when demand for these precious metals is reaching an all time high fueled by both the Automotive Industry and the Electronic Industry. High demand and low supply means the price of platinum and palladium have nowhere to go but up.

For the Week of May 5, 1997

I look for continued volatility in the precious metals market, especially silver. Silver should continue its fall this week. Silver's decline is being driven by two forces that are converging to weaken the price of this commodity. First, the strong dollar serves as a detriment for industrial demand in the particular foreign countries where the dollar is strongest (inversely local precious metals rise). Second, if overall global demand slows (not due to any currency issues), the price of silver that is dollar denominated gets hit once again, only harder. *This convergence of a strong dollar and weakening demand should be enough to send the price of silver even lower this week.*

For the Week of May 12, 1997

There could be some real upward pressure on wheat prices despite the fact that the U.S. spring wheat planting season appears to be back on track. From the international front, the European Union is taxing wheat exports as a means of building up wheat supplies in Europe. While on the domestic front, the recent freeze across the United States may have destroyed anywhere from up to 10% of the U.S. wheat crop. *The combination of lower domestic supply because of weather and lower international supply because of tax policy should certainly serve as the fuel to push wheat prices higher* in the near term.

For the Week of May 19, 1997

Events in the United States and Germany will continue to have a major impact on the price of gold. *I expect gold prices to display extreme volatility this week.* From the United States perspective a weaker United States Dollar will continue to drive gold demand and thus gold prices higher. This is due to the fact that when the dollar falls, gold is now cheaper to buy in foreign denominated currencies. It is this strong demand for gold outside of the U.S. that will drive prices up. Meanwhile, events in Germany hang like a dark cloud over the gold market. Germany's Finance Minister, Theo Waigel, is considering a proposal to revalue The Central Bank's gold which is currently in its "books" at well below market value. By revaluing Germany's gold reserves closer to the market price, Germany could release billions of "hidden" reserves to fund government deficits and avoid raising taxes. Expect more details of this proposal to come forward this week. One thing is for certain, whenever the details are released, the price of gold will most likely over-react.

For the Week of May 26, 1997

Two separate events are converging together to drive up coffee prices. As a result, I look for coffee prices to continue to climb higher again this week. The two events impacting the coffee market are the weather and trade. First from the trade front, the coffee market will continue to absorb and analyze the impact of the Association of Coffee Producing Countries Agreement to limit coffee exports. Although there is currently an export limit in place, with the already large run-up in coffee prices since January, the market was hoping for more supply. *Add to this trade backdrop the recent concerns about weather and you will see why coffee prices will continue to go higher.* The largest producer of coffee, Brazil has two major weather stories that are impacting their coffee crop. First, there has been below average rainfall, which will have a negative impact on crops; and secondly, there is grave concern for a rare "frost" to potentially hit the already lack of rain weakened coffee crop. These two events could combine to send coffee prices to record levels, and send consumers to drink tea.

For the Week of June 2, 1997

It has been almost a year since the Sumitomo Copper scandal broke. It's time to close that copper chapter and move on as *I expect copper prices to rise sharply the second half of the year.* This rise in price will be fueled by the strong demand for copper from China (China currently accounts for over 10% of all copper consumption). Two events will serve to peak demand in China. First, the government is easing restrictions on the use of copper. Second, China's five-year economic plan focuses on two key industries, Construction and Telecommunications. Both of these industries happen to be major copper users.

For the Week of June 9, 1997

Friday the 13th could prove to be an unlucky day for coffee prices. That is the day that the U.S. Department of Agriculture has scheduled to issue its first forecast of the Brazilian coffee crop for the 1997–1998 season. Brazil's largest coffee cooperative already released its forecast that the country's coffee crop should reach 24 to 25 million bags (60 kg) in 1997–1998. This is down slightly from the final estimate of this year's crop which is projected to be around 27 to 30 million bags. Other Brazilian sources have pegged the 1997–1998 crop forecast at 20 million bags or below. *If the U.S. forecast is closer to 20 million than 24 million (which I expect it to be) expect a swift response from the commodity markets which will send coffee prices skyrocketing.*

For the Week of June 30, 1997

Look for the typical headline commodities of oil, gold and coffee to take a back seat again this week to Cocoa. *I expect cocoa to continue to become a very volatile commodity that could continue to surge to new record highs.* Two events are driving the cocoa markets to new highs. First, all of the technical indicators of this commodity are displaying bullish technical signs and a good deal of the traders in the commodities market follow these technical indicators religiously. Secondly, more importantly are the concerns of El Niño. El Niño is the name given to a freak weather phenomena that is caused by a weakening in the westward winds across the tropical Pacific, which in turn plays havoc with weather around the globe. Many respected scientists believe that El Niño will make a comeback in 1997. These forecasts that call for a recurrence of El Niño in 1997 turned the grain market upside down recently and now it's time to worry about the cocoa market. The combination of strong technical fundamentals and the scare of El Niño should combine to continue to push cocoa price higher.

For the Week of July 7, 1997

Even after Japanese Prime Minister Ryutaco Hashimoto's threat to sell off Japan's holdings in United States Treasury bills and switch their foreign reserves to gold, the price of gold continues to move downward. Do the commodity markets know something that our stock and bond markets do not? Did the commodity market see right through the Prime Minister's threat and realize that there would be no increased demand for gold from Japan? Maybe so, but the story of gold's falling prices has to do with a lot more than Japan. *I expect the price of gold to continue to fall, possibly breaking the landmark $330 an ounce level.* Fueling this seemingly endless free fall of gold prices are the gold mining companies themselves. In order to attempt to protect their profits, they are actually borrowing gold which they have not yet mined in order to sell now and avoid the lower gold prices in the future. This strategy has sent the gold lease rate skyrocketing and serves as a key indicator that the end of gold's price fall is nowhere in sight. Gold mining companies will continue to borrow gold and run up the level of the gold lease rate which will continue to exert downward pressure of the price of gold.

For the Week of July 14, 1997

Iraqi oil should soon be flowing again to the world's markets. *I expect the price of oil to drop dramatically this week as the final details of the Iraqi Oil for Food Deal is completed by the United Nations.* It's been almost six weeks since the United Nations has authorized a second round of over $2 billion dollars in Iraqi oil sales. The hold-up on why this oil has yet to hit the market is because Iraq and the United Nations could not come to agreement on exactly how all of the food and medical supplies that Iraq would purchase with the revenue from the sale of their oil would be distributed. Those few glitches will now be resolved and this new supply of oil could not be hitting the markets at a worse time. Crude oil supply is already 2% higher in the Untied States (which is the world's largest consumer of oil), and once Iraq steps up production of its 700,000 barrels a day under its United Nations Oil for Food and Medicine Deal, it will add an additional one percent to world supplies. This combination of already high inventory along with new supply from Iraq will certainly send oil prices downward.

For the Week of July 21, 1997

Coffee prices could continue to show signs of weakness over the next few weeks; however, this weakness will be short lived. ***By the end of the year, I look for a tremendous spike up in the price of coffee.*** This price scare will not be driven by labor problems. Rather, it will be the result of El Niño. The cyclical El Niño weather pattern is currently developing in the Pacific Ocean. This severe weather pattern which makes the dry season even dryer and the wet season even wetter, will peak in late 1997. Scientists are predicting that this El Niño could be worse than the El Niño of 1982–83 which, was the worst one of this century. While all coffee prices will spike higher, it is the Robusta coffee growing regions that will be impacted the most from El Niño. Tea anyone?

For the Week of July 28, 1997

The price of rice should rise sharply this week, driven by both short-term and long-term factors. First, in the long run, rice—especially Thai rice—is gaining popularity in Europe. Thai rice, which has always been very popular throughout Asia because it is naturally aromatic and somewhat sticky, is now one of the hottest food trends in parts of Europe. ***This increased demand from European consumers will force rice prices higher.*** Second, from a shorter term perspective, Typhoon Rosie, which is packing 120 mile per hour winds, will bring heavy rains to the western pacific, specifically Japan. The greatest impact on crops will be rice. Typhoon Rosie has the potential to destroy a majority of the rice crops which would send rice prices skyrocketing. This one-two punch of European demand and Typhoon Rosie destroying current supplies will turn the technical supply/demand fundamentals upside down, which usually means prices will rise.

For the Week of August 4, 1997

The story in the commodities market is really a story about the weather in the Midwest. The midwest weather has been very dry with no immediate prospects for change. The Midwest is home to a majority of this country's soybean crop. The dry weather becomes a major factor in how productive the soybean crop will be. Before the weather concerns, the soybean harvest was to yield forty bushels an acre; that revised forecast is now thirty-five bushels and falling. If we do not get any rainfall to improve these crops, the production could fall even lower. Overlay these weather concerns with the fact that one of the world's largest exporters of soybean, Brazil, is running on record low inventories and you quickly see that *the price of soybeans have nowhere to go but up*. Who ever thought that weatherman Willard Scott would hold the key to any market? If only we could trust his forecasts.

For the Week of August 18, 1997

The price of copper could face some downward pressure in the near term. In the summer months, demand typically slows for copper. When you combine this seasonal slowing demand along with the already heavy inventory levels of copper, we could see *this one-two punch move the price of copper lower*. While longer term I expect the price of copper remain flat—especially when the sluggish summer demand cycle is behind us—short term technical issues should drive this commodity lower.

For the Week of August 25, 1997

Oil prices should remain steady with the risk being an increase in oil prices, not a decrease. While most market watchers have been concerned that the Iraqi "Oil for Food" deal would flood the markets with billions of barrels of oil, and thus, continue to put downward pressure on oil prices, these concerns appear to be unfounded. The fundamentals of the market are just too strong to worry about Iraq. Forecasts regarding the demand for oil have been underestimated, while forecasts for the supply of oil have been overestimated. Thus, *these fundamentals will put pressure to move the price of oil not downward, but upward*. In addition, inventories of both gasoline and oil are below last year's already low levels. Also, don't forget that Iraq lost almost two months of oil exporting when it was arguing over the details of United Nations Resolution 986. Iraq doesn't have the production capacity to make up for this lost time. Remember the U.N. resolution calls for Iraq to export a certain amount of crude oil every 90 days. Thus the Iraqi impact has been greatly overstated. This development could bode well for Energy Industry stocks.

For the Week of September 1, 1997

I look for the price of coffee to continue to creep upward. The story in the coffee market is really a story about the weather. First, there is tremendous concern about possible extended dry weather seasons in the very important coffee growing areas of Brazil, Columbia, Indonesia and all of Central America, for that matter. Overlay the recent focus that El Niño is receiving and you can easily see why coffee prices will continue to inch higher. Remember, El Niño is a warming of the eastern part of the surface water of the Pacific Ocean. In the past, El Niño has caused a chain reaction and has caused disruption in weather patterns worldwide. This disruption has caused draughts in some parts of the world and severe flooding in others. The coffee market is worried about the weather without El Niño. With El Niño, coffee prices could move much higher than anyone expects.

For the Week of September 8, 1997

The commodity market is trying to steal center stage from the currency markets. Everywhere you look, there is a developing story in the now volatile commodity markets. From the copper front, I expect that metal to continue its plunge lower based on very weak market fundamentals along with the series of technical indicators that point to lower prices. From the aluminum front, I expect that metal to also continue to fall. Possibly the strongest bull in the entire commodity market continues to be oil. I see no short-term end in sight for the price of oil. Oil should continue its steady climb the remainder of the year. Perhaps the biggest story in the entire commodity market will come from the most watched of all commodities, gold. *I expect the price of gold to make a major move lower between now and the end of the year*. Several issues will fuel this development. First, there really is no upside in the price of gold. The upside is limited because of a combination of continued heavy gold production combined with Central Banks around the globe continuing to sell gold from their reserves. Now overlay our low inflation/no inflation environment globally, and you will quickly realize that no one is rushing to gold as a hedge against inflation. It is not out of the realm of possibilities to see gold break through the $300 an ounce by the end of the year.

171

For the Week of September 15, 1997

I think it's time to call Willard Scott to figure out where commodity prices are going. The weather, specifically El Niño, seems to be ruling the day. Many scientists are now claiming that this El Niño could be the climate event of the century. El Niño is the name given to an irregular appearance of warm surface water in the Pacific off the western coast of South America that affects worldwide wind, rainfall and weather patterns by making the wet seasons even wetter and the dry seasons even dryer. The latest tip from the weather front should have commodity prices moving in opposite directions as a result of El Niño. *I expect cocoa prices to weaken over the next few weeks* now that the consensus from the weather front has concluded that El Niño should not impact the West African cocoa growing regions at all. This increase in supply as a result of no El Niño offset will serve to weaken prices on supply/demand fundamentals. From the coffee front, just the opposite is happening. The weather consensus is now calling for El Niño to cut the coffee crop in Papua New Guinea by over 50% due to severe droughts. Even though that country's Coffee Industry Corporation has yet to release their official findings of the potential impact, it appears that a 50% loss may be the best we can hope for. *I expect coffee prices to inch forward* based on weaker supply level fueled by New Guinea. Whoever thought that CNBC and CNN would have to compete against the weather station for financial news!

For the Week of September 22, 1997

The recent rally in the gold market will be short lived as I expect the price of gold to continue downward. When gold broke the $320 an ounce level, that was a break of a major technical support level which brought some speculators into the market. The fundamentals of this market, however, will continue to push the price lower. There is continued pressure over Central Banks from around the globe selling gold to "free up" some financial assets. And the very strong equity market in the United States will serve as one more key reason why the price of gold will go lower not higher. When you combine the threat of Central Bank selling with our strong equity market and the current low inflation, no inflation environment, any rally in the gold market will be short lived.

172

For the Week of September 29, 1997

I look for Natural Gas prices to continue their strong run-up this week. This recent price run-up is almost entirely due to very low inventories across the board. Most electric utilities have been keeping their inventories of natural gas extremely low, betting on prices to come down so that they could replenish their inventory at a cheaper level. However, now we also have weak inventory at the wholesale level which is causing many of the electric utilities to become panic buyers of natural gas. This temporary disruption in the supply/demand fundamentals of the natural gas market will not develop into a long-term trend as I expect the price to trade back down by the middle to the end of October.

For the Week of October 6, 1997

I fully expect the drop in copper prices to continue for the next few weeks. The recent decline in copper prices was fueled by an increase in copper supply. The current inventory of copper stands at a two-year high, and I don't expect that inventory to be worked off quickly. This sudden increase in supply is being caused by a major step up in copper production at Rio Tinto's Kennecott, Utah smelter and Mexico's Mexicana de Cobre's La Caridad smelter. While the markets are busy trying to digest this heavy inventory of current supply, the future demand for copper also appears to be weakening. The Southeast Asian currency and Economic meltdown that began in Thailand may now be impacting the copper market. The sudden downturn of these Southeast Asian economies will be felt first in the delaying of big ticket purchases such as automobiles and electronic equipment. These big ticket items are heavy users of copper in the manufacturing of their products. The slowdown in Southeast Asia will have a ripple effect all the way to the copper market when it can least afford it.

For the Week of October 13, 1997

I expect coffee prices to move sharply higher based on the concern with Hurricane Pauline. *There is little doubt now that the unbelievable force upon which Hurricane Pauline hit Mexico means that, not only will this storm delay the coffee harvest in Mexico, it will also have a tremendous negative impact*. The almost non-stop two weeks of heavy

173

rains in the Chiapas and Oaxaca states (Mexico's coffee rich states) have already ruined almost 10% of the coffee crop to date. When you add Hurricane Pauline to that total, you can see why we could be in for a real run-up in coffee prices. Also, don't forget about El Niño. The severity of Hurricane Pauline was fueled by El Niño. As the Hurricane stayed on the coast and moved northward, it continued to "feed" off the Pacific's warm waters caused by El Niño, which enabled the Hurricane to intensify. This event will only serve to add more fuel to the fire regarding the inflation potential of El Niño. Maybe the only way to offset this concern is to have a cup of tea.

For the Week of October 20, 1997

They're baaack! The Russians are at it again, turning the palladium market upside down. Don't look for this concern to end anytime soon as *I expect the price of palladium to rise sharply higher in the upcoming weeks*. What has caused this commodity market to go on edge is the fact that Russia has not brought any new supply to the market, which historically has meant that Russians have run out of or are very, very low on palladium. During the first six months of the year, Russia didn't export any palladium; and as a result, palladium prices soared to 20-year highs. Remember Russia is the palladium market. They are the world's largest producer, by far, of palladium. This shortage will be felt immediately across numerous industries with the most serious impact on semi-conductors, which are one of the largest industrial users of palladium. Nine months ago, Russia didn't bring palladium to the market in an attempt to shrink supply and let prices rise. Today, Russia is not coming to the market because these inventories have been depleted and there is nothing left to bring. Either way, the price of palladium has nowhere to go but up.

For the Week of October 27, 1997

Gold simply does not matter anymore as a barometer for financial assets. With markets crashing around the globe, including the United States equity market, one would have expected one safe haven to be gold. It wasn't and it never will be. Our global financial markets have left the gold standard in the dust. *Not only will the price of gold not increase during this Southeast Asian currency and economic crisis, I think that the price of gold can break through the landmark $300 an* *ounce level within the next year.* Think about it for a minute, if the events in Southeast Asia can't get investors flocking to gold, what, if anything, can? . . . Add to this the events in Switzerland and you will see the price of gold has nowhere to go but down. Switzerland is considering changes to its constitution to abandon the gold standard. Switzerland is the last developed country to insist on a gold backing for its currency. That gold standard will be dropped from 40 percent to 25 percent on November 1 of this year. Switzerland's plans to flood the gold market will cause a knee-jerk reaction from other central banks (like Germany) from around the world that were exploring liquidating some gold reserves. The pressure is clearly on them to do it now before the Switzerland plan becomes reality. I'm convinced we will see $250 an ounce before we see $350 an ounce.

For the Week of November 3, 1997

Look for coffee prices to continue to fall as production is coming in at levels higher than expected. While the recent rally in coffee prices has been fueled by the concern with El Niño, the reality is that El Niño will have a greater impact on next year's prices, not this year's prices. *The run-up of coffee prices because of the fear of El Niño is over. The supply of coffee is plentiful and larger supply means lower prices. I think that the price of coffee will trend lower the remainder of the year.* The current coffee supply numbers are staggering. Peruvian coffee producers are now predicting coffee exports of $415 million for 1997. This, by the way, would be a record. Also, the Guatemala National Coffee Association is calling for record coffee exports. Meanwhile on the demand front, Japan's importing of coffee (green coffee) was down a whopping 21% this past month from the levels of a year ago. Heavy supply and lower demands mean lower coffee prices no matter how much is written about the potential impact of El Niño.

For the Week of November 10, 1997

If you thought it was a wild ride in the stock market the last two weeks in terms of volatility, what lies ahead for the price of oil will make the recent events in the stock markets appear mild. *I expect dramatic swings both ways with the price of oil fueled by the brewing crisis with Iraq and the United States.* This made-for-television soap opera will swing from appearing at one point that we are on the verge of nuclear war to the next point where all economic sanctions will soon be lifted on Iraq. Expect these games to go on until December 5th. That is the date of the United Nations vote on re-certifying the Iraq oil for food deal. Until that date, I expect Iraq and Saddam Hussein to be headline news around the world threatening war and raising fear of both chemical and biological warfare. This high profile media confrontation will cause the price of oil to become the most volatile commodity for the next few weeks.

For the Week of November 17, 1997

This could be a pretty wild week in the commodity market regarding coffee prices. While the consensus of technical market watchers are calling for a major correction in the price of coffee, the weatherman just won't give up. *The fundamental concerns regarding coffee supply driven by weather factors will continue to push the price of coffee higher.* The Mexican coffee crop has been severely damaged by Hurricane Rick. Meanwhile in Indonesia, El Niño's impact is having a major negative impact on that country's coffee production as well. And even though all of the technical signs are pointing to this market as being overbought, I simply do not see a correction any time soon. I feel that the real story in the coffee markets for the next six months will be determined more by the weather than it will by any charts that technical analysts hang on their walls.

For the Week of November 24, 1997

I expect the price of oil to continue to fall this week due to the resolution of the crisis in Iraq. With the return of United Nations personnel which included United States nationals on the United Nations' teams, the likelihood of any military action has all but disappeared. The price of oil over-reacted to the potential crisis in Iraq which began with Iraqi threats to engage United States planes performing United Nations maneuvers in Iraqi air space and ended with the expulsion of United States inspectors from Baghdad. Although this crisis could always heat up again, the short-term crisis is behind us for now, which means the oil for food deal is again back on track, *which in turn means more oil to hit the markets along with no thoughts of any oil supply disruptions due to war or the threat of war in Iraq. This all adds up to lower oil prices.*

For the Week of December 8, 1997

I expect the downward pressure to remain on the price of gold. We have seen it above $300 for the last time this year and it very well may not see the $300 level all of next year. Two factors are converging to keep gold below the $300 an ounce level. First, because there clearly is no inflation and for the most part, not even any fear of inflation, who has any need to buy gold as a "hedge" against inflation that is non-existent. The second factor is the fear of Central Banks around the world liquidating some of their gold reserves. With the prospect of the European Monetary Union beginning to take center stage again, the threat of Central Banks selling gold in order to get their country's economic and fiscal house in order is a very real threat that will be with us for a long time (at least two years).

For the Week of December 15, 1997

I look for cocoa prices to continue to soar for the next few weeks as key supply/demand fundamentals will continue to push this commodity higher. From the supply front, it's bad news from both sides of the globe. In Brazil, their cocoa crop is being destroyed by a disease called "witches' broom," which is a rapid spreading fungus. This disease will cut Brazilian cocoa production by one third. And it's not just Brazil, in both Indonesia and Malaysia, unusually dry weather there has lead to a rash of forest fires that have taken their toll on cocoa supplies in both of those countries. Meanwhile, from the demand front, we are heading into the peak time of the year for cocoa demand fueled by chocolate makers. This tremendous surge by the chocolate makers starts after Thanksgiving and continues through the Easter holiday season. This one-two combination of weakened supply at the peak demand time for cocoa may push cocoa prices into record levels.

7 GLOBAL PERSPECTIVE

OVERVIEW

The dominate story in the global markets was the Southeast Asian currency and economic meltdown.

However, investors have to realize that no matter what the event is, it will create both winners and losers in the markets. A bad or negative event doesn't create all losers in the markets nor does a positive event make all industries winners.

Before I jump right into winners and losers, let me step back and give a frame of reference regarding what happened as a result of this crisis. There were four outcomes: slower growth, damaged banks, new trade flows and political unrest. Let me briefly touch on all four, beginning with slower growth. There was slower growth in the economies of Thailand, Indonesia, Malaysia, Singapore, South Korea and the Philippines. This slowdown can be explained by a very simple cause/effect relationship. The Central Banks in those countries are raising interest rates as a means of protecting their currency. Rising interest rates in turn means that there will be less capital, or I should say less affordable capital for expansion. In turn, if there is no expansion, there will be no growth or at the very best, slower economic growth. So now we know that there will be slower growth; let's move on to the second of four outcomes, damaged banks. As the local economies slow, it puts pressure on local businesses to keep their bank loans current. Also, when a local economy weakens, the real estate market usually takes a major hit. Because banks are the major real estate lenders, they will get hit here as well. To top it all off, while local businesses and real estate are failing, the banks own dollar denominated borrowing comes due. And because of the major currency devaluation, these loans will cost the banks much more than they budgeted. Okay, now we know that there will be slower growth and that there will be damaged banks; now let's move on to my third of four outcomes, new trade flows. Make no mistake about it; exports from these countries will surge. However, if we just focus on these countries, we are only getting half the picture. Multi-national companies from around the globe will look to maximize and expand their operations in these Asian Tiger economies in order to profit from cheap labor and plants as well. Let's move to my fourth and final point, political unrest. This political unrest will be tied to the standard of living. As this crisis continues to intensify and lowers the rising standards of living in these countries, I expect the masses to rise up against the current political leadership and demand changes. You see, once you've tasted the good life, it is difficult to go back.

With that background, I'm going to give you two losers and two winners. The first loser is Hong Kong. While everyone was worried about China screwing up their golden economic "Goose," it wasn't China at all; it was the Asian Tigers. The lone Asian currency to withstand the Asian onslaught has been Hong Kong. Even though Hong Kong has been able to protect the value of the Hong Kong Dollar, the Hong Kong economy will now suffer. Because of the tremendous devaluation of other currencies in the region, their products will be cheaper and much more competitive in the region. The Hong Kong economy will not be able to withstand the tremendous new source of export competition from its fellow Asian Tigers. The first real loser in the Asian currency crisis will be the Hong Kong economy.

My second loser is really the biggest loser in this crisis and that is Japan. To fully appreciate how this will impact Japan, we first must keep in mind what is going on in the Japanese economy today. The story of the day is exports. The domestic economy of Japan has been strangled by the recent increase of their "value-added tax," which is the international term we give to a sales tax. Within that export market in Japan the largest increase over the last ten years has been to the Asian Tiger economies of Thailand, Indonesia, Malaysia, Singapore and the Philippines. In 1987, exports to these Asian Tiger economies accounted for only 20% of Japan's total exports. Today that amount has more than doubled and currently accounts for more than 40% of Japan's total exports. As the economies of the Asian Tiger countries slow down, exports from Japan will slow down and in turn the Japanese economy will be crushed. In addition to the export crisis Japan will face, two other forces will combine to throw Japan a knock out punch. The first is regarding direct lending. Japan has one of the largest financial exposures of loans to the Asian Tiger economies. This direct lending will come under severe pressure as the Asian economies slow down. The timeliness of the repayment of this direct lending will become highly questionable. Now the second force, in addition to the direct lending, is equity exposure. Japan has also been one of the single largest investors in the individual equity markets of those Asian countries. The value of those assets has greatly diminished which will put another added pressure on financial balance sheets all over Japan. The combination of slowing exports, untimely payments on direct lending and equity value deterioration will combine to make Japan the biggest loser of all.

My two winners are U.S. multi-national "Blue Chip" consumer companies and U.S. banks. First let me start with the multi-national "Blue Chip" consumer companies who sold off in the wake of this crisis over concern that the slowing economies of the Asian Tigers will greatly deteriorate these consumer giants' earnings. The simple answer is they won't. And the reason is because these Asian Tiger economies are still at the very early stages of their economic development and are not yet major global consumers. If you want to worry about something, worry about the economy in the United States, a real global consumer. Let me put this Asian Tiger economic slowdown in perspective for you from our multi-national consumer companies. If the entire economies of Thailand, Indonesia, Malaysia, Singapore and the Philippines not only slowed down but actually stopped completely and totally disappeared to nothing it would have the same impact as the U.S. economy losing 6%. A slowdown in the Asian Tiger economies will not have a major impact on U.S. multinational consumer companies, because globally those markets simply don't consume. In addition, I expect these companies to go on sale from a price/earning's perspective as the media hype regarding this crisis will have people throwing out the baby with the dirty bath water once again.

Finally, I feel that major U.S. banks could eventually be the big winners in the southeast Asian currency crisis as the focus shifts to the Banking Industry. There is no overall southeast Asian Banking Industry impact; it varies country by country. To no one's surprise, Thailand's banking system is in the worst shape of any of the Asian countries. It is estimated that over 20% of the total loan portfolio of the Thailand banking system will be classified as bad debts that will not be collected. Though clearly not as bad as Thailand, Malaysia and Indonesia are close behind. These Asian communities in desperate need of a new source of cash infusion, may be willing (or forced) to open their markets to United States banks (as well as other foreign banks). Even before the first sign of the Thailand Baht crisis appeared, discussions were already underway in the World Trade Organization to look at ways to open up the Asian banking market. The United States, specifically United States banks, will now have a clear upper hand in these negotiations. High on the list of countries in which United States banks would love to gain concessions from are Indonesia, Thailand, Malaysia and the Philippines. Those countries are also at the top of the list as the ones that need the most help now. If the major U.S. banks can get the doors open now, when these Asian Tiger economies turn around in 18 months to two years the biggest winner of all just might be these major U.S. banks.

Fasten your seat belt and try to enjoy the ride as I recap with you how the issues and events that drive my global market outlook evolved on a week by week basis from Tax Day (April 15th) through the end of 1997.

For the Week of April 14, 1997

As the May 1st date for Britain's general election is quickly approaching, expect no reaction from the financial markets regardless of who wins. While there was a time when the markets were very concerned about what would happen if the Conservative Party's John Major were defeated by the Labour Party's Tony Blair, that concern has diminished. ***Blair has reversed his stand regarding de-privatizing certain sectors*** and having the government take over the operation. This potentially massive government growth is what had the markets spooked. Blair is a savvy politician and he has calmed the financial markets by moving "to the center" just like Bill Clinton did last November in the United States. . . . Prospects for the European Monetary Union (EMU) are back on track thanks to Germany. Chancellor Helmut Kohl announced the EMU platform as the cornerstone to his re-election bid. While there remains a great deal of doubt whether Germany can achieve the Maastricht Treaty's 3% deficit to GDP ratio (I personally feel that it will be impossible for them to do so), Kohl's renewed support will find a way to make the EMU work. If you had to pick one European politician to spearhead EMU to reality, it would be Kohl. It's still too early to tell exactly who will be in or out of the EMU but with Kohl's political clout, the EMU will happen.

For the Week of April 21, 1997

At some point in time maybe the economists will realize that in a global marketplace, higher economic growth does not always mean higher inflation. Just look at what's happening in China, the world's most dominant growth investment theme. China's inflation rate fell to 3% for the first quarter of 1997. In a global marketplace, could it be possible to achieve accelerating economic growth accompanied by decelerating inflation? China's growth story is real. For nervous international investors ***the safest way to invest in China's high growth, low inflation environment may be through the Hong Kong market.*** Even with the expected short-term volatility in the Hong Kong market due to all of the tensions surrounding China's upcoming Most Favored Nations Trade status debate, it's still a safer place to bank your money in the long run.

For the Week of April 28, 1997

On the Russian front, while the Russian economy continues to show positive improvement, that country's budget crisis now looms as their biggest problem. *I expect the Russian budget crisis to get worse before it begins to get better.* Russia is currently collecting under 40% of the tax revenue it had budgeted. Unless Russia can collect its taxes, there is no way it can pay the unpaid wages it currently owes workers that now totals approximately $9 billion dollars. While the strong economic signals coming out of Russia could certainly push that country's inflation rate below the 20% level it had last year down to the low teens, the economic gains won't matter if a credible plan is not developed to resolve the budget deficit crisis.

For the Week of May 5, 1997

As the prospects of a heated and prolonged debate over China's Most Favored Nation trade status materializes, the impact on both the stock and bond market become crystal clear. On the equity front, *many multinational corporations that dominate the key indexes of the markets, will be under pressure as investors will begin to question their growth projections ex-China.* The bond market will have its own problems. Any trade war with China is going to be fought with higher tariffs on imports from China. Higher tariffs on Chinese imports would have tremendous inflationary impacts for domestic U.S. consumers. The bond market certainly doesn't need any inflation problems from China. . . . *The Japanese banking crisis should get worse before it gets better.* The Japanese government has made it very clear that they are not going to let any of the major banks collapse due to bad loan problems. On the surface, this appears to be good news until you realize that someone has to pay for these bad loans. That someone will be the banks that are in sounder financial condition with fewer bad loan problems. Thus, before this industry improves, we are likely to see the overall industry converge down to the lower tier of the Japanese Banking Industry. Overall, things will certainly get worse for the Banking Industry before they get better.

183

For the Week of May 12, 1997

Britain's new Labour party has jump started its reputation in the global financial markets by boldly privatizing the interest rate setting process. ***I expect the U.K. markets to reap the rewards of global market support and acceptance over the next few weeks.*** Deregulation and privatization are themes that, when properly implemented, will attract capital from around the globe. Rates used to be set in England based upon the outcome of a monthly meeting between the Chancellor of Exchequer and the Governor of the Bank of England (only if the government approved). Over the past six months, the Bank of England has been calling for a rate increase, however, the Chancellor would have no part of it. All of that has changed now. Instead of a monthly meeting with the Chancellor, the Governor of the Bank of England (The Central Bank) will now be part of a nine member monetary policy committee at The Central Bank. The committee will decide on all rate changes by a majority vote. I expect the U.K. markets to outperform as the global markets will continue to cheer this bold privatization move.

For the Week of May 19, 1997

The upcoming U.S. trade policy debates will drive the markets in China, Hong Kong (what impacts China now also impacts Hong Kong) and Mexico. ***Passage of China's Most Favored Nation (MFN) trade status is in doubt.*** Several factors highlight why China's MFN may fail. First, there are very strong and vocal lobbying forces against granting China's MFN. These lobbying forces are led by: human rights activists, anti-abortion activists (protesting China's one child policy), and Christian conservatives and pro-Taiwan activists. Second, the current campaign finance controversy surrounding Asian money will stop any politician from taking a high profile to support this issue. Any high profile support will result in the spotlight being turned on that politician to look for Chinese campaign finance ties. . . . President Clinton must assess the first three years of the North American Free Trade Agreement (NAFTA) and send that assessment on to Congress which will then set a series of hearings on this matter. I fully expect all of the Ross Perot NAFTA bashers to come out of the woodwork and beat up on Mexico regarding drug, environment and labor policies. ***I do not believe that there will be any changes of substance to NAFTA,*** as I also look for President Clinton to stick with his pro-NAFTA stance. So it's good news for Mexico and bad news for China. . . . It is important to remember not to tie these two major trade issues together. China MFN is not NAFTA. Just because President Clinton championed and will continue to support NAFTA doesn't mean that he will do the same for China MFN. There were no campaign funds (that we know about anyway) that were linked to Mexico unlike the campaign finance problems President Clinton currently faces regarding Chinese contributions.

For the Week of May 26, 1997

Right now all of the focus in Mexico is on the upcoming major elections that will determine who will control Congress and who will be elected (previously appointed) Mayor of Mexico City. The reason for all of this focus and concern is that the last time there was a major election in Mexico, (which by the way was the 1994 elections for President) that country exploded with bad news and the markets were punished. *I think the markets will be surprised by how calm and uneventful the elections in Mexico proceed.* And more importantly, once the elections are over, the markets will again begin to focus on what's important to Mexico's continued recovery. Strong economic growth with low inflation and a stable currency are the keys to long term economic success. Right now Mexico finds itself in a period of good economic growth with declining inflation, while the peso has been very well behaved. Investors haven't noticed, however, because of all of the political focus. *The second half of the year looks very bright for Mexico.*

For the Week of June 2, 1997

Recent events in Germany and France may have the greatest impact on Italy. Germany's decision to revalue its gold assets and receive an immediate profit from these hidden reserves will greatly increase the risk of delay in the European Monetary Union. Meanwhile in France, the elections have changed the political landscape and caused even more questions to be raised about EMU. It is countries that find themselves "on the fence" regarding eligibility into EMU that show the greatest volatility as the markets swing between whether EMU will or will not happen. Right now Italy is the high profile fence sitter. *I expect extreme volatility in the Italian markets in the near term as the prospects for EMU are crystallized.* Adding to the Italian market's volatility are comments from the various political factions in Italy that question the need for any further sacrifices just for Italy to get into EMU. . . . Problems in North Korea could rattle the world's financial markets. The food shortage in North Korea has reached a crisis level and the entire country is on the verge of famine. Now in order to divert attention from this national government problem, rumors have begun circulating that North Korea is considering starting a war with South Korea. These rumors take on heightened credibility as the United Nations Nuclear Watchdog continues to sound alarms regarding plutonium that is still missing from a nuclear reactor believed to have been extracted when it was briefly shut down in 1989. *While I believe the actual risk of war in Korea is slim, the perception of war is greater than it has ever been, and the financial markets move based on what they perceive is going to happen.* I expect the Korean market, specifically, and the entire Asian market, generally, to experience increased volatility in the coming months.

For the Week of June 9, 1997

The global landscape continues to evolve as both politics and policies appear to change almost daily. Elections have changed the political landscapes in Britain, France, Canada (even though Prime Minister Chretien's government was re-elected with a paper thin, 155 of 301 majority, expect major changes) and Iran. While in Germany, the on-again, off-again policy plan to re-value its gold reserves (this ill-conceived plan almost cost Finance Minister Waigel his job) in order to meet the criteria for membership in the European Monetary Union appears off again. The global political and policy landscapes are becoming like the Chicago weather—if you don't like it, wait a day, it will change. In these times of political change and uncertainty, what people say becomes more important than what they do. With that, global speakers alert in mind, there are three events on the global calendar to keep on the radar screen this week. First, on Monday in Luxembourg, the European Union Economic and Finance Ministers meet to discuss, among other things, preparations for introduction of a single currency. Then on Tuesday, in Brussels, the European Monetary Committee meets. The entire world will be looking for clues from these meetings to try to figure out what is going to happen with the European Monetary Union. *I expect the comments from these meetings regarding EMU to be negative.* . . . Meanwhile, on Thursday in London, Chancellor or the Exchequer Gordon Brown gives the Annual Mansion House Address to London's financial community. I fully expect Chancellor Brown to drop a bombshell. The problem is that we just don't know which one will be dropped. I expect the extreme volatility in the global markets to continue this week as the evolution of new politics and policies continues.

For the Week of June 30, 1997

The eyes of the world will be glued on China and Hong Kong when at the stroke of midnight on Monday, June 30th, Hong Kong reverts back to China. *I do not expect any terrorist action at this time to spoil the transition of Hong Kong from Britain to China.* While the markets will be very nervous, the real concern should not be for the week that Hong Kong is handed over to China. The concerns are in the weeks ahead as both China and Hong Kong try to figure out how to survive with two distinct systems of government in one country. The first sign to watch for trouble in this transition is "Brain Drain." Talented business leaders and entrepreneurs have served as the real back bone for the Hong Kong economy. If China attempts to disrupt the business process in Hong Kong, the resulting brain drain could have serious long term ramifications for Hong Kong. Stay tuned, this story has only begun to unfold.

For the Week of July 7, 1997

Expect the global financial markets to cheer Chancellor of the Exchequer Gordon Brown's five year financial plan to reduce Britain's budget deficit. Although the plan still has to be implemented and has plenty of potential pitfalls, Britain has finally developed an action plan that the markets will clearly embrace. *As a result, I expect the United Kingdom to become a magnet for foreign capital looking for a home to invest somewhere in Europe.* With Gross Domestic Product forcasted for over 3% this year and slightly under 3% next year combined with inflation forecasts over the next three years of under 2.5%, you have a formula being developed similar to the United States—steady growth, low inflation Goldilocks' economy. When you combine these economic elements with the financial strategy that earmarks the windfall tax on privatized utilities to be allocated to the welfare system's work program, you quickly see why the financial markets will continue to reward Britain. Like any major fiscal plan, as the details evolve over the next few weeks, there will be some bumpy spots on the road to fiscal recovery.

For the Week of July 14, 1997

There is a lot more downside than upside currently in Thailand. Even though Thailand's government abandoned pegging Thailand's currency, the Baht, to a basket of other major currencies, effectively letting the currency float, Thailand's problems are far from over. After Thailand let their currency float on July 2, it was immediately devalued by 15 percent. While this is a good first step, it will not solve Thailand's problems quickly. ***I expect Thailand to dramatically under-perform the global markets the remainder of the year.*** Remember, when a currency is devalued, things always get worse before they get better. Now that the baht has been devalued, next up for Thailand will come slower economic growth, and slower economic growth always leads to declining tax revenues and higher interest rates. In addition, even though a weaker currency will help jump start Thailand's weak export sector, it does nothing to address the two biggest problems in Thailand's economy. First, there continues to be a lack of skilled labor. The economy simply can't grow without skilled labor. Second, the financial sector is in shambles. Their crisis is of the same magnitude of the savings and loan crisis disaster in the United States in the early 1980s. Until these two issues are addressed, Thailand will not be able to turn its economy around regardless of what they do with their currency.

For the Week of July 21, 1997

The hidden gem of the global market place in the second half of the year just might happen to be our next door neighbor. And I'm not talking about Mexico. ***Even though all of the recent focus regarding the political report card on the North American Free Trade Agreement has been spotlighted on our neighbors south of the border, it's our neighbors north of the border, Canada, that are positioned to take off the second half of the year.*** The rebound in Canada is being fueled by their improving employment picture. Canadian employment rose over 50,000 in June. This marks a steadily improving job creation picture in Canada for the past twelve months. Secondly, unemployment is falling. It actually dropped 56,000 in June. This drop almost pushed unemployment below the 9.0% level. It currently stands at 9.1% which is down sharply from last month's 9.5% level. This 9.1% level marks the lowest unemployment rate in Canada in the past two years. Canada's economy is about to turn the corner. The more people that are employed, the more consumers spend in the economy. When consumers spend more, businesses tend to expand, which in turn, creates even more jobs, which takes unemployment even lower, which makes the consumer even stronger. It's a great story. One of the greatest global opportunities in the next six months just may be a stone's throw away.

For the Week of July 28, 1997

As France attempts to make financial strides to meet the criteria to join the single European currency, it may soon become apparent that sometimes the "ends" doesn't justify the "means." In this case, the "means" was sharply raising taxes. *I expect the French financial markets to be very volatile this week with all of the risks on the down side.* Even though the French government did cut some government spending along with increasing corporate taxes in order to comply with the Maastricht Treaty, which sets forth the conditions of the European Economic and Monetary Union, the focus was on raising taxes. France already has some of the highest corporate tax rates in Europe. Now the rate moves even higher from 36% to 41%. In addition, the new "leftest" government is more than doubling the corporate Capital Gains Tax rate from its current 20% level to 41%. While the markets certainly applaud France's effort to move toward the common currency guidelines, getting there on the backs of business will not only damage corporate profits in the short-run, but in the long run, it simply gives business one more reason to flee France.

For the Week of August 4, 1997

I expect the German financial markets to underperform in both Europe and around the globe as a result of their failure to complete their tax reform package. The financial markets will make Germany pay a higher price than usual because of all of the global focus currently on tax policies, driven in a large part by the United States' balanced budget and tax cut deal that is receiving rave reviews from the financial markets around the globe. For as good as things are for the United States, they couldn't get worse for Germany. Chancellor Kohl's major tax reform program was to cut corporate and personal income taxes by over $16 billion. As a result, this major reform plan would have added close to a full percentage point to Germany's Gross Domestic Product. Instead, there is no tax relief and more importantly, no boost to the economy. The best the markets can hope for now is that after the federal elections in 1998, this major tax reform package will reappear in some fashion in 1999. Quite frankly, that is too little, too late and the German financial markets will be punished as a result.

For the Week of August 18, 1997

While much of the focus regarding the European Monetary Union (EMU) over the past few months has been on Germany and France, with an occasional glance at Italy, ***the markets may be overlooking the real gem, Spain***. Inflation remains very subdued and the recent run up had more to do with what was happening in Britain than in Spain. The recent spike-up in the British Pound-Sterling has turned the British population into tourists as they quickly find out that their strong currency can buy more in other countries. Well, the biggest beneficiary of this tourist movement has been Spain. This increased demand for goods and services has served as a real source to inch inflation higher, in the short run. However, don't lose sight of the fact that these tourists will have a very positive impact on the overall Spanish economy. Based on the back of a stronger economy, Spain's 1997 deficit will be under the 3.0% ceiling mandated by the Maastricht Treaty. Imagine that, solving budget problems on the back of a stronger economy; I think we may be developing a global trend.

For the Week of August 25, 1997

Keep a close watch on the Bundesbank, as Germany's Central Bank still may change the landscape of global interest rates. While there remains strong support to raise German interest rates to support the German Mark against the U.S. Dollar, there are other factors, both inside and outside of Germany, that are weighing heavy on the Bundesbank. First, inside Germany, even though the economy is showing some signs of picking up, unemployment is still at record highs. Thus, any interest rate hike would slow down an economy that many Germans already feel is too slow. Second, outside of Germany, the convergence of European yields due to the march toward the European Monetary Union (EMU) would slow down if there were a Bundesbank rate hike. The Bundesbank does not want to be accused of harming the EMU movement in any way. With the tremendous pressures both inside and outside of Germany, the Bundesbank is taking a page out of Alan Greenspan's jawboning strategy, that being threatening to raise interest can have the same impact as raising them. However, you can only cry wolf so often.

For the Week of September 1, 1997

Major United States banks could eventually be the big winners in the Southeast Asia currency crisis, as the meltdown of both the currencies and stock markets continue in Southeast Asia from Thailand to Indonesia to Malaysia to Singapore to the Philippines. The real focus will now shift to the Banking Industry. There is no overall Southeast Asian Banking Industry impact; it varies country by country. To no one's surprise, Thailand's banking system is in the worse shape of any of the Asian countries. It is estimated that over 20% of the total loan portfolio of the Thailand banking system will be classified as bad debts that will not be collected; though clearly, not as bad as Thailand, Malaysia and Indonesia are close behind. These Asian communities, in desperate need of a new source of cash infusion, may be willing (or forced) to open their markets to United States banks (as well as other foreign banks). Even before the first sign of the Thailand Baht crisis appeared, discussions were already underway in the World Trade Organization to look at ways to open up the Asian banking market. Those discussions are now moving at break-neck speed. The United States, specifically United States banks, will now have a clear upper hand in these negotiations. High on the list of countries in which United States banks would love to gain concessions from are Indonesia, Thailand, Malaysia and the Philippines. Those countries are also at the top of the list as the ones that need the most help now. Timing is everything.

For the Week of September 8, 1997

I think that possibly the most important development in the entire global market this year is not what happened in Thailand, but rather what happened in Indonesia. While all of the headlines continue to focus on all of the negative events surrounding Thailand and the surrounding Pacific Rim economies and markets, something very positive with tremendous long-term ramifications occurred in Indonesia. The Atlantic Richfield Company has announced that it will spend over $3 billion to develop a natural gas field in Indonesia. The basis of

191

this development is Atlantic Richfield's discovery of the Wiriagar field which has preliminary estimated reserves of over 13 trillion cubic feet of gas. If the development comes anywhere near that level, it will be Atlantic Richfield's largest development outside of the United States. Much more important than size, however, is the fact that it will make Atlantic Richfield a major global player in the liquefied natural gas business. Liquefied natural gas is gas that is liquefied through cooling so it can be specially stored and shipped. Even though the process is very expensive, it is the only way gas can get to remote locations where distribution by a pipeline is not economically feasible. Liquefied natural gas will be the wave of the future in Asia and the development of the Wiriagar field will clearly put Atlantic Richfield in competition with Mobile Corporation and Total SA of France, the two leading firms who currently dominate the liquefied natural gas business. Even though this is clearly great news for Atlantic Richfield, it is even greater news for global inflation. For massive capital projects like this to work, they need long-term sales contracts to insure that someone will buy what they produce. Right now all of the major developers are pursuing the same markets in Japan, Korea and Indonesia. It's clearly a buyer's market. These buyers have a chance to enter into long-term energy contracts that will be more deflationary than inflationary. *This simply serves as one more example of how, in our high-tech global economy, inflation just doesn't stand a chance.*

For the Week of September 15, 1997

Possibly the most intriguing aspect of what's occurring on the global marketplace is the maturity of the emerging markets. Investors have finally come to realize that just because there is a problem with one region of the global emerging market's landscape, that does not mean that all emerging market securities are bad. As proof of the markets' maturity, consider what happened a few years ago in Mexico with what is happening in the Pacific Rim today. In 1994, when the Mexican Peso was devalued and that country's economy and markets started a nose dive, it took all emerging markets from around the globe down with them. While today, the Pacific Rim crisis which started in Thailand, has had some effect on the emerging markets of Latin and South America, the impact has not been in the same order of magnitude as the emerging markets in the Pacific Rim. Consider what occurred just last week. As the concerns of Thailand, Indonesia, Philippines, Korea and virtually all of the emerging markets in the Pacific Rim are leading to capital fleeing those regions, other emerging markets are freely accessing that global capital. The Republic of Venezuela launched an unbelievably successful $4 billion global bond offering. The success of this offering was based on the solid turnaround in the Venezuela economy the past two years. During the Mexican crisis, you could not sell $4 dollars of emerging market debt to anyone, let alone $4 billion. *I look for the emerging markets of Latin and South America to continue their strong showing, despite the ongoing Thailand crisis.*

For the Week of September 22, 1997

The meltdown in the Pacific Rim, which started in Thailand and then spread to the other emerging markets of Indonesia, Malaysia, Singapore and the Philippines may present the greatest problem for a non-emerging market economy, namely Japan. *I feel that the greatest impact of the Emerging Market Pacific Rim crisis will be felt by Japan.* First of all, remember that the only thing that Japan's economy has going for it is its exports. Domestic consumption has been strangled by the recent increase of Japan's Value Added Tax. Japanese exports to fellow Pacific Rim countries has exploded over the past ten years by actually doubling exports from 20% to over 40%. As the economy of these emerging Pacific Rim countries slow down, so will Japan's exports. Also the Banking Industry in Japan has been one of the leading direct lenders to the Pacific Rim emerging markets. This direct debt is now in some jeopardy of being paid in a timely fashion. Also, Japan has extensive equity holdings in the Pacific Rim Emerging Markets. The value of these holdings will also greatly deteriorate. These events will all combine to make Japan the biggest short-term loser in the Asian currency crisis.

For the Week of September 29, 1997

The recent German elections in Hamburg will add volatility to the global markets as the results presented both good news and bad news for the European Monetary Union (EMU). Even though the Social Democrats won the state election and will continue to govern, Chancellor Kohl and his Christian Democratic Union enjoyed a 6% boost over the prior state election in Hamburg. With Chancellor Kohl's unappointed position as the "champion" of the EMU movement, this election certainly bodes well for the prospects of the EMU. A closer look at the elections, however, reveals the possibility that there was also some bad news for EMU proponents. While the Christian Democrats enjoyed a 6% gain, the Social Democrats watched their support drop 4%. This drop will force the Social Democrats to join forces with the Green Party Coalition to take on Chancellor Kohl and his Christian Democrats in next year's national election. That means that the Social Democratic Chancellor's candidate must be a consensus builder to align the Social Democrats with the Green Party (if that's possible). The most likely candidate is Gerhard Schroeder. Gerhard Schroeder has long been one of Germany's biggest skeptics regarding the need for EMU. *With the forum for the benefits and cost of EMU being Germany's national elections, this additional high profile focus will increase volatility in the European market.*

For the Week of October 6, 1997

It will be an extremely volatile week in the Italian financial markets with tremendous risk of further asset declines. As a result of the Communist Refoundation vote disapproving the 1998 budget, a formal verification of the Prodi government's majority in Parliament has been set for a Tuesday debate. That gives precious little time for a political compromise. And while in Italian politics, anything is possible, I feel a compromise is very unlikely because the battle really isn't over the budget, it's over the future of the Communist party in Italy. Fausto Bertinotti hopes that this last ditch political stand will somehow arouse the Italian labor unions which have recently become less radical. The real plan behind this defiant budget vote is to attempt to rally the unions in a radical front, positioning them for combative negotiations with the government in the near future. The stakes are very high and while a miracle is not out of the question, political and financial motives don't always mix. Thus, I think we are in for more bad news before anything good comes out of this standoff.

For the Week of October 13, 1997

Is it two down and three to go or is two enough? Now that Indonesia has been added to the list along with Thailand as two countries whose currency and economic crisis were so great that they had to be bailed out by the International Monetary Fund, the focus now becomes who's next? While many global strategists attempted to convince the markets that the crisis in Thailand was an isolated incident, we now have proof that it was not. In fact, the problems in Indonesia, I feel, are even greater than we are being told. *For Indonesia to ask for assistance only six months prior to the assembly to select the President, these problems had to be nuclear in nature in order to get President Suharto to agree to seek "outside help."* I still think that we are only seeing the tip of the iceberg. High corporate debt levels are strangling Indonesia. Now when you combine those high corporate debt levels along with the plunging currency, you have a deadly one-two punch that will take years to recover from. Also, remember when the International Monetary Fund steps in, things actually get worse before they get better. That's because in the short run, the International Monetary Fund will require drastic policy changes that will cut growth and further weaken the buying power of the citizens. This in turn could create political turmoil as well. In the long run, it will be the best thing that ever happened to Indonesia; in the short run, however, the worst is far from over. Will the bleeding stop here or will Malaysia, the Philippines or Singapore need to be bailed out by the International Monetary Fund as well? From my perspective, it's two down and at least one more to go. *Malaysia will need to be bailed out by the International Monetary Fund within three months.* The short term prospects for Southcast Asia just couldn't be worse. Remember, two is never enough.

For the Week of October 20, 1997

Sometimes the greatest "wars" are fought without a single bullet ever being fired. Such is the potential for this latest version of the United States-Japan trade war. The U.S. Maritime Commission decided to block all Japanese cargo vessels from unloading at any U.S. port. The Commission has ordered Coast Guard and Customs Service to keep Japanese-flagged ships from entering U.S. ports as well as detaining any ships that are already in U.S. ports. How this particular issue is ultimately resolved misses the real issue. *Trade tensions between the United States and Japan are explosive and Japanese companies and the Japanese economy could be the biggest loser.* This Maritime Commission issue is simply one more glaring example of our trade problems with Japan whereas the industries seem to change, never the problem . . . from automobiles to commercial airlines and now to shippers. This latest showdown could not have come at a worst time for Japan. Its entire economy is dependent upon the Export Industry. Domestically, there is simply nothing going on in Japan; the Japanese consumer is non-existent.

This explains why the entire economy is dependent upon exports. This crisis takes on even greater significance for Japan when you consider what is happening to its exports to other Southeast Asian economies. Japan's exports have doubled over the past ten years to Thailand, Indonesia, Malaysia, Singapore and the Philippines. Today, those economies are in the mist of the Southeast Asia currency and economy meltdown which means little, if any import demand.

For the Week of October 27, 1997

The Southeast Asian currency and economic meltdown will continue, especially in Thailand, Indonesia, Malaysia, Singapore and the Philippines. While each of these countries are at different stages of this crisis, the blue print for what to expect has become very clear. First comes slower economic growth. This is caused by Central Banks raising interest rates to defend their local currency. When you raise interest rates, it will mean that there is less capital available for business expansion, which means slower economic growth. Second, the Banking Industry will be damaged. Once the local economy begins to slow, local banks loan repayment in a timely fashion are called into question. Also, as the real estate market declines, it will have an adverse impact on the Banking Industry. Finally, right in the middle of all of this happening to them, the Bank's dollar denominated borrowing comes due and the money that they have set aside in local currency to pay off this debt is now not enough due to the tremendous currency devaluation. Third, there will be new trade flows. Exports will surge as a result of the currency devaluations which will potentially open all markets to new lower priced competition. Fourth, and finally, there will be political unrest. ***When this crisis begins to impact the standard of living of these countries, you can expect major political uprisings to follow.*** Once you have had your standard of living improved, you never want to go back again. A room at the Holiday Inn is 100 times better than sleeping in your car; however, after you stay at the Ritz Carlton, the inside of your room at the Holiday Inn looks as small as the inside of your car.

For the Week of November 3, 1997

I was in Toronto, Canada, last Friday speaking at an Investment Advisors Conference. While the current focus in Toronto seems to be on their teacher's strike, which by the way is the largest-ever teacher's strike in North America, the real focus should be on the Asia currency and economic meltdown. While most investors have been so worried about the impact the Asia crisis would have on our stock market, we forget about asking the question, what impact will it have on our neighbors to the North? *The single greatest loser in North America as a result of the Southeast Asia currency and economic meltdown will be the Toronto Stock Exchange*. Consider these facts; nearly one-third of the entire Toronto Stock Exchange is comprised of natural resource companies. Add to that the astonishing fact that somewhere between 40% and 50% of Canada's natural resource exports go to Asia. Combine these facts with the economic reality that when economies slow down (like the ones in Southeast Asia will be doing over the next year to eighteen months), the first import to take a major hit is natural resources. While all the headlines in Toronto are on the teacher's strike, the real story will be the impact that the Southeast Asia crisis will have on the Toronto Stock Exchange (by the way, there were a lot more kids roaming the streets on Friday).

For the Week of November 10, 1997

The recent American and Chinese summit will dramatically change global trade patterns which will in turn favor several United States industries. When the ink finally settles, the big winners in order of magnitude are: number one, the Nuclear Utility Industry which will now find the $50 billion Chinese nuclear power market open to it. Number two is technology and telecommunications. *China will now be a part of the Information Technology Agreement. This in turn means that Chinese tariffs on computer and telecommunication equipment must now be eliminated*. Number three, a new round of major aircraft orders will be a boom to the Aerospace and Defense Industry. And finally, there was even something left over for the Entertainment Industry, specifically the media. While the details still need to be hashed out, financial news services will be given more latitude to operate in Chinese markets going forward. While most of the headlines were on the "human rights" issues surrounding the Chinese visit, the real story lies with the United States industries that are clearly poised to benefit from this recent summit.

197

For the Week of November 17, 1997

The eyes and ears of the entire global markets will be on Manila this week. On Tuesday and Wednesday, the Asian Deputy Finance ministers are meeting to strategize regarding the creation of an Asian monetary fund to combat attacks against Asian currencies. Deputy Treasury Lawrence Summers and Federal Reserve Board Governor Laurence Meyer will attend on behalf of the United States. Finally, it appears that we are going to address this Southeast Asian crisis with an integrated policy response. What has been lacking from this crisis is any policy direction to resolve this issue. Unlike the peso currency crisis in Mexico where the United States quickly stepped up to the plate in a leadership role to formulate the necessary policy issues to solve the problems, there is a real void in leadership regarding this Southeast Asian crisis. The most likely leader, Japan, finds itself in such economic turmoil that it not only comes up short in terms of financial resources to "bail out" Southeast Asia, it has serious credibility issues to face as well. Looking beyond Japan, the next obvious leader is the United States and I do not expect that to happen. Bailing out Mexico was one thing; Southeast Asia is another. I look for the United States to participate, not lead. That leaves us with the Pacific Rim to develop a coordinated leadership and policy response on their own. This is exactly what is transpiring this week in Manila. ***This very well could be the most critical stage of the entire Southeast Asian crisis to date***. The stakes are very high and it is very important that this crisis be contained in Southeast Asia. The Pacific (ex-Japan) accounts for $3 trillion of a $24 trillion global economy. Japan accounts for another $3 trillion. If the crisis is contained here, we are talking about focusing on ¼ of the world's economy. It is critical that it does not spread to South and Latin America which accounts for another $1 trillion and to parts of Europe which account for $8 trillion. It is easy to see how ¼ of the world's economy could quickly spread to ⅓ or greater. Years from now we may look to this meeting in Manila as the key turning point in the Southeast Asia crisis.

For the Week of November 24, 1997

Regardless of what ultimately happens in Japan, the global markets are cheering the discussion of the Japanese government even considering a "bailout" of the weak Japanese banking system. While I can almost assure you that it will not be of the same magnitude as our government's bailout of our savings & loans, the amount of the bailout is not as important as the focus. *Simply the fact that the discussion and debate on the government bailing out the troubled financial systems signals to the global markets that Japan truly understands the magnitude of the problem.* They also clearly understand that there are truly only two options to fix the banking system. One would be to stimulate the economy by cutting taxes. This would indirectly provide the banking system with the financial support it needs. The problem with this option, however, is that it is politically unacceptable to Prime Minister Hashimoto's goal of raising taxes and cutting government spending as the way to eliminate Japan's budget deficit. That leaves us with option two, which would be a public bail out of the Japanese bank. I think the final solution will be more like 1½. It will combine moderate tax cuts with a partial government bailout.

For the Week of December 8, 1997

Our U.S. equity market has clearly reestablished itself as the global leader again. Over the past month, no one was sure who was leading and who was following. Was Europe following the Asian markets or the United States' reaction to the Asian markets? Was Asia really leading or was it following the United States markets? Global leadership has been clearly reestablished and our markets are the barometer for the world. *This leadership will be put to the test next week when Janet Reno and FBI Director Freeh testify before Congress regarding the Justice Department's decision not to appoint an independent counsel—the greatest risk in these hearings are not political, but rather global.* You see, if you think people in our own country have a hard time figuring out what's going on politically, just think of the daunting task for the global investor. If these hearings turn into a circus, the ramifications could be on the entire global marketplace, as the search for leadership begins anew.

For the Week of December 15, 1997

The eyes of the world will be on Japan this week as two key events will have global ramifications. First, on Monday the "Tankan" Report will be released. I expect that this report will show that the Japanese economy is in worse shape than most investors had previously feared. *This Tankan Report could push the Nikkei below the benchmark 16,000 level*. Second, the final details of Prime Minister Hashimoto's economic recovery plan will be developed this week. I expect no surprises which is a kind way of saying that I expect no creativity from Prime Minister Hashimoto's government. In order to jump start the economy, the Prime Minister needs to propose major tax cuts, not just at the corporate level, but at the personal consumption tax level as well. Also, another way to start the economy is to let government spending lead the way. Prime Minister Hashimoto's focus on the deficit will not allow him to propose any increase in government spending. The combination of worse-than-expected Tankan Report and a "boring" economy recovery plan will put a great deal of downward pressure on the Japanese markets this week.

8 POLITICAL PERSPECTIVE

OVERVIEW

Clearly the biggest political event of the year was the Balanced Budget Agreement and Taxpayers Relief Act of 1997.

I want to stay with my theory that every event creates winners and losers, who are the winners and losers as a result of this landmark legislation, starting with the winners.

There are several winners. First of all, the Defense Industry. With all of the focus on balancing the budget and cutting government spending, the Pentagon's budget came through the entire process virtually untouched. In fact, annual spending will rise steadily from $269 billion in 1998 to $289 billion in 2002. This will be a huge positive for defense contractors, especially in the Aerospace and Defense Industry. Secondly, high technology companies should stand to benefit. The budget deal renewed the research and development tax credit which is a huge boost to the High-Tech Industry. Capital intensive industries were also big winners. The rules were changed on the depreciable life of assets which clearly favors the Mining, Chemical and Steel Industries. In addition, the super-fund excise tax was not reinstated. This tax cost the Chemical and Oil Industry close to $1 billion annually. Finally, the Retail Industry should prosper, not because of anything that specifically happened to it, but rather what happened to its consumers. The "Kiddie Tax Credit" and the Education Hope Tax Credit as well as the Education Interest Deduction together will combine to boost the income of consumers, which in turn, should boost retail spending.

The two biggest losers were the Airline Industry and the Tobacco Industry. In the Airline Industry the entire ticket tax and fee structure has been revamped. And even though this restructuring has placed a greater burden on discount carriers, it is a negative for the entire industry. It will cost the overall industry an additional $3 billion in taxes over the next five years to pay for this restructuring. Specifically this restructuring scales back the ticket tax to 7.5% from 10%, imposes a $3 fee on each airport to airport segment and establishes a $12 international departure and arrival fee. The Tobacco Industry was also a big loser. Although they didn't get hit as badly as some experts thought that they would, the fact remains that they still got hit bad. The tobacco tax will increase by 10¢ in the year 2000 and another 5¢ in the year 2002. This will bite into both sales and profits.

Another loser is the Hospital Industry. The Hospital Industry really takes a one-two punch from cuts in Medicare and Medicaid. The budget deal lowers the Medicare payments to hospitals over the next five years as well as reducing the Medicaid payments paid to hospitals that treat the poor. The biggest loser, however, just might be the Home Oxygen Industry. This industry faces a 25% reduction in their reimbursement rates from the Federal Government next year and an additional 30% reduction the following year. As if this is not bad enough, buried deep in this legislation is a provision that allows the Clinton Administration to cut an additional 15% off the reimbursement rates for all "durable medical equipment." You guessed it, Home Oxygen is part of the Durable Medical Equipment category.

There are other investment opportunities or themes as a result of this budget and tax compromise. I think that there may be one developing as a result of the Capital Gains Tax relief for real estate. The first $500,000 of profit from selling your principle residence now escapes taxation. For singles, it's the first $250,000. I think that this provision will cause a flood of existing homes to hit the market, thus slowing down new home sales. Think of what happens when more existing homes are sold than new homes. There tends to be more things that need to be fixed up in the home that you buy if it is an existing home. When you buy a new home, everything is always new and perfect; however, when you buy an existing home, chances are you will soon be off to the hardware store, building outlet store, garden store, etc., to fix up that existing home you just bought.

Finally, focusing on the stock market, there are asset classes that should do better and worse as a result of this deal.

Small-cap stocks are clearly a big winner. With the lower Capital Gains Tax rate, investors will be focusing on asset classes that generate most of their returns in the form of capital gains which reward small cap stocks. The other end of the spectrum will be helped as well, namely large-cap stocks, as if they need any help. With the recent run up in the stock market, investors will now flood even more money into the large-cap "blue chip" stocks, especially now that these great gains will now be taxed at a lower rate. The asset class with the most to lose are the high-dividend stocks. As the gap between the Capital Gains Tax rate and the ordinary income tax rate widens, dividends that are taxed at the ordinary income tax level become less attractive.

And finally regarding the attractiveness of Variable Annuities. I'm quite certain that the new IRA Plus Accounts are not going to replace

Variable Annuities. These IRAs have a $4,000 annual limit while most Variable Annuities start with investments around $40,000. Second, 8% is not that great of a tax break and, after you add in the state taxes, what you have to pay as an investor just might put you right back where you started. Also, investors in annuities have a long-term perspective and don't overreact to short-term events. Our tax code could change another five or six times over the next ten to twenty years and no one really knows what those changes will be. Don't lose sight of the fact that the real reason that people invest in Variable Annuities is tax-deferral, and that hasn't changed at all. People who are focusing on tax-deferral are less concerned about differences in tax rates and, remember, when an investor finally takes money out of a Variable Annuity, they are usually retired. And, retirees tend to be in a lower tax bracket than when they were employed. In other words, the difference between ordinary income and Capital Gains Tax levels may become much less material at the time of withdrawal.

Also, look for the tax reform debate to take the center stage in the next Presidential election. The Capital Gains Tax was the start of something not the end of anything. The one thing that this current legislation did not address was making our tax code any simpler; in fact, it actually made it much more difficult. We already have the most complex income tax system in the world and now it was made even more complex. Think about it; the top rate on capital gains drops to 20% from 28% for assets held at least 12 months and sold after May 6, 1997. Effective, July 29, 1997, assets must be held at least 18 months to qualify for those rates. Starting in 2001, the lowest rate falls to 8% for assets bought this year or later and held five years, provided you fall within a certain income level. And in the year 2002, the top rate falls to 18% for assets bought in 2001 or later and held for at least five years. No wonder Albert Einstein quipped "The most complex system in the entire universe to understand is our income tax system."

Sit back now and enjoy the ride as I recap with you how the issues and events that drive my political perspectives evolved on a week by week basis from Tax Day (April 15th) through the end of 1997.

For the Week of April 14, 1997

With Newt Gingrich now firmly on board, it appears that the most popular bi-partisan game in Washington today is China-bashing. The combination of the political contribution scandal along with the upcoming debate over renewal of China's Most Favored Nation (MFN) status could spell selected trouble for the financial markets. While no one expects rejection of MFN (I certainly don't, and it doesn't really mean that much anyway) a heated high profile debate could lead to *a great deal of volatility in the overall Hong Kong* market as well as a sell off of U.S. companies that derive significant revenues from their China operations. . . . *The balanced budget is gaining steam again.* Even though there is a lot of work to be done, political compromise now seems to be the order of the day as both parties work toward agreement. While political realities will stop it short of doing everything that is needed, progress on this issue will be viewed as a real positive by the financial markets. . . . Listen up, the financial markets will be trying to read between the lines this week as *three Federal Reserve Bank Presidents hit the speaking circuit—* McTeer of Dallas on Monday, Stern of Minneapolis on Tuesday, and Hoening of Kansas City on Thursday.

For the Week of April 21, 1997

With the May 8th deadline for the Federal Communications Commission to unveil its Universal Service/Access Charge Reform component of Telecommunications Reform, don't expect many clear cut investment themes to emerge. These new guidelines will be so detailed and complicated to understand it will make Health Care Reform look simple. When all is said and done, *I expect the Long Distance Carriers to be the big losers with the Local Telephone Companies the winners.* While no one in the industry will end up getting exactly what they hoped, the political scale seems to always tilt to the Local Telephone Companies because Washington politicians want to avoid being associated with local telephone rate hikes at all costs. . . . With the very light economic calendar this week, the economic speaking circuit could have a greater impact on the market than any of the economic releases as *three Federal Reserve Bank Presidents and the Vice Chairman hit the speakers circuit this week.* Vice Chairman Alice Rivlin kicks things off for the week followed by Moskow of Chicago, Hoening of Kansas City and Jordan of Cleveland.

For the Week of April 28, 1997

The race is on to see how long the confirmation process of the two new Federal Reserve Board Governors nominees will take. The stakes are very high for the markets in this very critical and time sensitive process. At issue is whether or not Alan Greenspan and Co. will be able to raise rates at the upcoming May 20th Federal Reserve Board meeting. It is always difficult to determine in advance what the likely voting patterns of any new Fed nominees will be in the long run; however, in the short run I can promise you one thing about Roger Ferguson and Edward Gramlich, neither of these two candidates would have been nominated by President Clinton unless he felt that they would not support any immediate rate hikes. Thus, the race is on. If the approval process drags on, Alan Greenspan will view this as his last window of opportunity (I think he will increase rates 50 points) before the dynamics of a new Board are in place. *If, however, the political process moves quickly and Federal Reserve Board Governors Elect Ferguson and Gramlich attend the May 20th meeting, the likelihood of a rate increase diminishes to a less than a 10% chance*. There is just no way that you are going to get two new Federal Reserve Board Governors to approve a rate hike before they even figure out where the washroom is. . . . Watch out for Alan Greenspan's comments this week! *In what may be the most unique speaking schedule of the year, Alan Greenspan is speaking both the day before and the day after Friday's all important employment releases.* Talk about three strikes and you're out. One, he talks in Chicago before the most important release date of the month; two, we have the actual employment releases; and three, he talks in San Diego after the most important release date. Unlike baseball, in the financial markets it's one strike and you're out (or down).

For the Week of May 5, 1997

For the first time this entire year, political news out of Washington this week could actually cause the markets to rally. The Federal deficit, which stood at $290 billion four years ago before shrinking to $107 billion on the eve of President Clinton's re-election, is now projected to end this fiscal year at $60 to $65 billion dollars. The Clinton Administration's official forecast is still $127 billion. Needless to say, this extra $60 billion dollars can go a long way toward making any balanced budget deal more balanced. The real engine behind this deficit reduction are the very strong tax receipts that are the result of our strong and growing economy. ***I think that great progress will be made toward a balanced budget***, but I don't think it will have anything to do with financial issues (the reduced deficit); it will have everything to do with political reality. The facts are clear. First of all, President Clinton is still searching for his legacy (Whitewater, Paula Jones, FBI-gate, Travel-gate, Indonesia-gate. . . .). A balanced budget deal could give him the cornerstone that he so desperately needs. Second, the Republicans have to do something. They have retained control of both the House and the Senate, now it's time to do something. For different political reasons, both parties might move quickly to negotiate a balanced budget deal. . . . With President Clinton in Mexico the middle of the week, all emerging markets securities will be holding their collective breath. Mexico is still the bellwether of emerging markets. ***If Clinton's visit does not go well, its impact could be felt financially well beyond Mexico's "emerging markets" border.***

For the Week of May 12, 1997

The new battle lines have been drawn as a result of the balanced budget agreement. ***It's no longer Democrats vs. Republicans, it's Democrat & Republicans vs. Alan Greenspan***. In the past, Democrats have proposed balancing the budget by raising taxes, while Republicans have proposed balancing the budget by cutting spending. Nothing new here. The only two options appeared to be either increase taxes or cut spending. Then along comes our strong economy and with it, bloated tax receipts to balance the budget. Thus, instead of the traditional tax increase or major expenditure cuts, we are now going to balance the budget on the back of the economy. Thus, any interest rate move by the Fed to slow down the economy will actually have a negative impact on the balanced budget deal. Both political parties want this deal very badly. Expect a great deal of political pressure to be placed on the Fed to leave rates alone. It's one thing if a rise in interest rates increases mortgage payments for voters, it is another if it breaks the landmark balanced budget agreement. Politics at the Federal Reserve Board is now spelled with a capital "P."

For the Week of May 19, 1997

All eyes in Washington remain focused on getting the balanced budget deal through the legislative process as soon as possible. A closer look at this deal reveals just how much the budget is balanced on the back of the strong economy. ***The balanced budget projects that the revenue windfall of $45 billion that they found this May will reappear again every year for the next five years***. The budget also assumes saving over $25.2 billion over the next five years due to lower interest rates which will in turn reduce the overall dollar amount needed to pay interest. The budget also grants the Federal Government a "fiscal dividend" of $76.8 billion over the next five years. This fiscal dividend assumes that interest rates will come down even further over time based upon the adoption of a "credible and sustainable" balanced budget plan. I sometimes wonder who in the world comes up with these bizarre concepts like "fiscal dividend." Furthermore, how could anyone in their right mind think that this balanced budget plan was "credible or sustainable" when it fails to address the two biggest problems that we face in government today, namely Social Security and Medicare.

For the Week of May 26, 1997

Last week's special election in New Mexico cannot be used as a barometer for the upcoming 1998 Congressional elections, although, I'm sure Republicans will try. The election was held to fill the Congressional seat left by U.S. Ambassador to the United Nations, Bill Richardson. The Republican candidate won an upset victory in a predominately Democratic district. The Republican, however, can thank the up and coming state-wide "Green" party for this victory. The Green party garnered 17% of the vote, the Republican candidate, 42% and the Democratic candidate, 40%. Most of the traditional Democratic voters supported a Green party candidate instead of a moderate Democrat. The center of the Congressional District is in Santa Fe, home of a very liberal and strongly pro-environmental electorate, the exact profile the Green party is targeting. Remember there aren't many Santa Fe's across the U.S. . . . . *Congressional approval of any industry-wide settlement with the Tobacco Industry appears slim*. Even though the Tobacco Industry appears to be making progress, the issues are so complex and our legislative process so cumbersome, most of the litigation would wind its way through the courts and be settled before any settlement gets through Congress.

For the Week of June 2, 1997

When the dust finally settles, the biggest loser as a result of the Supreme Court decision regarding the Paula Jones sexual harassment litigation, will be China. The Supreme Court's decision not to delay the sexual harassment charges against President Clinton until he leaves office will re-focus Washington insiders of both political parties on this highly partisan negative issue. The working relationships across party lines that developed during the balanced budget negotiations will be a thing of the past. The new focus will be on Paulagate, which will in turn resurface Whitewater, Filegate, Travelgate, Coffeegate and all of the other "gates" that enclose the potential scandals hanging over the Clinton Administration. Regarding China, the President has already picked his side when he announced that he would extend China's Most Favored Nation (MFN) trading status for one year. The next move is up to Congress and I expect that the Republican members of Congress smell blood as a result of the Paula Jones suit. It will now make them fight even harder against China's MFN status. First, it's very high profile and second, it gives them a chance to show that they are very different from President Clinton on this important issue. The longer the debate drags on, the greater the likelihood that the Indonesia illegal political contributions get discussed. This Paula Jones issue has put President Clinton on the ropes, the Republicans will try to use China as the knockout punch by tying the Asian fundraising scandal into the approval of China's MFN. I look for the political battle lines to be drawn very, very deep. The ramifications of the Paula Jones decision go well beyond a sexual harassment suit. *This recent decision could be a key determinant in the outcome of China's MFN status. And it doesn't stop there, if China's MFN fails, all bets are off regarding the already promised Capital Gains Tax and Estate Tax Relief.* Who would have ever thought a hotel room in Little Rock, Arkansas, could change the world.

For the Week of June 9, 1997

It becomes more clear every day that, at least from a political perspective, *Congress will not approve any global Tobacco Industry settlement.* Two factors best highlight why it will never happen. First just consider who would have to agree or sign off on the legislation. The Tobacco Industry, the State Attorney Generals and key public health advocates are just the beginning, not the end of the proposed settlement participants who would have to sign off. It would also have to have broad political support across both political parties, this cannot be a partisan settlement. In addition, it would have to have the White House's seal of approval and to get that, means that the general public would have to be supportive of the settlement. I don't think you could even get this diverse group to agree on what day of the week it is, let alone, details of a global settlement. If by some miracle you did, the settlement still would never happen. That is because of my second factor, our complex Congressional process. It was not designed for global settlements like this. Just think for a minute now, this settlement will fall under the jurisdiction of several committees and sub committees in both the House as well as the Senate. You can expect each and every committee to hold their own Congressional hearings and propose their own amendments. What finally comes out of this process would not even be recognized let alone supported by the settlement teams that sent the deal to Congress. . . . *I expect the political pressure on state pension systems regarding divesting of all tobacco investments to intensify* if the Washington State Investment Board follows the recommendation of one of its subcommittees to dump all $250 million it has currently invested in tobacco stocks. The Washington State Pension System will make a final decision regarding tobacco stocks in mid July. Currently, only two state pension systems (Maryland and Florida) prohibit any investment in tobacco stocks. Two down, one leaning that way and forty-seven to go.

For the Week of June 30, 1997

The count down begins toward July 8th. That is the day that Senator Fred Thompson conducts his Congressional investigation and hearings into the Clinton White House's illegal campaign donations. For historical purposes, it should be noted that the Congressional hearings will be conducted in the exact same Russell Senate hearing room used for the Nixon Watergate investigations. . . . Meanwhile, Whitewater just refuses to go away. Last week's Supreme Court decision that First Lady Hillary Clinton's conversations with government lawyers aren't protected by attorney-client privileges should shed new light on this affair and most certainly push it up to the next level. . . . The Paula Jones case also continues to move along. Although I feel that this case is probably the weakest in terms of its legal merits, it most certainly could be the most damaging and embarrassing from a political perspective for President Clinton. Even with all of these scandals hovering over him, Bill Clinton does have an ace up his sleeve—the strong economy. The fact of the matter is people care more about getting jobs and getting paid than they do about anything that's going on in Washington. ***For any of these scandals to seriously damage President Clinton, the economy must slow down first*** in order to get the eyes of the voters glued on Washington and not on their paycheck.

For the Week of July 7, 1997

The U.S. Senate returns from their short Fourth of July holiday break on Monday while the U.S. House of Representatives resumes action on Tuesday. At the top of the agenda is working out the details of the tax bill, which in its various proposed forms currently stands as the largest potential tax reform legislation since 1986. The focal point will become the Capital Gains Tax cut. The House of Representatives wants the tax cut and they want it indexed for inflation. The Senate wants the tax cut but gave up on indexing for inflation. President Clinton does not want the Capital Gains Tax cut for upper income wage earners and wants no part of indexing Capital Gains Tax. ***Despite all of the political rhetoric that you will hear in the coming weeks, President Clinton will not veto the tax bill.*** Instead, he will try to weaken what eventually comes out of the Senate/House conference. Even though President Clinton does not want to provide tax breaks to the "rich," I think he will give in on this in return for removing the indexing provision from the Capital Gains Tax. Everyone in the administration hates Congressman Archer's indexing idea and as such they can all rally around this concept of a victory against the Republicans. But make no mistake about it, a compromise will be reached and President Clinton will sign it. He really has no choice. You see from a political perspective, if President Clinton were to veto the tax bill, the entire budget balancing process and budget bills would also quickly unravel. President Clinton desperately wants to hang on to the positive legacy as the President that balanced the budget. If this comes apart, it will simply be added to the current list of Health Care Reform, Whitewater, Travelgate, Paulagate and so on. President Clinton's focus on needing something positive for the history books to say about him will not allow him to veto the tax bill.

For the Week of July 14, 1997

President Clinton's nomination of Edward Gramlich and Roger Ferguson to the Federal Reserve Board should have no problem winning Senate approval. *I expect both of the new Federal Reserve Board nominees to be confirmed by the full Senate in time to join the Board before its next Federal Open Market's Committee meeting on August 19th.* Two issues will help these nominations sail through the confirmation process. First, it was way back on April 21st that President Clinton announced his intentions to nominate Gramlich and Ferguson. Over the past 90 days there have been no complaints from any constituency group regarding either of these two nominations. It has also given the White House plenty of time to double check and make sure that neither of the nominees has ever slept in the Lincoln bedroom. There is simply no "political baggage" with either of these candidates. Second, it is in Congress's own self interest to appoint these new federal Reserve Board Governors as quickly as possible. The whole Balanced Budget Accord is dependent on a strong economy. In essence, the budget is balanced on the back of the economy. Right now, if Alan Greenspan wanted to strike with one more pre-emptive rate hike against inflation, he would only have a five-member Federal Reserve Board to convince. Once Gramlich and Ferguson are on board, he would have to convince seven members, not just five. I simply can't imagine either of these individuals winning President Clinton's support unless they pledged to fight against future rate hikes. Thus, if the Senate wants any chance of balancing the budget on the back of the economy, their best bet is to confirm Gramlich and Ferguson now and remove the threat of a pre-emptive rate hike to slow down the economy. . . . The Senate Governmental Affairs Committee continues its hearings on alleged campaign finance violations. It would be a major mistake for the markets to underestimate what might come out of Senator Fred Thompson's hearing. *Possibly the greatest risk to the financial markets in the second half of the year lies in what is uncovered at these Indonesia-Gate hearings.* Remember, the markets hate uncertainty, and these hearings have the potential to create a great deal of uncertainty, especially when we throw terms like "treason" around, just like "apple pie."

For the Week of July 21, 1997

The greatest risks that the financial markets will face this entire year will come this week from Alan Greenspan's Humphrey-Hawkins testimony. The markets continue to try to convince themselves that nothing new will be disclosed by Alan Greenspan at his semi-annual Humphrey-Hawkins testimony to Congress. Yet Alan Greenspan, who in addition to being the most influential financial figure in the world is also a pretty shrewd politician, has recently used this high profile forum to deliver some critical messages to the market. Remember it was the last Humphrey-Hawkins testimony where the term irrational exuberance was coined. Those two words caused the stock market to sell off for the next eight weeks. ***This very well may be the most critical speech Alan Greenspan has ever given to Congress***. He finds himself at the economic crossroads. The tone of Alan Greenspan's speech must take one of two tracks. On the one hand, he can embrace this so-called "new era" economy. The new era economy almost makes the business cycle obsolete. Because of the tremendous technology and productivity improvements we have made over the past few years, our economy can grow much faster than we thought and still have no inflation. When you overlay the impact of the global marketplace to this new era economy, it is possible to consider 5% economic growth with 2% inflation. If this is the track Alan Greenspan takes, it will fuel a tremendous rally in the markets. On the other hand, Alan Greenspan may choose to focus on "Keynesian" economic theory where he raises the concern that low employment and high capacity utilization could combine to cause inflation, and even though there are no signs of inflation, the Federal Reserve Board needs to be pro-active and have a bias to tighten before inflation shows up. In addition, *I truly expect him to make some comment regarding the "bubble" in our stock market*. If he was concerned with irrational exuberance at 6,200, what can he be thinking with the markets now at 8,000? While no one knows exactly what Alan Greenspan will say for sure, traders should keep a Thesaurus close at hand when Alan Greenspan tells Congress what kind of exuberance the market is displaying at 8,000. My personal leading candidates to cause the next Greenspan inflicted market correction are imbecilic exuberance, fatuous exuberance or fallacious exuberance.

> *Note: Special Thesaurus "Clue for the Week"*
>
> imbecilic = stupid
> fatuous = dim-witted
> fallacious = misleading

For the Week of July 28, 1997

The fall-out of the recent "over-throw" attempt by Republican Congressional rebels to oust House Speaker Newt Gingrich could touch everyone. . . . in their pocket book. The Republican congressional leadership is in such dire straights, it can't even overthrow a leader. With egg clearly on their face, there is still one more chance to get Newt. You see, the way you "get" a leader is to prove that he can no longer lead. The battle ground just may be the Gingrich sponsored tax bill which includes the Capital Gains Tax relief. *If these House Republican rebels align themselves with Congressman Gephardt's "no tax cut" liberal wing, they can easily kill Newt Gingrich's tax cut bill.* If all they have to hurt is every investor in America in order to "get" Newt, I think that they just might do it. After all, their re-election is still sixteen months away, and according to political calendars, that's a lifetime. So much will happen between now and then it most likely will have no impact on the 1998 Congressional elections. After all, if the market falls a couple hundred points because we can't get a tax bill approved, investors will in turn have a couple of hundred points less of capital gains to worry about avoiding to pay taxes on. While Main Street is trying to figure out if the glass is half empty or half full, Washington just may decide to break the glass and eliminate the argument.

For the Week of August 4, 1997

With the balanced budget and tax cut plan accomplished, what in the world will Washington politicians become involved in next? I think that there will be three key issues between now and the remainder of the year. The first issue will be the tobacco settlement. *I continue to believe that our political process alone makes it nearly impossible to reach a global tobacco settlement,* so don't hold your breath. Second, Senator Thompson's campaign-finance hearings will now receive top billing. It's time for the committee to put up or shut up. I still believe that there is something there, I am just not sure that these campaign-finance hearings will be able to prove it. Finally, the real problems of our government will finally start to be addressed, that being Social Security reform and Medicare reform. I do not look for anything to happen with these entitlements this year, however, I do expect these issues to now be at the top of everyone's political agenda.

For the Week of August 18, 1997

With both chambers of Congress on summer vacation, we have limited the political risks to the financial markets in the near term. . . . Two events could possibly throw the markets a curve this week. First, even though I firmly believe that the Federal Reserve Board will not raise interest rates this week, that is only half of the FOMC risk. The bigger risk is not the actual meeting on Tuesday, but what happens on Thursday. The detailed minutes of the last FOMC meeting held July 1 and 2 are released to the markets. *Any signs of division among the members of the FOMC could be all the markets need to sell off.* . . . The second event that we have to worry about is on Friday from Texas. On that day in San Antonio, Federal Reserve Bank of Dallas President, Robert McTeer, speaks. For the past two Fridays the markets experienced a major setback. If the market has a setback on Friday of this week, it can probably be traced to something said in Texas.

For the Week of August 25, 1997

When both chambers of Congress return from summer recess after Labor Day, I expect "trade" issues to dominate the agenda. Congress will look to the White House to take the lead on just how far President Clinton is willing to go to push for "Fast Track Authority." President Clinton's own timetable set early September as his deadline to send Congress a Fast Track Trade proposal. Clinton's reluctance to send the proposal to Congress is his fear that House Minority Leader, Dick Gephardt, will use this as a grand standing issue to separate him from President Clinton and more importantly, Vice President Al Gore. Gephardt and Gore will most likely square off for the Democratic Presidential nomination for the year 2000 election. This will be a very volatile issue for the Democrats. Gephardt will push for very tough labor and environmental standards and President Clinton knows that the inclusion of those standards will do nothing but insure that the Republicans will not support it. This will be a very high profile battle that has as much to do with personal political ambitions as it does with free trade. *As the debate heats up, it could put some stock price pressure or investor nervousness on companies that derive a majority of their revenues internationally.*

214

For the Week of September 1, 1997

The United States Congress reconvenes on Tuesday. *I look for a stepped-up focus on the campaign finance problems of Teamsters President, Ron Carey.* Republicans have been trying desperately to tie the Indonesian campaign contributions directly to President Clinton; and for the most part, have not succeeded. They have fresh meat in Ron Carey and I expect them to go for the kill. One of the problems with going after the Asian money laundering scheme was that some Republicans also were tainted by Asian money. That is not the case with the Teamsters Democratic money. The biggest guessing game in Washington continues to be who or what will bring the Clinton Administration down? Whitewater, Travelgate, FBI Filegate, Paula Jones-gate, etc., etc. In my opinion, move Ron Carey to the top of the list. I expect this one to get real ugly before it's over.

For the Week of September 8, 1997

Washington will throw the financial markets mixed signals in the coming weeks. On the positive front, I look for both Congress and President Clinton to begin to make some progress on the long-term entitlement crisis that we have in this country. With the balanced budget agreement and Taxpayers Relief Act of 1997 behind them, I look for the powers in Washington to finally start to address our real problems, namely Social Security and Medicare. I expect President Clinton to push forward with his commitment to establish a blue-ribbon bipartisan commission to develop recommendations on how to solve our Social Security and Medicare crisis. The financial markets will rally at the mere thought of Washington finally addressing our biggest problems . . . On a somewhat related front, the Democrats are now breaking rank in their support (or lack of support) by allowing the Social Security Trust Fund to invest in the stock market. Senator Bob Kerrey, a Democrat from Nebraska and a leading expert on our Social Security system is now leaning toward supporting investing in the stock market. The fact that he is both very well respected in the Democratic circles as well as a potential year 2000 Presidential candidate will certainly serve to push this concept forward . . . Now for the bad news, *I expect some high profile political battles between the Washington establishment and Alan Greenspan.* As the Federal Reserve Board moves ever closer to raising interest rates, I expect political leaders from both political parties to voice their displeasure. The politicians do not

215

want to see the economy slow down heading into their 1998 re-election. Also, these politicians realize that most of their major accomplishments were the result of one thing, our strong economy. Anyone or anything that attempts to slow it down will face their political wrath. Hold on; this could be the mother of all political battles.

For the Week of September 15, 1997

Pretty soon you are going to need a score card to figure out who said what to who as the scandals in Washington, D.C., are starting to boil. We are now being told that Vice President Al Gore was advised that his fundraising actions violated Federal law. Al Gore claims his actions did not violate Federal law. Meanwhile, Joseph Sandler, the Democratic National Committee's general counsel is stating that he did not advise and/or train fund-raiser John Huang regarding campaign finance laws. This, by the way, is in direct conflict with what the Democratic National Committee's finance director recently testified before Congress. Who said what, to who, when? When the stories start to change by the people who are supposed to be on the "same side," pay close attention; there may be a crack in the dam . . . ***Possibly the most intriguing battle involves Teamsters President, Ron Carey and President Clinton***. While on the one hand Carey is being investigated by Federal officials for a possible illegal money laundering scheme between the Democratic Party and his Teamsters re-election campaign, on the other hand, he is attacking President Clinton and any Democrat that is considering supporting Free Trade Fast Track legislation. It's rare to see the president of a powerful labor union doing public battle with a Democratic president. As I've said before, Ron Carey could be a dangerous wild card in President Clinton's future. If Carey sees his world crumbling, don't expect him to go down alone as some of Clinton's loyal followers may have done with Whitewater. Carey will go down with both guns blazing, hoping to take President Clinton along with him.

For the Week of September 22, 1997

Look for the Fast Track Trade legislation to take center stage on the political front. This debate has great impact for our markets. The underlying strength of the recent bull market has been driven by the powerful forces of global free trade. Anything that we do politically to improve the global free trade landscape will be viewed as a positive by the markets. The most immediate impact of Fast Track legislation will be on Latin and Southern American emerging markets. With Fast Track legislation in hand President Clinton could extend the North American Free Trade Agreement beyond Mexico to include Brazil, Chile, Venezuela and others. Our multinational companies that export to these countries would also be poised for great things. Since the adoption of the North American Free Trade Agreement (NAFTA) in 1994, United States exports to Mexico and Canada have grown 34% which far outpaces all of our other trading partners. Fast Track Trade legislation is not just a political debate; it is a debate that will have its greatest impact on the financial markets.

For the Week of September 29, 1997

The biggest event from the political front will be this week's Federal Open Markets Committee (FOMC) meeting on Tuesday. *The FOMC will take no action at this week's meeting.* Even though there almost appears to be unanimous market consensus regarding no FOMC rate hike, the markets are always apprehensive leading up to the actual announcement that we made it through another meeting. I expect all of the financial markets to give out a collective sigh of relief realizing that they don't have to worry about rates again until November 12th, the date of the next FOMC meeting . . . While I expect no action at the FOMC meeting, there could be some fireworks contained in the FOMC minutes from the August 19 meeting. The official minutes from that meeting will be released to the markets on Thursday. Any signs of a lack of consensus from the FOMC could cause the markets to sell off . . . As if we don't have enough to worry about on this very hectic week, Federal Reserve Chairman, Alan Greenspan is speaking Sunday morning at the American Bankers Association's annual convention in Boston. Even if we survive all of the events of the week, remember in the opera, it's not over 'til the "fat lady sings," while in our markets, it's not over until Alan's done speaking.

For the Week of October 6, 1997

The Tobacco Industry settlement is not only dead for this year, it may be dead for next year as well. The combination of President Clinton not supporting the current settlement proposal and Congress's intention to recess for the entire year by the first week in November, make it absolutely impossible for anything to be accomplished this year. The bigger issue becomes what are the prospects for a global settlement next year. Based on President Clinton's analysis of the current proposed settlement, I would put the odds on passage next year at slim to none. Remember, even though the President paid lip service to the idea of a global settlement, his three lynch-pins will make it impossible for the existing settlement to be modified enough to gain presidential approval. President Clinton's three keys are first, if youth smoking reduction targets are not met, cigarette prices would be drastically increased. Second, the President is demanding that the tax-deductibility of any youth smoking penalty payments be removed, as well as the removal of any upward annual limits. Under the current proposed settlement, annual youth smoking penalties would be capped at $2 billion. Third and finally, the Food and Drug Administration must be given complete and full control with no strings attached to control tobacco. Maybe President Clinton doesn't even really want a tobacco settlement. While everyone is busy looking at the numbers in the proposed settlement, maybe President Clinton has his eyes on another set of numbers. The number of adults who smoke in the United States is larger than the number of votes President Clinton received when he was re-elected. This lame-duck president just might be more worried about his legacy and popularity than about any global settlement.

For the Week of October 13, 1997

The greatest political risk to the markets is not Indonesia-gate or Paula-gate or Travel-gate; it's Speakers-gate. I'm not talking about House Speaker, Newt Gingrich; I'm talking about all of the "Speakers" at the Federal Reserve Board that whip-saw the markets with their speeches. Last week it was Alan Greenspan on Tuesday in front of Congress saying one thing as the Chairman of the Federal Reserve Board, then the next day we had Alice Rivlin, the Vice-Chairperson of the Federal Reserve Board saying something else on CNBC. Well, if you think last week was crazy, *this week's edition of Speakers-gate, I feel, may present the single greatest risk to our markets*. On Tuesday, Federal Reserve Board Chairman, Alan Greenspan speaks at a Cato Institute Conference. Cleveland Federal Reserve Bank President, Jerry Jordan, also speaks that same day at that same conference. Meanwhile, back in New Jersey on that same day, the Federal Reserve Bank of Philadelphia President Edward Boehne speaks. On Wednesday, it's

Greenspan again, this time in Minneapolis; while in Massachusetts, Federal Reserve Governor Susan Phillip talks about the ten-year anniversary of the stock market crash (I can hardly wait). Another day, another speaker; on Thursday, it's Federal Reserve Bank of St. Louis President, Thomas Melzer then, finally on Friday, it's Federal Reserve Bank of San Francisco President, Robert Parry, also talking about the crash of 1987. Speakers-gate will make this one of the hardest weeks to figure out where the markets are headed.

For the Week of October 20, 1997

Fast Track Trade legislation this year is dead. As President Clinton parades and politics through Latin and South America in an attempt to gather steam and support for "Fast Track Trade" legislation, it is issues here at home that will kill this legislation. First of all, let's be clear on what Fast Track legislation exactly is. Under Fast Track legislation, the President would be allowed to seek Congressional approval of future trade agreements without the threat or possibility of any Congressional amendments. Congress would simply be forced to approve or disapprove the trade deal as it is presented to them. As you can imagine, most trading partners are almost requiring this as a pre-requisite to negotiate any trade deal with the United States. After all, they don't want to spend months hammering out the details of a deal only to have Congress change all of the details. *I think that the recent discovery of video tapes regarding White House fund-raisers will prove to be the ultimate killer of the Fast Track Trade proposal.* While it is still unclear whether any of these tapes will ultimately led to any criminal indictments, they have certainly lead to a higher level of uncertainty regarding the Administrations dealing with foreign contributors. While most Americans are lost in trying to connect John Huang and "Charlie" Trie and The Lippo Group and so on and so on, they are certainly not lost in connecting "something just doesn't seem right." Sometimes it's the perception or appearance of a problem that can be greater than the problem itself. These new video tapes once again highlight the concern of President Clinton receiving contributions from foreign sources. With that cloud that's hanging over his head getting bigger and bigger, there is simply no way Congress is going to give him what the American public perceives as even a freer hand to negotiate with foreign officials. Based on perception, impeachment hearings are more likely than Fast Track Trade hearings.

For the Week of October 27, 1997

In case you need one more reason why the Federal Reserve Board will not be raising interest rates anytime soon, U.S. Senate Republican Leader, Trent Lott, has just given you one (actually two). Senator Lott has decided to stop holding President Clinton's nominations of Edward Gramlich and Roger Ferguson to the Federal Reserve Board hostage over campaign finance reform battles and will now schedule a vote on these two nominations. *Once these two new members are confirmed (which they will be) it will be impossible for Alan Greenspan to deliver a preemptive strike on inflation by raising interest rates.* Today, if Alan Greenspan wanted to strike with one more preemptive rate hike against inflation, he would only have a five-member Federal Reserve Board to convince. Once Gramlich and Ferguson are on board, he would have to convince all seven members, not just five. I simply can't imagine either of these individuals winning President Clinton's support unless they pledged to fight against future rate hikes. After all, if President Clinton has any hopes of a political legacy, it will be to balance the budget. If the budget is balanced before he leaves office, it will be on the back of our robust economy. Any rate hike will not only slow the economy and eliminate the chance of balancing the budget sooner rather than later, it will also remove President Clinton's last chance for a legacy. . . . Two weeks ago, everyone was worried what Alan Greenspan was going to say on Wednesday, October 29, 1997, when he testified to the Joint Economic Committee of Congress on "The Economic Outlook and Monetary Policy" now no one really cares. The powerful Fed Chairman has finally met his match with this Asian meltdown. It really doesn't matter what he says on Wednesday; the global markets will not allow him to raise rates.

For the Week of November 3, 1997

Tuesday is election day here in the United States and we can expect the markets to try to interpret the results to determine what they might mean for the 1998 Congressional election as well as the Presidential election in 2000. First off, on the ballot are the Governor's office in New Jersey and Virginia, mayoral races in most major cities as well as one special Congressional election in New York. *I expect the trend in Tuesday's election will be the exact same trend that we see in 1998 and that is incumbents will rule the day (and that's good news for Christie Whitman).* Given the choice, voters will always vote with their pocketbook. They really don't care about this Democrat vs. Republican thing or this liberal vs. conservative argument, what they really are concerned about is their own pocketbook. If they have a job (which most now do with unemployment levels at twenty-five year lows) and if inflation is not eating away at their paycheck, they will usually vote to keep things the way they are. Unless we have a major economic downturn, which I do not expect, incumbents will rule the day this November as well as November 1998 . . . This Friday could develop into a very strange day. It is the first time in recent memory that both the Federal Reserve Board Chairman and the Vice Chairperson are both giving public speeches on the same day in different locations. Vice Chairperson, Alice Rivlin is speaking in Washington, while Chairman Alan Greenspan is speaking in Germany. (I wonder who got first choice?) The markets shouldn't worry, however, because of the time difference, Vice Chairperson Rivlin will be able to absorb all of Greenspan's comments before she ever steps behind the podium. It should be the end of a great week.

For the Week of November 10, 1997

All eyes in Washington will be on the Federal Open Markets Committee which meets on Wednesday. If ever there was a non-event, this is certainly one of them. ***There is simply no way that the Federal Reserve Board can hike interest rates.*** These inflation fighters have done such a good job that the new fear in the markets is not inflation, but deflation. In a deflationary environment Central Banks ease interest rates, they don't tighten them . . . One fly in the ointment "The Shadow Open Markets Committee." This informal committee made up of influential economists that critiques (second guesses) the Federal Reserve Board has dramatically shifted direction and has now said it's time to hike interest rates. If all the influential economists agree it's time to raise interest rates, then I'm 99.9% sure that the Federal Open Markets Committee won't raise rates . . . Whitewater could heat up again, as the result of a $27,000 check dated 1982 from the failed Madison Guarantee Savings and Loan made payable to President Clinton, which was found in an abandoned car in a junkyard in Arkansas. This check reintroduces the testimony of President Clinton in which he stated he did not receive a loan from the bank. Stay tuned, this thing just gets crazier by the day.

For the Week of November 17, 1997

With the most recent defeat of President Clinton's Fast Track Trade legislation, this marks the beginning of the end of his policy influence in Congress. The term lame-duck president now has a capital "L." When you are a Lame-duck President, you lose both the support within your political party as well as the continued political shots from the opposition's political party. ***Thus, this recent defeat of Fast Track Trade authority now means that the political scandals will once again take center stage.*** I look for Whitewater to heat up again especially in light of the check found last week made out to President Clinton. Also, the December 2 deadline for Attorney General Janet Reno to call for an independent counsel regarding illegal fundraising in the White House is fast approaching. And don't forget what's right around the corner. Live, from Little Rock, Arkansas, the Paula Jones sexual harassment trial is set to begin on May 26, 1998 . . . Analyzing the aftermath of the November election, the story I feel is in the losers not the winners. Even though Republicans are pointing to their sweep of the Governors' races in New Jersey and Virginia as a sign of things to come, the real sign of things to come can be found in the losers. ***All across the United States, the big losers were tax increases.*** Despite a tremendous economy, with unemployment at levels we have not seen in the past quarter of a century, voters still said no to new taxes. If you can't get voters to increase taxes when times are good, it will never happen when times are bad. Look out; major tax reform might be just around the corner.

For the Week of November 24, 1997

You can circle November 20, 1997 on your calendar as the date that Social Security Reform officially began. Alan Greenspan who has constantly thrown cold water on the idea of privatizing Social Security has now become the strongest advocate for Social Security reform. Alan Greenspan is the one individual who has the respect and influence to move a politically sensitive issue forward. His support and endorsement of this issue will place it at the top of the political calendar for 1998. This discussion has tremendous ramifications for the stock market. Any movement at all towards a privatized or a partially privatized system means that more money will ultimately flow to the stock market. This issue also has global ramifications. Many of the social public retirement systems in Europe, specifically Germany, France and Italy are also in serious financial straits. These European countries, however, have been looking to the United States for a clue on how to solve this public retirement system crisis. *As we begin the move to privatize Social Security, look for it to cause a chain reaction all across Europe. And once again the biggest winner will be our stock market which currently accounts for over 50% of the entire global equity market.*

For the Week of December 8, 1997

The decision by the New York Stock Exchange to leave the trading triggers unchanged will clearly stir up some action at the Securities and Exchange Commission as well as Congress. *The New York Stock Exchange's decision to stay in the dark ages on these market triggers just might result in an onslaught of investor wrath.* The stock market after all doesn't belong to Wall Street anymore; it belongs to Main Street. These outdated triggers only serve to put panic in the eyes of everyone on Main Street, while the insiders on Wall Street realize that there is nothing to worry about. Their lack of action represents a breach of trust with the investors on Main Street, USA. This issue will not go away. I look for someone in Washington to latch on to this key issue and force the New York Stock Exchange to wake up and smell the roses. In 1987, triggers like 350 points and 550 points made sense. In 1987, the only triggers that make sense are 10% and 20% declines. Stay tuned; this issue is far from dead.

For the Week of December 15, 1997

The political highlight of the week is Tuesday's meeting of the Federal Open Market's Committee (FOMC) to determine what to do with interest rates. For the first time in the past two years, this meeting has been rendered a non-event. *It is absolutely impossible for the FOMC to move rates one way or the other.* A rate hike is out of the question. The economic crisis in Southeast Asia and the impact that it will have on economics around the globe will not allow the FOMC to take action on their own to slow our economy. Keep in mind; a rate hike also serves as a magnate for foreign capital searching for yield. Thus, any increase will have serious global market liquidity ramifications. On the other side, any thoughts of a rate decrease to make up for the Southeast Asian crisis are history. The unbelievably strong November employment report guaranteed no easing. If you can't raise rates and can't lower rates, why even meet? . . . Maybe there will be some fireworks contained in the FOMC minutes from the last meeting on November 12 which will be released this Thursday. The markets have to worry about something. If we don't have to worry about this month's meeting, why not worry about last month's. Who knows, maybe Alan Greenspan coined a new term to replace his overused "irrational exuberance."

9 COMMENTARY ON KEY INVESTMENT ISSUES THAT EVOLVED IN 1997

There were numerous issues and events that evolved in 1997 that will have long lasting impacts on all types of investments. As these issues continue to be debated on Wall Street and Main Street, they will add increased volatility to an already volatile financial marketplace. The top of the list of investment issues that will continue to impact our markets are Capital Gains Tax cuts, the strength of the dollar, the European Monetary Union, revising the Consumer Price Index, the Federal Deficit, Hong Kong's reversion back to Mainland China, the United Parcel Service strike and finally, Fast Track Trade authority.

CAPITAL GAINS TAX RELIEF

While Wall Street hung on to every word and phrase from Federal Reserve Board Chairman, Alan Greenspan, during his recent Humphry-Hawkins testimony to Congress, Main Street was more interested in the first question Congress asked Mr. Greenspan. Consider the setting: As Alan Greenspan, arguably the most powerful and influential financial figure in the world, is winding down his Congressional testimony regarding inflation, economic growth and the markets, the very first question he was asked by Senator D'Amato was "tell me again why our Capital Gains Tax rate should be zero." Talk about a question from left field. I wonder why the Chairman of the Senate Banking Committee is so focused on Capital Gains Tax relief? The answer may be in the question itself. Could Washington finally be coming around to a major policy shift by dramatically cutting our Capital Gains Tax? The answer is yes! Any major policy change always draws two questions from Wall Street. First, what will this public policy change mean for the financial markets and second, are there any investment opportunities or themes that this public policy shift will create?

Let's first look at the impact on the market. Opponents to reducing the Capital Gains Tax over the years have been warning individual investors that any reduction in the Capital Gains Tax rate will immediately cause investors to liquidate their investments and with more "sellers" than "buyers" the stock market will undergo a major correction. *(It is interesting to note that this myth is probably the reason Alan Greenspan is supporting a major Capital Gains Tax reduction—it is clear that Mr. Greenspan feels valuations are simply too lofty.)* Opponents point to history as their proof, focusing on the last two times this country had a Capital Gains Tax cut (1981 and 1978) and the ensuing sell-offs or market corrections that followed. While history can sometimes be a good guide, in this case, it misses the most dramatic shift in our industry—demographics. The aging of the baby-boomers is creating long term investors focusing on establishing a nest-egg for retirement, not trading opportunities or short term tax strategies. While the temptation will clearly be there for the baby-boomers to liquidate their investment at the lower Capital Gains Tax rate, the bigger question for them becomes what do I do with the money then? The combination of the aging baby-boomers focusing on longer term investing and the explosion of the retirement 401(k) market should supply an ample level of buyers to the market. While I am sure that any Capital Gains Tax reduction will cause a temporary "tax correction" in the market, the correction will be short lived, and savvy investors will view it as a "blue light special" buying opportunity.

Second, does this public policy shift create any investment opportunities or themes? The answer again is yes. Investors are becoming more and more aware of how public policy issues can impact the financial markets and can no longer be viewed in isolation. Recent history shows us what the perception of a public policy issue—healthcare reform, can do to an entire industry—pharmaceutical stocks—in the financial markets, even if it is never approved.

While no one can predict exactly what will be included or excluded in the final Capital Gains Tax plan, one thing appears certain, Capital Gains Tax relief for residential real estate is now a lock with broad based support from both political parties. As we draw closer to the time that Capital Gains Tax relief is adopted for residential real estate assets, look for the following opportunity to evolve. The sale of existing homes will probably slow down as sellers will pull back in anticipation of a reduction in Capital Gains Tax. When the Capital Gains Tax is then finally approved we can expect the markets for existing home sales to explode. This should create a surge in the Home Improvement and Home Furnishing Industries. The sale of existing homes is typically followed over the next six months with major expenditures in both home improvements and home furnishings. Thus, a cut in the Capital Gains Tax rate could create a short term resurgence for both of these industries.

Capital Gains Tax relief should be viewed as the beginning not the end. As we continue to down-size our government, we can also continue to down-size our taxes and our tax code on an incremental basis. Capital Gains Tax relief is the first step. For investors with a long term investment perspective the future could not look brighter. (*3/97*)

THE DOLLAR

Hardly a day goes by that someone, somewhere is not commenting on the problems caused by the strength of the Dollar. Currency market debates were once left only to the most savvy and experienced broker. But now, because of the evolution of the global marketplace and a highly educated investor community, currency markets (especially the value of the Dollar) are almost discussed with as much frequency as the overall stock and bond markets.

It is important to keep in mind that even though the Dollar has strengthened a great deal over the past two years, it has a long long way to go to get into the record books. The most common measurement of the strength of the United States Dollar is the German Mark and the Japanese Yen. These two currencies are always used as the frame of reference because the German Mark currency is the benchmark for all of Europe and Japan is our major trading partner. The low water mark, you may recall, for both the Japanese Yen and the German Mark since World War II both occurred in 1995 when the Japanese Yen fell to 79.85 and the German Mark fell to 1.340. On the high side, in 1963 one Dollar purchased 362.98 Japanese Yen while the high side for the German Mark was in 1957 when the U.S. Dollar traded at 4.200 Marks.

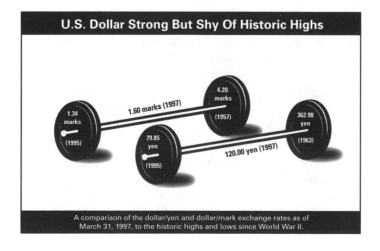

A comparison of the dollar/yen and dollar/mark exchange rates as of March 31, 1997, to the historic highs and lows since World War II.

The negative focus of the strength of the Dollar hit new highs on the investment community's radar screen when the Group of Seven Major Industrial Countries (G-7), Finance Ministers and Central Bankers met in Berlin and announced to the world that the Dollar had risen far enough and should now stop. The problem however, was that they had no plan of action to implement their desire to weaken the Dollar. And thus the Dollar has remained strong.

Why in the world is everyone so worried about the strong Dollar and why is a strong Dollar perceived to be negative by the financial markets? The answer is what I refer to as E^2 (Exports and Earnings). Well over 10% of our entire economy is accounted for by exports to other countries. The strong Dollar in essence makes these United States products somewhat less competitive globally because they now cost more abroad because of the currency exchange. A weakening of global market share will impact earnings as demand for your products weaken. Also, when overseas earnings in foreign currency are exchanged into United States Dollars for profit reporting purposes, earnings again can be reduced. So the real concern isn't a strong Dollar, it's E^2; Exports and Earnings. Now I would be the first person to agree that the strong Dollar could influence exports and trade, however, exports have more to do with global economics than they do with exchange rates. With a global economy expected to grow at 4.0% in 1997, the highest level in the past decade, I just don't see the strong Dollar stopping export demand. Second, it is absolutely mind boggling to me to think that some investors actually think that the Chief Executive Officer or Chief Financial Officer of a multi-national company do not have a currency strategy or hedge to offset the potential currency fluctuations. The impact on earnings may not be as great as everyone fears.

Let's not forget that there actually is a positive side to the strong Dollar that we must not lose sight of; it provides a one-two knock out punch to inflation. First, a strong Dollar lowers the cost of all imports into the United States. Second, these lower priced imports in a global economy make it very difficult if not impossible for U.S. companies to raise their prices. If the price of foreign imports are lower and domestic producers match those prices, it's tough to see how you can expect any inflation.

The ultimate value of any currency is a reflection of the country's economy that stands behind the currency. Thus, the value of the Dollar is a direct reflection of the perceived "value" of the United States economy. If you have a strong economy (which we do) and have low to moderate inflation (which we also have) along with low interest rates (ditto) it is virtually impossible not to have a strong Dollar.

Capital always has and always will flow to the highest economic returns. The strength of the Dollar is helping the United States win the race for global capital. In the end, whoever has the money wins. From a global perspective, driven in part by the strength of the Dollar, when international investors say "show me the money" it's the United States financial markets that are opening investors' eyes. Sometimes the greatest investment opportunity can be right under your nose. *(4/97)*

THE EUROPEAN MONETARY UNION

EMU-4-U. No, this is not the license plate of a hit-and-run driver. However, you may feel like you've been run over by a truck even if you only invest domestically in the United States if you are not paying attention to EMU or the European Monetary Union.

The European Monetary Union has dominated the headlines in recent weeks, especially in light of the changing political landscapes in Europe. Britain, France and now Ireland which all, to one degree or another, have undergone tremendous political ideology shifts as the result of election upsets. With each passing election, the final commentary always touches upon what the impact will be on EMU. As a domestic investor, it is important not to get lulled to sleep during all of this European political debate. EMU could have a tremendous impact on your investments too, especially if you are a fixed income investor.

It happened before and it will happen again. This is not the first attempt at a monetary union in Europe, nor will it be the last. In fact, there have been five monetary unions in Europe during the 19th Century, none, however, were of the scale and magnitude of the current proposal. France, Italy, Belgium and Switzerland formed a currency zone linked to silver in the 1860s. Even the countries of Scandinavia tried to form a monetary union in the late 1800s. What happened back then was that by the late 19th Century, most countries moved onto the gold standard and thus, the focal point of their exchange rate policy was a global monetary standard, not a regional one. The current EMU is attempting to create a zone of regional monetary stability within the framework of an international financial system where exchange rates will remain flexible.

Why would Europe launch such a massive change you may ask? First, with EMU the exchange rate risk within Europe will be eliminated. That in turn, will simplify and promote trade and investment.

And trade and investment will promote growth and employment. Second with EMU, prices in EMU countries can now be easily compared with one another. Third, travel within the EMU will no longer entail any currency conversion costs, and fourth and most importantly, as the financial borders in Europe disappear, competition will become more intense. This increased competition will ultimately benefit both companies and consumers.

Along with the establishment of a single European currency, the euro, EMU will create a single broad bond market in which European governments and corporations will issue debt beginning January 1, 1999. Thus, EMU will create the first liquid and highly traded bond market approximating the size of the U.S. market. In fact, many investors who have shied away from the relatively small individual European bond markets in favor of U.S. Treasuries will, for the first time, have a choice of venues in which to buy bonds. As an investor, it will be a whole lot easier to sleep at night knowing that you are investing in all of Europe through EMU rather than investing solely in Italy or Spain. And the ultimate impact on the treasury market would continue to increase as the EMU bond market developed and offered a variety of coordinated maturities and yields. Don't forget, issuers of debt could also choose to go to the EMU market. If the euro develops into a popular currency, global investors may now see it as a suitable compliment to the dollar, especially from a diversification standpoint. Thus, any diminution of the dollar's strength would likely weaken the demand for dollar denominated securities, especially U.S. bonds. As if all of these factors aren't enough to impact our fixed income markets, just think of their political perspective. Our bond market could be held hostage in future global negotiations.

Just think about future trade negotiations with Japan or human rights negotiations with China. And as these negotiations begin to break down as they always do, China and/or Japan could threaten to move their investments from the U.S. bond market to the EMU. Our bond market could become a pawn in global political negotiations as a result of EMU. It is truly a global marketplace. What happens in Europe could have a greater impact on your U.S. Treasury Bond than any event in the United States itself. The EMU will be the single most important development in the U.S. fixed income market in the next decade. Don't forget to figure out what EMU means to U-2. *(6/97)*

REVISING THE CONSUMER PRICE INDEX

While the rage all around the country seems to bounce from martini and cigar bars at one end of the spectrum to exotic flavored coffee shops at the other, Washington is searching for the middle ground with a new Diet "COLA." Washington's version of Diet "COLA" is not made by Coke or Pepsi, however, it is made by Washington's politicians and a political Diet "Cola" is spelled *Cost Of Living Adjustment*. You see, the Cost Of Living Adjustments on individual benefits under all federal entitlement programs, which by the way, account for over one third of all Federal Government spending (Social Security and Medicare to name just a few) are actually determined by the Consumer Price Index. Thus, if you want to reduce the Cost Of Living Adjustments, in other words, make them smaller, a Diet COLA so to speak, you would do so by reducing the Consumer Price Index which serves as the foundation for all Cost Of Living Adjustments. Thus, all of the political jockeying and high profile bi-partisan debates regarding revising the Consumer Price Index was really about creating a new Diet COLA which would save the Federal Government over $70 billion dollars over the next five years.

NOTE: *What a 0.5 percent reduction in the Consumer Price Index would mean over five years.*

231

Last year the Senate Finance Committee appointed a Special Commission headed by Stanford University economists Michael Boskin (dubbed the Boskin Commission) to study, analyze and make recommendations regarding the Consumer Price Index. The findings of that Blue Ribbon Commission were that our current Consumer Price Index overstates actual inflation by a full 1.1%. As a result, the Boskin Commission has recommended that Congress adjust any Cost of Living Increase that is being driven by the Consumer Price Index, downward by a full 1.1%. The Commission's recommendations would also have an impact on federal tax brackets by lowering the income adjustments to the tax code levels (inflation induced increases in tax rates is commonly referred to as "bracket creep"). Remember, the lower the actual tax income levels, the greater the number of taxpayers that will fall into that category and thus with more taxpayers come more tax receipts.

COMPONENTS OF THE CONSUMER PRICE INDEX

The Consumer Price Index represents all goods and services purchased for consumption by households. Expenditures are classified into over 200 different categories that fall into 7 major groups. Here are the seven major groups including examples of the categories that fall within each group:

Groups	*Categories*
Food and Beverages	Coffee, Beer, Cookies, Restaurant Meals
Housing	Rent, Fuel Oil, Televisions, Local Telephone
Apparel	Women's Dresses, Men's Suits, Jeans
Transportation	Airline Fares, New & Used Cars, Gasoline
Medical Care	Hospital Room, Drugs, Eye Care
Entertainment	Movies, Newspapers, Toys
Other Goods & Services	Haircuts, College Tuition

The Consumer Price Index was established by Congress back in 1972. It is interesting to note that even back then, it was widely recognized that the Consumer Price Index will actually overstate inflation. Congress pushed ahead anyway, feeling that a flawed inflation index is still better than no inflation index at all. While there are numerous technical and statistical issues that converge to overstate inflation, the basic fundamental reason that the Consumer Price Index overstates inflation is because the Consumer Price Index does not take into account the retail consumers' behavior regarding changes in prices.

Think about it, when the price of peaches rises faster than the price of bananas, most consumers will simply put more bananas in their fruit salad and less peaches. The kids can expect bananas cut up over their cereal instead of peaches. In other words, people will actually change their buying habits because of price and buy more bananas than peaches. That doesn't mean that the consumer is spending more on food even if the price of peaches is rising dramatically. These indexes simply don't understand the psychology of retail price consensus shoppers. These indexes assume that a consumer that wants a peach will buy a peach at any cost; in reality, that simply is just not so.

THE CONSUMER PRICE INDEX IMPACTS EVERYONE	
The Consumer Price Index is used to adjust consumer's income payments so that inflation does not erode the consumer's purchasing power. Here is a sample of who the Consumer Price Index touches:	
43.1 Million	Social Security Beneficiaries
22.6 Million	Food Stamp Recipients
3.9 Million	Military and Federal Civil Service Retirees and Survivors
24.2 Million	Children who eat lunch at school
2.8 Million	Workers who have their Collective Bargaining Agreement tied to CPI

While most of the focus to date regarding the revision of the Consumer Price Index has been on the reduction that revision will mean to Social Security benefits, the actual ramifications are much broader than Social Security. Currently, the annual adjustments in spending for over one third of all federal outlays are determined by the Consumer Price Index. And this isn't just a government issue, think of the impact it will have in the private sector. Currently, in the private sector, most contracts and most of the private workforces' wages will be increased annually according to increases in Consumer Price Index. A reduction in the Consumer Price Index would fall right to the bottom line of most companies by reducing the annual amount of increases in payroll costs. This would certainly be bullish for the stock market. Meanwhile, the benefits to the bond market are even more obvious. Fixed income investments get eaten away by inflation, thus the lower inflation is, the better fixed income investments appear. Expect both the stock and bond markets to rally if the Consumer Price Index is revised. While the political obstacles can't be underestimated, don't forget that the baby boomers are a health conscious force and when the time is right, these baby boomers just might order "A Diet COLA, please!" *(5/97)*

THE FEDERAL DEFICIT

As the "Men In Black" rescue the universe from destruction by alien forces in the blockbuster hit movie, "Men In Black," I already know what the sequel will be titled. It will be called "Here Come The Men And Women In Black." And instead of saving the universe from destruction by alien forces, these men and women in black will save the United States from destruction by eliminating our Federal Government deficit. You guessed it, our new super-heroes, the men and women who got us into the "black" and out of the "red ink" are our very own members of Congress. We have 435 men and 62 women in the United States Senate and the United States House of Representatives that put our country back in the "black" from a financial perspective. (All right for all of you political science majors, these numbers don't add up because there is currently one vacancy in the House of Representatives—Susan Molanari resigned effective August 1, 1997.)

In order to understand the true significance to this landmark "deficit reduction," balanced budget agreement, it is helpful to put it into some historical perspective. Budget deficits in the United States are nothing new. In fact, our Federal Government generated its first ever deficit when our country was just a teenager. A short sixteen years after our country was founded in 1776, we had our first budget deficit in 1792. Since that first-ever budget deficit, there have been over one hundred occasions where the Federal Government ended the year in the red. The real ballooning of our Federal Government deficits did not begin to occur until the late 1930s. Two things were forcing the deficits higher. First of all, we had to pay for President Franklin D. Roosevelt's "New Deal" and, the second, the outbreak of World War II mandated enormous expenditures in military spending.

The next ballooning of our Federal Government deficit did not occur until the 1980s. Again, just like the 1930s, a tremendous increase in defense spending was part of the reason. However, in addition to increased defense spending, there were major cuts in income tax rates, meaning Federal tax revenue was reduced. However, there were no offsetting cuts in Federal programs and thus, the deficit skyrocketed. If this wasn't bad enough, the recession in our economy in the early 1980s also reduced tax receipts. In addition, interest rates were rising so not only did we have more debt, but we were paying more in interest cost for the debt that we had.

While keeping track of our deficit is important, how we keep track of it has become equally important. It is not enough to just look at the deficit in isolation; the deficit should be looked at as a percentage of Gross Domestic Product (GDP). This is the most important way of looking at the deficit because it reflects our economy's ability to absorb the federal deficits. This is one reason why one of the key economic measurements for a country to become eligible for membership in the European Monetary Union (EMU) is that their deficit, as a percent of GDP, must be 3% or less.

To give you some frame of reference to what that 3% level would mean in the United States today, consider this. The current projection of the Congressional Budget Office shows our Federal Government ending this fiscal year (September 30) with a deficit of approximately $30 billion. With a $7.1 trillion economy, our deficit could balloon a whopping seven-fold from its current level, and we would still have a $3 billion cushion before we wouldn't meet the deficit criteria for admission to EMU.

Measuring our deficit as a percent of GDP provides us with an interesting analysis. When we look at our deficit as a percentage of GDP, the highest level that our deficit has ever reached was in 1943 when it was an unbelievable 31.1% of GDP. The highest level that our deficit has reached in the last fifty years was back in 1983 when it stood at the high water mark of 6.3%.

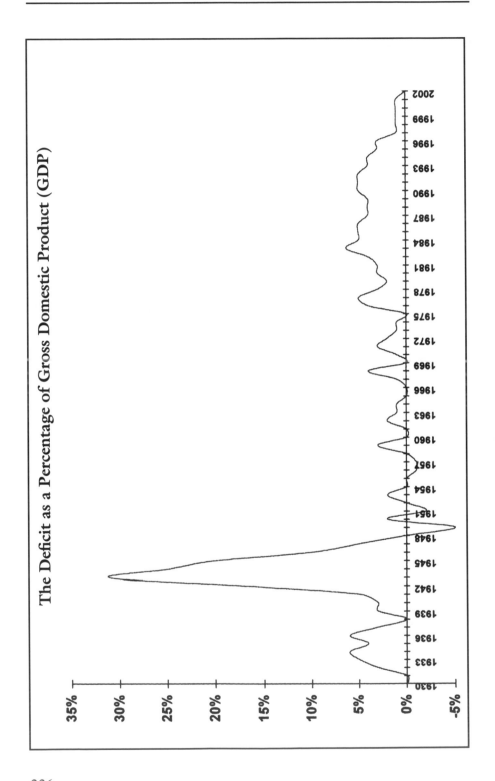

The Deficit as a Percentage of Gross Domestic Product (GDP)

While lowering the Federal Government's deficit is good news for the overall financial markets, it is especially good news for the bond market. The lower the deficit, the less debt (treasury securities) the government has to issue to fund the deficit. Our balanced budget agreement means that we will be issuing less debt and this decrease in future supply will increase the current value of the debt that is outstanding. It doesn't matter what you are buying, whether it's luxury cars, coffee or treasury securities, if there is less supply, the value or price of what is available goes up. For anyone that was waiting for a sign from outer space to invest in bonds again, your sign has just arrived.

I wonder who will play Newt Gingrich in this made for TV drama? *(8/97)*

HONG KONG'S REVERSION TO MAINLAND CHINA

International investors around the globe are holding their collective breath hoping that the return of Hong Kong to China will not disrupt the global financial markets. Its importance transcends all markets as Hong Kong has become the benchmark of what every economy and every market around the world would like to become. And while many have tried to mirror Hong Kong's success, no one has been able to do it.

It was 13 years ago that Britain and China agreed that all of Hong Kong would revert back to Chinese rule. At that time (1984) the Hong Kong stock market was valued at $30 billion dollars. Today the Hong Kong stock market is capitalized at almost $500 billion dollars. One reason that no one will ever duplicate Hong Kong's success is that the Hong Kong story is so unique it can never be duplicated. It was the confluence of three factors that fueled Hong Kong's success and no country on earth can duplicate those three factors.

The first factor is that age old real estate key; location, location, location. Hong Kong is right next door to both the largest source of labor in the world as well as the largest consumer market on the face of the earth (China). Hong Kong is able to tap into both of these unbelievable benefits without paying any of the costs. You see, Hong Kong does not have to pay any of the social costs of sustaining the world's largest labor and consumption market. That problem as well as all of the costs associated with it are China's problem to bear. Second, Hong Kong found itself in the unique position of not expending any of its precious financial or economic resources on national defense. Because Hong Kong was a British colony, national defense was Britain's problem to worry about and Britain's problem to fund, not Hong Kong's.

237

Hong Kong Time Line

1842 - At the end of the Opium War the Treaty of Nanjing cedes Hong Kong to Britain in perpetuity

1898 - New territories (the current mainland portion of Hong Kong) as well as 235 nearby islands are leased by China to Britain for 99 years (lease ends 1997)

1949 - Chiang Kai-Sheks forces flee to Taiwan after being defeated by communists

1984 - Britain and China agree that Hong Kong will revert back to China

1997 - British colonial rule ends and China and Hong Kong become "one country, two systems"

Third, as a result of the first two factors, Hong Kong's tax burden is among the lowest anywhere around the globe. Think about it for a minute. If as a country you don't have to worry about huge social problems and you don't have to worry about national defense, you don't need higher taxes.

Do not worry about this unique and truly unbelievable economic miracle that Hong Kong has put together. It will be just fine under Chinese rule. China will not destroy the golden economic goose.

Now that does not mean that there will not be major bumps in the road regarding the free and honest flow of financial and political information. And it doesn't mean that there will not be potential pitfalls as the civil service system evolves and changes. And the "human rights" issue will be with us for a long time to come as will the fear and memory that the next demonstration will turn into another Tiananmen

Square affair. While all of these may be legitimate short-term issues, none will stop the successful transformation of Hong Kong and China into "one country, two systems."

Nervous investors around the globe are still searching for clues about what the future will hold for the Hong Kong market now that China has regained control of Hong Kong, ending 156 years of colonial rule by Britain. Perhaps the biggest clue to the future of the re-unification of Hong Kong with China can be found in the past, in the title of the 1950s Doris Day movie "Tea for Two."

You see that real reason that the re-unification of Hong Kong will be successful is because it is not just about Hong Kong, it's about Taiwan as well. Hong Kong is only the first step in getting what China really wants and that is reuniting with Taiwan. Unless the Hong Kong re-unification is a rousing success, China can never hope to get Taiwan to the table to talk about re-unification with China. While the celebration over the re-unification with Hong Kong fulfills a dream of every patriotic Chinese, that dream is only halfway complete. Taiwan is what they are really dreaming about.

Once investors realize that China's ultimate goal never was just the re-unification with Hong Kong they will quickly realize that despite potential problems in the short run, in the long run China will not allow this re-unification with Hong Kong to fail. After all, who wants to have a tea party with only one guest (Hong Kong)? It's much more fun having Tea for Two (Hong Kong and Taiwan). *(7/97)*

THE UNITED PARCEL SERVICE STRIKE

The recent Teamsters strike against the United Parcel Service (UPS) was the highest profile labor movement in this country in the last quarter century. The air traffic controllers in 1981 and the baseball strike in 1994 may have had similar media coverage, however, their impacts on the economy and the markets pale in comparison. This strike, which at some times appeared more like a made for T.V. soap opera, clearly had something for everyone. And in the end, there were some good things that came out of the strike and there were some bad things that came out of the strike. In addition, there may be some real ugly things that come out in the future. In order to analyze the impact that this event will have on our economy and our markets, let's take a closer look at the United Parcel Service strike by identifying, with all due respect to Clint Eastwood's classic western "The Good, The Bad and The Ugly."

At first blush, it's hard to imagine anything good coming out of tense labor battles that impact a wide cross section of the American public, however, there were some good things that happened as a result of this labor stand-off. First, this deal is certainly good news for the salary of part-time workers at UPS. Over the next five years, a part-time employee at UPS will watch their wages increase from $11.00 an hour to $15.00 an hour. This will amount to an annualized increase of 7% a year for the next five years. This good news for part-time wage earners will also spill over into the economy as employees find themselves with more disposable income which will benefit the overall economy. The second good thing was that this agreement actually has something for inflation watchers to cheer about as well. While most of the focus has been on the fate of the part-time workers, it's important not to lose sight of the implications of the agreement with full-time employees. A full-time UPS employee will watch their wages increase from roughly $20.00 per hour today to $23.00 per hour five years from now. This works out to less than a 3% wage increase annually over the next five years. When analyzing this strike from strictly the full-time employees' settlement, it is clearly not inflationary at all. The third good thing that came from the strike and the settlement is increased competition in the Parcel Post Delivery Industry. While there is very little doubt in my mind that UPS will remain the dominant company by a wide margin in that industry, this strike will certainly change the competitive landscape of the industry by opening up doors that, before the strike, were closed. Companies that were negatively impacted by the strike now realize how vulnerable their business was to one company, namely UPS. I think that there will be a major move to diversify at least some small portion of their shipping as sort of an insurance policy against future work stoppages at UPS. It's simply not good business practice to have the entire fate of your business to be determined by another company that you have absolutely no control or influence over. No matter how you get there, increased competition is a good thing; whether it's driven by deregulation or, in this case, driven by a strike, the positive benefits are the same.

WAGES AT UPS
(average hourly wages)

	Today	UPS Proposal (wages at end of contract)	Teamster Proposal (wages at end of contract)	Final Agreement (wages at end of five-year contract)
Part-time	$11.00	$13.50	$14.60	$15.10
Full-time	$20.01	$21.51	$22.61	$23.11

As with every strike, the only thing for sure is that when everything is all said and done, there will probably be as many bad things that come from the labor conflict as there are good things and this strike is no exception to that rule. The first bad thing is the impact on small business. Small businesses were dealt a one-two punch by this strike. First, the greatest negative economic impact of the strike was felt by the small business community who simply could not operate without their much needed deliveries and shipments. As if this was not bad enough, the second punch is being delivered to them now that the strike is over. Small business will no doubt be expected to pay the brunt of the increased costs associated with the settlement. UPS will make sure that their biggest and best customers (who have some leverage over UPS) stay happy which means once again, no one cares about the "little guy" and because small businesses have never really organized as a united front, their voice will be left crying in the wind as they will be expected to pay for the bulk of this new labor agreement. The second bad thing to result from the strike is contaminated economic releases. With nervous markets, the last thing that we need is tainted economic releases which is exactly what we are receiving. The UPS strike impacted a broad range of economic releases. As we were heading into the strike, there was a build-up in supplier deliveries which in turn slowed down the order "pipeline." Typically when there is an order "pipeline" backup, inflation soon follows. Will that happen this time? Then you have to consider how many striking workers found other jobs. How many competitors' delivery companies went on a hiring binge to take care of new demand? How many companies laid off workers knowing supplies and equipment would not be delivered? And finally, what does all of this do to the quarterly Gross Domestic Product number? It will be extremely difficult for economists and

241

nearly impossible for individual investors to sort out all of the distortions that the UPS strike has placed upon the next round of economic releases. The third bad thing is that the profits of the express carriers and even the Trucking Industry could come under severe pressure. This would occur if UPS does indeed lose some of its market share permanently as a result of the strike. If this occurs, because UPS is such a dominant leader in the industry, they very well may respond by slashing prices. If that happens, it would very quickly develop into a full-scale price war that would transcend the entire Parcel Post Delivery Industry and all of its components. While the ultimate consumer will benefit, corporate profits in the Parcel Post Delivery Industry will clearly suffer if such a price war breaks out.

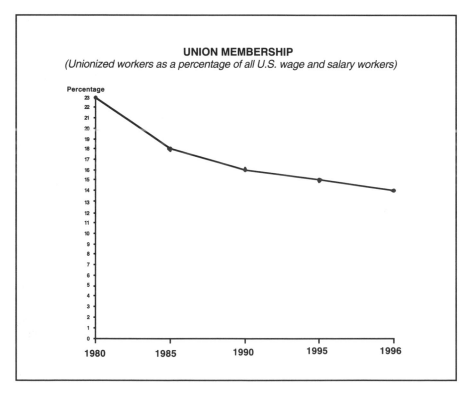

UNION MEMBERSHIP
(Unionized workers as a percentage of all U.S. wage and salary workers)

Almost without fail, every strike ends up with some good things and some bad things. What's unique about this strike is that in addition to the good and the bad, it also may have something very ugly for our markets in the future. Without a doubt, the greatest potential impact that this strike will have is the feeling that it shifts the balance of power back toward labor unions and the U.S. work force. Remember, Teamster President Ron Carey summed up the settlement this way, "a historic turning point for working people in this country." The psychology of the markets are now expecting wage inflation. Going forward, we can expect labor unions to draw a deeper line in the sand demanding higher wages. While this will certainly be ugly in the short-term, the UPS strike did not shift the balance of power back to unions. First, union membership has been on a steady decline for the last 15 years and currently represents less than 15% of the total work force. Second, even if labor negotiations get very hostile in the short-run, negotiators will quickly realize how unique the UPS strike really was. There are very very few, if any, companies that enjoy as dominant a role over their industry as UPS does over the Parcel Post Delivery Industry. Thus, UPS was willing and able to settle in a way very few other companies could or will. We may be in for some real ugly times on the labor front as unions try to leverage this high profile strike into major labor victories across the board. However, six months from now, the markets will finally realize that the UPS strike did not shift the balance of power to labor unions. The psychological impact will be much greater than the actual one. *(9/97)*

FAST TRACK TRADE AUTHORITY

President Clinton's decision to pull the plug on Fast Track Trade authority (officially known in Washington as the "Export Expansion and Reciprocal Trade Agreement Act of 1997") rather than watch it be defeated in Congress is by no means the end of this issue. This is not just about partisan politics; there may be no more important issue next year for our stock market and the global economy than passage of Fast Track Trade authority, and as such, not only will this issue not go away next year, it very likely will become the highest profile political "investment" issue for the remainder of the Clinton Administration. Let's get prepared for the upcoming debate by exploring the 3 Ws of Fast Track Trade authority—WHAT (exactly is it anyway?), WHEN (did this whole thing get started?), and WHO (*benefits?*). Fast Track Trade authority just might be the fuel needed to take our stock market to the next level. Next stop, 10,000!

Both the President and Congress share authority for issues involving international trade. The President, as set forth in our Constitution, has the authority to negotiate international trade agreements. Congress however has the exclusive authority, also granted by our Constitution, to set tariffs and enact legislation governing international trade. Thus, if the President negotiates a trade agreement that requires any change in U.S. tariffs or in other laws that govern international trade issues, the matter must be submitted to Congress in the form of legislation for their approval.

Fast Track Trade authority is nothing more than a streamlined or expedited procedure for Congress to consider trade agreements. With Fast Track Trade, Congress simply votes yes or no on the entire treaty. They cannot change it in any way; no amendments are allowed. This process eliminates special interest groups lobbying Congress to amend the deal to help them. Because of this procedure, there are no delays or gridlocks debating over changes. That's actually how it got the name "Fast Track."

Thus without Fast Track Trade authority the President's credibility as a trade negotiator is greatly diminished, because in theory everything that he negotiates could be changed or amended by any of the 535 members of Congress. This takes on added importance in the area of trade because there is a great deal of give and take and countries agree to give up certain things because they received other things in return. Thus, the final negotiated deal strikes a mutual balance for all parties. If Congress is allowed to change one facet of the agreement, it could tip the entire balance of the trade agreement one way or the other and unravel the entire deal. Also, foreign governments are very skeptical about supporting any "final" deal knowing that it could be amended again and again and again by Congress.

In order to negotiate the best deal possible, the President needs to guarantee that the final deal will be considered in its entirety within a short period of time. It is interesting to note that this is exactly what we require of our trading partners before we do a trade deal with them.

In 1934 Congress enacted the First Reciprocal Trade Agreements Act. That act gave the President authority to negotiate mutual tariff reductions with our trading partners. Congress has renewed that tariff reduction authority repeatedly over the years. Numerous Presidents used this authority to dramatically reduce tariff barriers around the world.

"Fast Track" was first put into place under the Ford Administration to expand the President's authority beyond just tariff reductions. Under "Fast Track" the President, in addition to negotiate away foreign tariff barriers to United States products can also negotiate on non-tariff barriers as well. Foreign governments have been substituting non-tariff barriers such as quotas and subsidies to replace tariff barriers. Thus, the "Fast Track" authority enables the President to negotiate regarding all barriers: tariff and non-tariff.

Fast Track Trade authority Lapsed in 1994 at a time when the United States was not engaged in negotiations that required any Congressional action.

The entire economy benefits from Fast Track Trade authority. Specifically small business in this country may actually be one of the biggest winners. In reality, one of the key reasons that our overall economy has done so well the past few years is because small business is on a roll. The reason that our unemployment rate is below 5% and hovers at the lowest levels in the quarter of a century is because of small business. Almost all of the "net" job creation in the 1990s has come from small business. From 1992 through 1996 companies with 100 or fewer employees created 85% of the net gain in new jobs. During that same time period firms with 1–19 employees expanded employment by 11.4% level which is truly remarkable. If small businesses are going to keep up this remarkable pace, they need greater access to the international markets because that is where most of the growth potential lies. In the last two years the number of small sized businesses that get at least 10% of their sales from exports has astoundingly doubled to now stand at 50% of all businesses. What's even more important to our economy about these small businesses that do business internationally is that they pay wages 10%–20% higher, they generate more new jobs and are less likely to go out of business than those not engaged in global trade.

TOP TEN EXPORTING INDUSTRIES IN 1996

1. $112.0 billion - Industrial Machinery and Computers

2. $96.6 billion - Transportation Equipment

3. $94.9 billion - Electric and Electronic Equipment

4. $59.6 billion - Chemical Products

5. $37.1 billion - Agricultural and Livestock Products

6. $34.8 billion - Scientific and Measuring Instruments

7. $27.6 billion - Food Products

8. $21.9 billion - Primary Metals

9. $17.1 billion - Fabricated Metal Products

10. $14.2 billion - Paper Products

From an industry perspective, the clear winners from Fast Track Trade authority would be the industries that currently export the most. The immediate impact would most likely hit the top ten export sectors first and thus they would be the greatest beneficiaries. At the end of 1996, the top exporting industries in the United States were: Industrial Machinery and Computers, Transportation Equipment, Electric and Electronic Equipment, Chemical Products, Agricultural and Livestock Products, Scientific and Measuring Instruments, Food Products, Primary Metals, Fabricated Metal Products and Paper Products. I would expect these industries that already have a truly global focus to continue their expansion and truly begin to dominate world markets. *(12/97)*

10 BRADY COMMISSION REFORM

Mention "The Brady Bunch" today and most people flash-back to the popular sitcom of the '70s starring Florence Henderson. This hit series was modernized in 1995 with the launching of "The Brady Bunch Movie" which was an updated version of the original. The setting however, was in the '90s not the '70s. This modernized Brady Bunch film did so well, the very next year "A Very Brady Sequel" was released. We can all rest easier knowing that we have updated and modernized The Brady Bunch from the '70s to the '90s, and they are now ready for the next millennium. It's the "other" Brady Bunch that I'm worried about getting updated and modernized for the next millennium. This other Brady Bunch was from the '80s not the '70s and the star was Nicholas Brady not Florence Henderson. This is the same Nicholas Brady who went on to become Secretary of the Treasury. This other Brady Bunch was formally known as The Brady Commission.

The Brady Commission was a task force created by President Reagan charged with determining what caused the "Black Monday" stock market crash of 1987 and how or what can we do to stop it from occurring again.

The final report on the Brady Commission was almost one thousand pages long. Within those pages were numerous recommendations and ideas on how to stop Black Monday from occurring again. Only one major change was ever instituted as a result of the Brady Commission. That change was the implementation of "triggers" or "circuit breakers" by the New York Stock Exchange that would actually stop all trading on the New York Stock Exchange if prices fell a certain amount within a certain time frame.

The Brady Commission's circuit breaker concept was adopted by the New York Stock Exchange in 1988 and has been updated only once since that time; that update occurred in February of 1997.

Here is how the circuit breakers work today. If the Dow Jones Industrial Average drops 350 points from the prior day's close, the market stops trading for one half hour. When the market resumes trading, if the Dow Jones Industrial Average were to fall a total of 550 points from the prior day's close, trading would stop for one full hour. When these circuit breakers were originally established in 1988, the levels were 250 points and 400 points respectively. Back then the market was scheduled to close for one hour when the first trigger was hit and for two complete hours when the second trigger kicked in.

While Gray Monday certainly re-focused attention on the circuit breakers that were established as a result of the Brady Commission's recommendations, sometimes lost in the shuffle is the fact that four different levels of trading restrictions were actually established by the New York Stock Exchange as a result of the Brady Commission's work. (See Table A—Trading Restrictions of the New York Stock Exchange.)

TABLE A

	TRADING RESTRICTIONS OF THE NEW YORK STOCK EXCHANGE	
Trigger Event	**Trading Restriction**	**Description**
±50 Points	Collar	Program Trading Restriction
±100 Points	Sidecar	Increased Program Trading Restrictions
-350 Points	First Circuit Breaker	30 Minute Trading Halt
-550 Points	Second Circuit Breaker	60 Minute Trading Halt

The first restriction is called a "Collar." This program trading collar is also commonly referred to as the uptick-downtick rule. It is put in place if the Dow Jones Industrial Average is 50 points greater or less than the prior day's close. This restriction stays in place until the Dow Jones Industrial Average returns to within 25 points of the previous day's close or until the end of the trading day (4:00 p.m., Eastern Standard Time), whichever comes first. This collar rule only applies to Program Trades. The New York Stock Exchange defines a Program Trade as either a basket of 15 or more stocks from the S&P 500 or a basket of stocks from the S&P 500 valued at $1 million or greater. Once this collar restriction is put in place, Program Trading sell orders can only be executed on an up-tick. Meaning that the last trade was executed at a higher price than the trade before it. At the other end of the spectrum, Program Trading buy orders can only be executed on a down-tick. Meaning that the last trade was executed at a lower price than the trade before it.

The second restriction is called a "sidecar." This restriction is put in place when the S&P futures contrast is 12 points above or below the days opening level. Twelve points on the S&P 500 futures contract is approximately 100 points on the Dow Jones Industrial Average. When this sidecar is enforced, all program trades are held for at least five minutes. After five minutes, the orders will only be executed if they can be done so without causing the market to trend up or down.

The third restriction is circuit breaker number one. If the Dow Jones Industrial Average falls 350 points (no restriction if it rises 350 points), trading is halted on the New York Stock Exchange for one half hour.

The fourth restriction is circuit breaker number two. If the Dow Jones Industrial Average falls 550 points (again no restrictions if it rises 550 points), trading is halted on the New York Stock Exchange for one hour.

It is important to note that all of the other United States Stock Exchanges, as well as the options and futures exchanges, have amended their rules to correspond to the New York Stock Exchange restrictions so that all markets remain coordinated.

These circuit breakers have outlived their usefulness. Like the original Brady Bunch, these circuit breakers need to be modernized and updated to prepare our markets for the next millennium. These circuit breakers that, in theory, were established to prevent the stock market from "crashing," in reality, caused such an investor panic that the real reason behind Gray Monday (October 27, 1997) was not the Hong Kong market but rather the panic induced selling as a result of these outdated circuit breakers. As the market decline moved toward the first trigger, panic selling set in as investors rushed to sell before the stock market would close down on them. To many investors this was reminiscent of the Savings and Loan crisis of the early 1980s where the front doors of the S&L were bolted shut. The circuit breakers bolted shut the doors of the New York Stock Exchange to investors. If they weren't worried before, they were certainly worried now. When the market finally opened up after a one half hour halt, it took exactly twenty-two minutes for the market to plunge an additional 200 points and cross the second trigger at 550 points. All closing down trading of the New York Stock Exchange did was create a sense of panic, which in turn created "pent-up" demand. Think of it this way; if your child is eating Halloween candy and all day long is putting one M&M after another into his mouth, you finally have enough and scream, not another single M&M goes in your mouth for the next half hour (the parental circuit breaker). During this break, the child continues to place the M&Ms one at a time into his hands but never into their mouth. As the half hour is almost over, the child's hand is overflowing with M&Ms. You then tell your child that the cooling off period is finished and they can resume eating again, to which the child immediately takes the entire handful of M&Ms and places the whole thing (pent up demand) in his mouth. The fundamental flaw with the circuit breakers is that because they are based on actual index point movements instead of a percentage basis, we are creating panic when in fact the market did not even move that much.

Here's the simple crux of the problem. The stock market closed the Friday before Black Monday in 1987 at 2,246. Using that stock market level as a basis here is what the Brady Commission's circuit breaker recommendation meant in terms of percentage moves in the markets. If the stock market would drop 250 points from the 2,246 level, that would be a percentage drop of 11% before the first circuit breaker would kick in. If the market were then to drop a total of 550 points from the 2,246 level, that would be a percentage drop of 18% before the second circuit breaker would kick in. With the "unofficial" definition of a market correction on Wall Street being a 10% decline, it's easy to see where these levels came from. (See Table 1—1987 Circuit Breakers.)

TABLE 1

1987 CIRCUIT BREAKER COMPARISON	
Black Monday—October 1987	
Dow Jones Industrial Average closing price the prior day	2246
Brady Commission recommendation for first circuit breaker	250
Actual percentage move to trigger circuit breaker	*11%*
Brady Commission Recommendation for second circuit breaker	400
Actual percentage move to trigger second circuit breaker	*18%*

Now let's look what happened on Gray Monday. The Friday before Gray Monday, the Dow Jones Industrial Average closed at 7,715. After the market dropped 350 points, the first circuit breaker kicked in. The problem however stems from the fact that we shut down the New York Stock Exchange after the market only dropped 5%. Even though it fell 350 points on a percentage basis, it was a mere 5%. When trading resumed, the market continued to drop and when the total fall elapsed 550 points, the market then shut down for the second time. The problem here is a 550 point drop from a 7,715 market level on a percentage basis is only 7%. (See Table 2—1997 Circuit Breakers.) And while on the surface a 500 plus point drop in 1997 could seem like a

500 plus point drop in 1987, however, there is truly no comparison to these two events.

TABLE 2

Gray Monday—October 1997	
Dow Jones Industrial Average closing price the prior day	7715
Brady Commission recommendation for first circuit breaker	350
Actual percentage move to trigger circuit breaker	5%
Brady Commission Recommendation for second circuit breaker	550
Actual percentage move to trigger second circuit breaker	7%

On Black Monday when the market dropped 508 points from 2,246 to 1,738 it lost 22.6% of its market value. While the market dropped 554 points from 7,715 to 7,161, it lost only 7.2% of its market value. The circuit breakers should have never even been triggered once let alone twice, with a market decline of only 7% in 1997. (See Table 3—Black Monday vs. Gray Monday.) Comparing absolute numbers instead of percentages can present a very misleading picture. A 500 point decline in 1987 with the market at 2,200 is much different from a 500 point decline in 1997 with a market at 7,700. Comparing 500 point market losses to markets at different levels is about as useless as comparing 50 pound weight losses of people who weigh different amounts. Consider this, "Black Monday" would be the same as a 220 pound person losing 50 pounds (22.6%) to now weigh in at the mean and lean level of 170 pounds. Dropping 50 pounds from 220 to 170 is a big deal. You in essence lost 22.6% of your body fat. Now let me tell you what Gray Monday was like in terms of weight loss. Gray Monday would be the same as a 715 pound Sumo wrestler losing 50 pounds (7.2%) to now weigh in at the still rotund level of 665 pounds. Getting equally excited about losing 50 pounds whether your original weight was 220 pounds or 715 pounds is about as ridiculous as getting equally excited about a market that falls 500 points whether the original level was 2,200 or 7,700.

TABLE 3

	Black Monday October 19, 1987	Gray Monday October 27, 1997
BLACK VS. GRAY MONDAY		
Dow Jones Industrial Average closing price from the prior day	2246	7715
Market Decline	-508	-554
Dow Jones Industrial Average Closing Price	1738	7161
Percentage Decline	22.6%	7.2%

My strong feelings about the need to modernize and update the Brady Commission is in no way meant to be a negative reflection on the findings of the Brady Commission. There is simply no way back in 1987 and 1988 anyone could have grasped the importance of having triggers at a percentage basis instead of absolute numbers. Throughout the entire history of the Dow Jones Industrial Average there had never been any ten year period where the market elapsed more than a single one thousand level milestone. (See Table 4—Dow Jones Industrial Average milestone by decade.) The first 1,000 level in the Dow Jones Industrial Average occurred on November 14, 1972. It is interesting to note that the Dow Jones Industrial Average crossed the 100 level on January 12, 1906, so it actually took 66 years spanning seven decades to get to that first 1,000 level. The next 1,000 level occurred in the decade of the '80s. On January 8, 1987, the Dow Jones Industrial Average crossed the 2,000 level. Look then what has happened in the decade of the '90s. In 1991 the Dow Jones Industrial Average crossed the 3000 milestone, in 1995 it crossed both the 4,000 and 5,000 level, in 1996 it crossed 6,000 and here in 1997 we crossed 7,000 and 8,000 even though the market ended slightly below 8,000. I am sure that if the Brady Commission had any idea that the Dow Jones Industrial Average would cross not one, not two, but five 1000 point level thresholds within the first decade after their recommendations were implemented, they would have placed the circuit breakers on a percentage basis not a index point basis. It's not too late. If we can modernize the original Brady Bunch with two movie sequels, we can certainly modernize the Brady Commission by changing the circuit breakers from an index point basis to a percentage basis.

TABLE 4

DOW JONES INDUSTRIAL AVERAGE
MILESTONES BY DECADE

Decade	Milestone
1900s	100
1910s	-
1920s	-
1930s	-
1940s	-
1950s	-
1960s	-
1970s	1000
1980s	2000
1990s	3000
	4000
	5000
	6000
	7000
	8000

One additional point that argues for the modernization of the Brady Commission recommendation is our media and technology explosion. Back in 1987 most people didn't find out about the Black Monday stock market's correction until they got home that evening and watched the evening news. Others didn't find out until they read the paper the next morning.

That is certainly not the case with Gray Monday. Investors knew what was happening every minute of the day via CNBC, CNN, FOX Cable, CNN*fn*'s website and the entire world wide web. This media and technology explosion let people know that the trigger was about to kick in, which added to the panic.

TABLE 5

TEN GREATEST SINGLE DAY LOSSES BASED ON POINT CHANGES		
Rank	**Date**	**Change**
1	October 27, 1997	-554
2	October 19, 1987	-508
3	August 15, 1997	-247
4	June 23, 1997	-192
5	October 13, 1989	-190
6	October 23, 1997	-186
7	March 8, 1996	-171
8	July 15, 1996	-161
9	March 13, 1997	-160
10	March 31, 1997	-157

The single greatest risk that our stock market faces as we head into the next millennium is not El Niño or the Year 2000 problem or the Southeast Asian currency and economic crisis, but rather a problem we created ourselves with the Brady Commission's circuit breakers on the New York Stock Exchange. These outdated restrictions create a sense of investor panic in the markets when, in fact, the actual movements in the market should not even cause us concern, let alone wholesale panic! While Gray Monday represented the greatest single day point drop in the history of the Dow Jones Industrial Average (see Table 5—Ten greatest single day declines based on index points), Gray Monday doesn't even crack the top ten if we look at it in terms of the greatest single day drops based on a percentage of market value. (See Table 6— Ten greatest single day declines based on market percentage.) Focusing on points instead of percentages does nothing but create unnecessary market panic!

TABLE 6

TEN GREATEST SINGLE DAY LOSSES BASED ON PERCENTAGE CHANGES		
Rank	Date	Change
1	October 19, 1987	22.6%
2	October 28, 1929	12.8%
3	October 29, 1929	11.7%
4	November 6, 1929	9.9%
5	December 18, 1899	8.7%
6	August 12, 1932	8.4%
7	March 14, 1907	8.3%
8	October 26, 1987	8.0%
9	July 21, 1933	7.8%
10	October 18, 1937	7.7%

Let's update and modernize the circuit breakers now by establishing the first circuit breaker at a 10% market decline from the prior day's close and the second circuit breaker at a 20% market decline from the prior day's close. These updated levels will insure that we never again have another Black Monday and more importantly, these levels that are based on a percentage basis will insure that investors never again think that we are having a Black Monday when in fact all we were having was a light Gray Monday.

One final thought, one of the theories behind these circuit breakers was to calm the markets down by closing it for a period of time. Here's my final idea on calming the markets. After we modernize our circuit breaker levels to 10% and 20% respectively, I suggest that the Federal Communications Commission adopt a new policy that once the circuit breakers are triggered, all signals from the financial networks—CNBC, CNN, MSNBC, CNN*fn*, etc., etc.—should be scrambled and forced to carry a TV episode of the original Brady Bunch. Can you imagine the sense of calm on the floor of the New York Stock Exchange when all the traders are whistling to the tune "Here's the story of a man named Brady . . . " *(11/97)*

11 Top 10 Investment Themes for '98

The popularity of David Letterman's Top 10 List is unparalleled in the Entertainment Industry. Not only are there a growing number of Top 10 "Junkies" that live for his nightly list, there are now radio stations as well as newspapers that replay and reference David Letterman's nightly Top 10 list, too. Well, the David Letterman bug has finally bitten me as well. As we head into the new year, I decided to develop my own Top 10 list for 1998. My Top 10 list comprises what I feel will be the Top 10 investment issues or themes for 1998.

Number 10: Weatherman discover that there is as much "hot air" coming from Washington D.C. in the Congressional election year as there is from El Niño and these two hot air forces counter-act themselves as the most hyped disaster in the past quarter of a century—El Niño—never comes to pass, and ultimately has no impact on our markets. That doesn't mean that every major snowstorm still won't be blamed on El Niño. What it really means is that this much hyped disaster is not going to cause commodity prices to skyrocket which would in turn fuel inflation fears that in turn would damage our markets. Pretty soon the only one talking about El Niño will be Willard Scott, not the traders on the floor of the New York Stock Exchange.

Number 9: Reform takes center stage in Washington D.C. as both major Tax Reform and Social Security Reform, meaning privatization, gets new life. This may be the single greatest opportunity for you to add value to your clients because, as these issues evolve, they will create a tremendous amount of uncertainty in the markets.

Alan Greenspan has been one of the strongest opponents to privatizing Social Security. He has reversed field 180%. Now he not only supports it, but he even has a specific plan on how to implement it. Greenspan is suggesting a two-tiered approach. First, younger workers would move to a new semi-privatized plan where they would be permitted to earmark a portion of their Social Security payroll tax for investment into stocks and bonds. Meanwhile, older workers could continue in the existing plan as is. Thus, over time, all workers would be covered by the new system. Here is what Alan Greenspan specially told a Congressional committee regarding his plan, and I quote "A privatized defined-contribution plan would, by definition, convert our Social Security system into a fully funded plan" end quote. When the most powerful and influential financial figure in the world speaks, you better believe that Congress will listen.

Number 8: The European Monetary Union comes together and is back on track as the political leadership in Germany, France, Italy and Great Britain finally realize the benefits and clout of a united Europe. With all of the negative international news that has dominated the investment headlines, progress on the European Monetary Union will not only be a welcome relief, it could provide a tremendous boost to our markets. While we still continue to worry from an international perspective about Thailand, Indonesia, Malaysia, The Philippines, Hong Kong, Singapore and South Korea, it is important to note that not one single one of these economies even rank in the top ten economies of the world. That's not the case with Europe. Most investors know that the number one economy in the world is the United States, followed by Japan at number two. Many investors, however, might be surprised by number 3, 4, 5 and 6. The third, fourth, fifth and sixth largest economies in the world are Germany, France, Italy and Great Britain. That's the same Germany, France, Italy and Great Britain that will be coming together to launch the European Monetary Union. This could clearly be a calming event for the international markets.

Number 7: In his last major accomplishment of his Presidency, President Clinton "brokers" a Congressional deal to get Fast Track Trade Authority approved. The reason that this issue is not going away until it is approved is because it's not just about politics, it's about our economy. With Fast Track Trade authority, our entire economy stands to benefit. Specifically small business in this country may actually be one of the biggest winners. In reality, one of the key reasons that our overall economy has done so well the past few years is because small business is on a roll. The reason that our unemployment rate is below 5% and hovers at the lowest levels in a quarter of a century is because of small business. Almost all of the "net" job creation in the 1990's has come from small business. From 1992 through 1996 companies with 100 or fewer employees created 85% of the net gain in new jobs. During that same time period, firms with 1–19 employees expanded employment by an 11.4% level, which is truly remarkable. If small businesses are going to keep up this remarkable pace, they need greater access to the international markets because that is where most of the growth potential lies. In the last two years, the number of small sized businesses that get at least 10% of their sales from exports has astoundingly doubled to what now stands at 50% of all businesses. What's even more important to our economy about these small businesses that do business internationally is that they pay wages 10%–20% higher, they generate more new jobs and are less likely to go out of business than those not engaged in global trade.

Number 6: The Year 2000 problem becomes one of the highest profile issues in 1998; however, our software gurus in Silicon Valley figure out a way to save us from disaster and the high profile of this issue actually fuels the technology sector by the end of the year instead of destroying it. I am not trying to over-simplify this problem; however, I truly believe that most computers will be fixed in time. Now that doesn't mean that there won't be some disruptions. I think that one of the biggest risks will be the "domino effect." In other words, could there be some adverse impact of non-compliance systems on compliant ones. Let me explain to you the basis of why I think this problem will be solved. This isn't a technical solution; it's a practical one. I want you to think back to last July. Last July we launched a space craft with the Sojourner explorer on board to Mars. We actually were able to watch video in our living rooms of the Sojourner explorer hunting for rock on Mars, being powered by solar energy with its actual movements being controlled back here on earth by officials at NASA. Now, here's my problem; think about it. We can send the Sojourner explorer to Mars, figure out how to power it from the Sun with solar energy and have someone sitting at their computer in NASA control the entire operation. And you want me to believe that these same software gurus can't figure out how to get our computers to read 20 instead of 19. Give me a break. I do firmly believe, however, that the biggest disruptions will be related to non-compliance government computers. Think about this, the Year 2000 problem just might be the trump card that causes Social Security privatization to happen. I am not sure how many people will rush to defend the current Social Security system when they fail to receive their checks or when the checks they receive are for the wrong amount, or when they disappear from the Social Security system altogether. When banks, insurance companies and mutual fund companies continue to operate without a hitch in the year 2000, someone is going to wonder just how smooth Social Security would be operating if it would be privatized.

Number 5: The Asian currency and economic meltdown remains the top story for all of 1998. Meanwhile Hong Kong successfully defends both its dollar and the stock market with the help of China, and all of the alarmist fears of Hong Kong being destroyed by China are finally put to rest. Let me make this clear, the Southeast Asian crisis is not going away anytime soon, so I would suggest that you take out a globe and figure out where these countries are located because your clients are going to continue to have questions about them. In my opinion, the benchmark economy that everyone will watch is Hong Kong. Both, because we have always held this economy in such high esteem in the United States, and second, because of our fear that after "rule" reverted back to "Mainland" China, Hong Kong would never be the same. Hong Kong will be just fine because the Hong Kong Dollar will be protected and here is why. Hong Kong's foreign exchange policy links the Hong Kong Dollar to the U.S. Dollar. What's important to note is that the Hong Kong Monetary Authority is a currency board and not a central bank, with the distinction that a currency board's main mandate is the maintenance of the currency value. A central bank typically has other mandates in addition to the currency, including growth, employment and inflation. As a result, Hong Kong's economic policy is conducted mainly through fiscal policy. And remember, three banks have the authority to issue currency in Hong Kong. To issue Hong Kong Dollars, these banks are required to submit U.S. Dollars to the Exchange Fund. The U.S. Dollar foreign exchange reserves at the exchange fund now stands at about $65 billion, which is equivalent to about five times the currency currently in circulation. In addition, Hong Kong has $88 billion in foreign exchange reserves and when you add in China's $122 billion, that's an additional $210 billion in reserves. Make no mistake about it; the Hong Kong Dollar will be protected. Also, don't underestimate the positive psychological lift that Hong Kong will have on the global markets.

Number 4: His past finally catches up with him as the Paula Jones sexual harassment case does what no other scandal, Whitewater, Travel-gate, FBI File-gate, Indonesia-gate, Teamsters-gate, is able to do; destroy the President's credibility and render him a "lame-duck" President the remainder of his term. This simply means that the political battle lines will be drawn much deeper now. It also means that our political landscape will appear somewhat unsettled. The greatest risk to the markets is that this political chaos could cause foreign investors to slow down their investments in the United States as they struggle to figure out what all of this political uncertainty means to the markets.

Number 3: Merger Mania dominates the global equity markets as everyone once again seeks to become a global player. Banks, insurance companies, asset managers and the whole spectrum of tele-communications, local phone companies, long distance phone companies, cellular phone companies, paging companies, cable television companies and all of the internet related companies. I think that you are going to need a score card going forward to keep track of the new names during this merger and acquisition frenzy. There are two tremendous outcomes from this activity. First, the new company that evolves from these mergers is usually bigger, stronger and more global. When you strengthen the individual parts that make up our stock market, that has tremendous long term positive ramifications for our overall stock market as well. Second, as merger and acquisition activity continues, it shoots a hole in the theory that our market is over-priced or that the stock market is too high. This continued acquisition binge is proof that our markets are not inflated. If they were, you would see merger and acquisition activity slowdown significantly.

Number 2: The yield on the benchmark 30-year Treasury Bond ends the year below 5.5% fueled by the continued strong deficit fighting in Washington D.C. and inflation disappearing as gold stays under $300 an ounce all year and oil tests $15 a barrel. Remember, in addition to these strong fundamentals, we will have unbelievable demand from both foreign investors seeking safety and liquidity as well as our own domestic investors re-balancing their portfolios with bonds to get their asset allocation strategies back in balance.

Number 1: The Dow Jones Industrial Average ends the year at 10,000 fueled by rallies at both ends of the capitalization spectrum: small caps and blue chips. You simply couldn't ask for anything more than getting a rally fueled by both ends of the capitalization spectrum. The small cap rally is going to be fueled by three things. First, the recent Capital Gains Tax cut is finally going to sink in and as investors realize that they will be paying less in capital gains, they will be seeking investments that provide them capital gains—namely, small cap stocks. Second, as the fear of an international meltdown continues to haunt investors, they will search for companies with little or no international exposure. Smaller companies tend to have less global exposure, again a positive for small caps. Third, the fear of an interest rate hike is a thing of the past. Rising interest rates have a much greater negative impact on smaller companies because they have less financial flexibility to deal with this change. The fact that expectation has now shifted to no rate hike is also a positive for small caps. On the other end of the spectrum, I think two factors are going to drive the surge in large cap, blue chip stocks. First, as our economy begins to slow down in the second half of the year, investors will begin fleeing to those large multi-national companies with a long and predictable profit and earnings' picture. In other words, everyone will be moving to the blue chip stocks. Second, as I said before, I don't see the crisis in Southeast Asia ending anytime soon; thus, I expect our markets to continue to be the beneficiary of a strong flow of funds from foreign investors. These foreign investors don't want to invest in some small cap bio-technology stock company that they can't even pronounce the name of. They want to invest in the big global companies that they already know, recognize and are familiar with. In other words, our large cap stocks. 1998 may prove to be a very volatile year for the stock market; however, when the dust settles, I am confident the Dow Jones Industrial Average will be above 10,000!

12 THE GREATEST INVESTMENT IDEA FOR THE NEXT MILLENNIUM . . . BOOMERNOMICS

William Shakespeare contributed 1,500 words to the English language, I would humbly like to introduce just one . . . Boomernomics. Boomernomics will be the most significant investment development in the next century! You've probably heard of Macro-Economics and some of you may even remember Reaganomics; now I'm going to tell you about the new world order, Boomernomics.

Let me begin by giving you my formal definition of Boomernomics. Boomernomics is the investment synergy that is created when the demographic trends driven by the Baby *BOOMERS* converge with the *ECONOMIC* trends driven by the end of the Cold War and the creation of the global marketplace.

You see, there are two types of investment events that drive the markets. I've classified these events as blizzards and icebergs. (You can tell I'm from Chicago, can't you!) Blizzards are the investment events that take a relatively short time to impact the markets. The lag between the event and the market impact is measured in weeks, days, hours and sometimes even minutes. When these events occur, the markets are bombarded with what seems like a blizzard of information about the event. Examples of "blizzard type" investment events are economic releases, interest rate hikes, earnings releases, and the newest addition to the blizzard events . . . an Alan Greenspan speech. Now blizzards are very difficult, if not impossible, to predict and when they finally hit, it is too late to do anything about it.

On the other hand, iceberg investment events take a relatively long time to impact the markets. The lag between the time we recognize the investment event and the impact on the markets is measured in years, decades and quarter centuries. Even though we see the iceberg coming, we question the impact it will have on the markets. The market in essence only sees the tip of the iceberg. Examples of "iceberg type" investment events are demographic shifts, global capacity and trade trends, or change in government ideology. Now icebergs, unlike blizzards, are very easy to predict. In fact, you can actually see them coming for years before they hit you. Boomernomics is an iceberg investment event centered on demographics.

Let me simplify this demographics thing for you. The term demographics tends to turn investors off. Instead of using the term demographics, use age characteristics. When you use age characteristics, it's easy to see how they will influence investments. First, age characteristics strongly influence four factors:

- *Consumption Patterns*—Age characteristics determine what we buy.
- *The Aggregate Level of Savings and Investment*—Our age characteristics will determine how much we save and invest.
- *The Composition And Number Of Household Formations*—Age characteristics determine both size and make-up of households.
- *Government Policies*—And to a large part, the age characteristics of a nation have a very strong influence on government policy.

Think about it for a minute—if you know what people are going to buy, what they are going to save and invest, how many houses there are going to be and how many people live in those houses, as well as what government policies are going to be, what in the world else do you need to know. In turn, these factors will determine the outlook for many industries and individual companies. Let me give you three quick industry examples . . . Discount Stores, the Pharmaceutical Industry and the Food Industry.

Let me start with discount stores. When discount stores first appeared on the scene, they were very volatile and marginally successful. This was due in part to their narrow target—that being the universe of buyers that were actually cost conscious.

Now, even though the underlying theme and target of discount stores has not changed, the people who fit into the cost conscious buyer category are greatly expanding. Fundamentally, two major shifts are happening on the demographic front. First, the buying power of the younger generation is no longer so young and free spending. This group now must start worrying about saving for the purchase of a home and for their children's college education.

Second, the older generation is now living longer on their same fixed income and as part of that aging process, they are becoming even more selective in their spending habits.

Both of these demographic shifts will create an expanding universe of potential customers for discount stores.

Let me switch gears now and move on to the Drug Industry. Children under the age of 5, on average, receive eight prescription drugs per year. That trend then declines for the next forty years. However, at age forty-five, the worm turns and that trend reverses itself and from that point on for the rest of our lives, the amount of prescription drugs we use each year accelerates. The trend peaks with individuals 76 and older who average 18 prescription drugs per year. And you think age characteristics don't dominate industries.

Let me quickly move on to my third and final example: the Food Industry. The Food Industry has been besieged by years of slow growth; however, look for consumer spending on ready made food to accelerate in the next ten years. This growth again will be driven by demographics.

There is a whole group of 18–24 year olds that represent the emergence into adulthood of the first generation who grew up with working mothers and consequently, "meals-on-the-run."

The Food Industry must reach out to this group who are much more proficient using microwaves than traditional ovens. This group favors drive through everything. Consumers are now passing up the meat and raw baking ingredients' aisles and instead are picking up prepared chicken and ready-made salads.

Listen to this, by the year 2005, over 50% of homemakers will have never cooked a meal from basic materials. This demographic shift will change the Food Industry forever.

People currently spend less than 20 minutes preparing a meal today; 50 years ago they spent over 2½ hours. Remember growing up as a kid, the way the Jetson's prepared meals on their Saturday morning cartoon seemed as if it was light years away? Well, guess what, it's almost here, only 19 minutes and 59 seconds away.

Let me give you a clear road map of what I want to cover with you regarding Boomernomics. I am going to focus on three things:

- First, we are going to look at the baby-boomer demographic trends.

- Second, we are going to explore what's happening in the economies around the globe.

- And then, third and finally, I want to tie together demographics and the global economies so that we can all get a peak into the future. I'll call this global demographics.

Let's begin with the baby boomers. First, to make sure that we are all on the same page, let me define exactly what a baby boomer is. Anyone who was born between 1946 and 1964 is a baby boomer. During that 19-year period from 1946 to 1964 there were 76 million babies born. To put the magnitude of this boom in perspective for you, in the 19-year period prior to 1946, that being 1927 to 1945, there were less than 49 million babies born.

Think about it in one 19-year period—1927 to 1945 we have less than 49 million babies, then in the next 19-year period—1946 to 1964—we have 76 million babies. That's a baby boom!

In order to understand the true impact of the baby boomers, you cannot look at them in isolation. In fact, there are three separate and unprecedented demographic trends that are converging together to actually turn the United States upside down.

These three trends that highlight the booms or bust scenario of demographics are:

- A senior boom
- Birth bust
- The aging of the baby boomers

It's the confluence of these three trends that is changing the way we live, the way we work and the way we invest. I want to briefly look at all three of these trends starting with the senior boom.

When this country was founded in 1776, a child born in America could expect to live to be 35. One hundred years later in 1876, life expectancy was only 40. Did you ever wonder why we didn't have 401(k)s or IRAs back then? You didn't need them. Everyone died before they could even think about retiring. Look what's happening now. A child born in 1997 can expect to live to be at least 76. So it took us 100 years from 1776 to 1876 to add an additional 5 years of life expectancy from 35 to 40. In the next 100 plus years, we have almost doubled life expectancy from 40 to 76.

Two thirds of all of the men and women who have lived to see their 65th birthday in the entire history of the world are still alive today. Think about it, throughout the entire history of time two thirds of all of the people who celebrated a 65th birthday are still alive today. And most of them by the way I think, are driving in Phoenix.

Throughout all of recorded history, only one in ten people could expect to live to the age of 65. Today, eight out of ten Americans will live past 65.

In 1983 we hit the demographic crossroads in the United States. The number of Americans over the age of 65 surpassed the number of teenagers for the first time in the history of our country. That trend will not reverse itself during the lifetime of anyone who reads this book.

We are no longer a nation of youths. There have been baby booms before, but there has never been a senior boom.

One of the best barometers of how important any social issue truly is, is the number of people who study it.

In the five years after the passage of Social Security in 1935, only ten scholars in the U.S. chose aging as their subject for doctoral dissertation.

In the last five years, there have been over 3,000 such studies.

In the decades to come, aging will become the fastest growing area of study, even surpassing technology! You see, when you are 65, you really don't care that the VCR is still blinking 12:00 o'clock, you just want a few more years to live.

And just in case you think that this senior boom won't have an impact on certain industries in the stock market, remember this:

- The average age of the buyers of American made luxury cars is 65.
- Grandparents buy 40% of all the toys sold.

Did you ever think that all those people with gray hair, driving around in a Cadillac with Toys 'R Us bags in the back might be sending you an investment message.

Let's now look at the second major demographic trend, the birth bust.

A decade ago, the fertility ratio in the U.S. plummeted to its lowest point in history, and it has been hovering there ever since, and it's not likely to change. The senior boom that we just talked about is not being offset by an explosion of children, and here is why. Twenty percent of the baby boomers will have no children at all, another 25% will have only one.

Everyone has a different theory as to why this birth bust is happening. Some point to the shrinkage of births during the Vietnam war years; others point to the shrinkage during the height of the "women's movement"; I don't feel that the birth bust has anything to do with either of those. The birth bust is about our economy, or I should say the evolution of our economy. I'll bet you're wondering how in the world am I going to tie birth rates into the economy.

Think about the evolution of our economy for a minute. It started out as an agricultural based economy, then it evolved to an industrial based economy and finally it has evolved to a service and information based economy.

Think about what this evolution means to birthrates.

In an agricultural based economy, the single most important asset you can have is cheap, unskilled labor. Can you think of a better source for cheap, unskilled labor than your own children.

Listen to me, a large number of healthy children was not just an advantage—it was an economic necessity. You couldn't survive in an agricultural based economy without a lot of children.

Now when you evolve from an agricultural to an industrial to a service and information based economy, children become an increasing economic hardship.

Children today do not add to the economy—they subtract from it. A child today represents tremendous long-term cost with no economic return.

This combination of my first two points, the senior boom and the birth bust is turning American demographics upside down.

The era of the U.S. as a youth focused nation is coming to an end, and it will not be seen again in our lifetimes.

Now, let's move on to our third and most dramatic trend, the aging of the baby boomers.

I know that there continue to be a lot of doubters out there that feel that the baby boomers really are not going to have that great of an impact. Well, to all those doubters, I simply say this:

Over ⅓ of all living Americans today is a baby boomer.

Let me repeat that . . . Over ⅓ of all living Americans are baby boomers.

At every single stage of their lives, the needs and desires of the baby boomers have become the dominant concerns of American business and political leaders. The only thing is, we just didn't give the baby boomers credit for all those changes.

Think about it though, in the 1950s when the baby boomers first arrived, out of nowhere popped up a Diaper Industry. We never had one of those industries before in the U.S. Now we not only had one, but it was making a lot of money. . . . Why?—Well, when you have 76 million babies, you better have a Diaper Industry.

Okay, let's fast forward from the 1950s to the 1960s. Now the boomers are teenagers. Do you know the one thing that every teenager loves to eat? French fries, well not just french fries, but fries, hamburgers, fried chicken. Think about it, in the 1960s on almost every corner up popped another fast food restaurant—You don't think it had anything to do with the quality of the food, do you? Absolutely not, the quality of the food didn't matter. It had everything to do with 76 million teenagers wanting to eat french fries and wanting to eat them fast. It's the baby boomers who made millionaires out of the founders of McDonalds and Kentucky Fried Chicken.

Okay, now let's fast forward to the next decade, the 1970s. In the 1970s the boomers wanted to settle down and buy a house. The real estate explosion in the '70s had absolutely nothing to do with the economy and it had even less to do with real estate agents. It had everything to do with 76 million baby boomers wanting to buy a home. With 76 million people chasing real estate, prices went up in every state in the United States in the '70s.

Let's quickly now move forward to the '80s. The boomers are now focusing on their careers and how to advance them. Publications like the *Wall Street Journal*, *Forbes* and *Fortune* entered periods of record growth. Financial news networks like CNBC and CNN came out of nowhere. All because the boomers were interested in deciding how to get ahead in the business world.

This is not rocket scientists stuff here. If you can anticipate the movement of the baby boomer generation, you can actually see the future.

Okay, now it's the '90s and guess what the boomer's #1 worry today is? . . . Retirement. And when you worry about retirement, you are really worrying about having enough money for retirement so you really start to focus on the stock and bond markets. This great bull market is only partly driven by low inflation or low interest rates or the new global economy. The great bull market is primarily the result of one simple fact. Seventy-six million boomers worrying about their retirement and realizing that the only way they can accumulate enough money is in the stock market.

Now I know that there are some skeptics out there that think this great bull run is over. They simply look at what the stock market has done already in the '90s and they are convinced it has to stop. You see the Dow Jones Industrial Average in the '90s has already blown through:

3,000 in 1991

4,000 and 5,000 in 1995

6,000 in 1996

7,000, 8,000, 7,000, 6,000 and 7,000 in 1997

(It was a volatile year in 1997; however, the direction was still up)

Remember, I told you in the beginning of this chapter that Boomernomics is an Iceberg Investment Event. Well, we don't even see the tip of the iceberg yet. The baby boomers haven't stopped driving the stock market to all time highs; they have just started. We're only at the tip of the iceberg.

Beginning January 1, of 1996, every single minute of every single day for the next 10 years, seven more baby boomers turn 50. Listen closely to this; beginning January 1st, 1996, every single minute of every single day for the next decade, seven more baby boomers turn 50. Think about it; since you started reading this chapter, there are now 70 more baby boomers over-the-hill at age 50.

And guess what, when the boomers cross that magical ½ century mark, they get even more worried about retirement and they will be putting even more money into the stock market.

And it's not just the overall markets. Think about this specific industry impact for a minute.

Boomers are probably going to be the most active 50 year olds who ever lived. One thing they are intent on is feeling youthful and not looking like their parents. Did you ever think of this—perhaps the four wheel drive sports utility vehicles are so popular because baby boomers are apprehensive about driving the station wagons their parents drove.

Before I close on the baby boomers specifically, and demographics generally, I need to quickly and briefly touch on a sub-set of the baby boomers.

The Echo-Boomers are the children of the baby boomers. Now the echo-boomers are not going to change the world the way the baby boomers did; however, they are becoming another significant force in our economy.

Even though the echo-boom is much smaller than the baby boom, there are enough of them to make a difference in our economy.

Let me help put the economic impact of the echo-boom in perspective for you.

Roughly ½ of all the 16–19 year olds have jobs that, on average, pay $50 per week. In addition, most teens receive an allowance averaging $30 per week.

Together, these two sources of income give teens aggregate spending power of more than $100 billion per year.

The economic impact of this money takes on even greater significance when we realize, because teens do not have to pay the mortgage or the heating bill, teenagers spend their rising income entirely on discretionary items like clothes, cosmetics, fast food and entertainment.

And unlike their parents, teens are not jaded, time-pressed consumers for whom shopping is a chore; on the contrary, going to the mall is actually a form of entertainment.

While teens are deciding what to buy, they are shaping *their personal appearance* and *personal identity* during a very formative period in their lives. . . . As a result *brands* matter to teens . . . a lot!

And in case you are wondering what impact this echo-boom will have on the stock market, consider this. . . . When teens were asked to identify the "coolest brands," the top 5 were:

- Nike
- Gap
- Guess
- Levi
- Sega

Now don't try to read into this; I'm not suggesting that you buy these stocks. I don't know if their P.E. ratios and beta's and capitalization levels are giving us a buy signal.

All that I know is that there is over $100 billion to be spent and I think that it's going to be spent on things that teenagers think are cool. Think about it, we've got aging baby boomers along with their echo-boomers to combine with the other two great demographic changes: the senior boom and the birth bust. Together these trends will converge to produce a historic shift in the structure and concerns of America.

Now move on to the second of my three major points: what's happening in the economies around the globe.

There was a time when investors in the U.S. didn't need to care about what was going on globally. You see, back in 1970 the U.S. stock market clearly dominated the world equity markets as it represented approximately 70% of the total world market capitalization.

That's not the case today. With the rapid growth of the equity markets throughout the world, U.S. equities now account for roughly ½ of that total.

Looked at another way, that means if you limit your portfolio only to U.S. stocks, you are forfeiting the chance to participate in 5 out of every 10 of the world's equity investment opportunities.

I want to briefly touch on three things with you regarding the global economies. First, I want to give you a big picture look at how the global landscape has changed and then I want to touch on two of the biggest global forces in the future, that being China and the European Monetary Union.

Let's start by taking a look at the global landscape. Think about it; the global landscape has changed dramatically since the end of World War II. In the early days of the post-war era the focus was simple and very parochial. You may remember it as to the victor's belong the spoils.

There were four investment themes that were driving the global markets. First, the U.S. was basking in a new industrial renaissance *unchallenged at home* and largely *unconcerned about vying for market* share abroad.

Second, in war ravaged Europe and Japan there was an obvious and urgent focus on reconstruction aimed at restoring the economics of income generation and wealth creation.

Third, global competition was not exactly encouraged in the early days of the post-war era. With the dawning of the Cold War, the world became quickly segmented into free market and communist regimes. The Berlin Wall was symbolic of a demarcation that kept more than 3 billion global citizens away from the free enterprise system.

Fourth and finally, to further complicate things in order to bootstrap their post-war recoveries, most of Europe and Japan embraced elaborate subsidy and regulatory schemes, thereby *limiting the impact of market* forces on their companies and their economies.

Even the United States was quick to seek comfort under the regulatory umbrella, shielding vast and rapidly growing Service Industries such as Telecommunications, Financial Services, Transportation and Utilities from competitive reality.

You need to understand those investment themes are gone forever. We have a new global landscape. The new global landscape has three new investment themes.

- The Cold War is over

- Regulation has given way to deregulation and privatization
- World Trade is surging

Like it or not, in this new global landscape it's financial capital not military or governmental capital that matters.

The market forces of globalization, driven by massive flow of foreign direct investment of capital have become the most powerful forces the world has ever known.

Now that we have a better understanding of the new global landscape, let's move on to my second point: one of the biggest forces globally today—namely China.

Almost 200 years ago, Napoleon said "when China awakes, it will shake the world"—Napoleon was right! And the world is shaking.

China is in the process of constructing the largest wealth creation engine in history. I want to touch on three things regarding China: the *poverty* level, *savings* rate and the *economy.*

Let's start with the poverty level because it will help put the size of this wealth creation machine in perspective for you. In the last 20 years alone, over 170 million Chinese have escaped or risen above the poverty level. That number is larger than Japan's entire population.

Let's now move the second point, savings. China, for the past 20 years, has averaged real growth of 10%. China's growth is fueled by its incredible 35% personal savings rate. China uses this pool of capital to finance productive capital investment. By the way, the U.S. savings' rate is under 3%.

Third and finally, look at China's economy. China will overtake number 2, Japan, and the number 1 global economy, the United States, within the first quarter of the next century.

Think about this for a minute. With a population five times larger than the United States, that means that China only needs to achieve per-capita production levels of just $1/5$ th of each American worker to outpace the United States.

If, however, instead of working at $1/5$ th the per-capita production levels of U.S. workers, Chinese workers instead match their major Asian market competitors in Taiwan regarding output per worker—which by the way I think that they will—look what would happen.

China's GDP would exceed that of all the rest of the industrialized world combined within the next 25 years.

(ASSUMPTIONS: U.S.—2.5%/CHINA 8.0%)		
	U.S.	*China*
1996	6.8 trillion	3.2 trillion
2021	12.7 trillion	21.9 trillion

Now I know that even with these *dramatic forecasts*, many of you not only don't want to invest in China, you don't want to invest in any emerging market—of which China is the biggest.

You may not have a choice before long—let me switch from forecasts and projections to reality and show you exactly where we are today with emerging markets.

Let me start with a quick definition of an emerging market so that we all have the same frame of reference.

The World Bank defines emerging markets as those countries with per capita income less than $8,956. Let me give you a frame of reference regarding this $8,956 per capita income level. In the United States, per capita income is $23,208. Looking at it on a state by state basis, our lowest per capita income in any state is Mississippi, with per capita income of $16,531, which is almost 2 times greater than the emerging market level.

Using that World Bank definition—today, right now over 85% of the World's population lives in emerging markets.

And right now over 65% of all of the world's natural resources come from emerging markets.

Still think you'll never invest in emerging markets? . . . Think again!

Now let's move on to my third and final point regarding the global economy—the European Monetary Union.

Several countries of Europe are committed to introducing a Monetary Union on January 1, 1999. This union is referred to as the EMU or European Monetary Union.

The scope of this monetary union proposal is unprecedented in both European and world economic history.

I want to briefly touch on three issues with you regarding EMU. First, I want to give you some historic perspective. Second, I want to touch upon why countries are pushing for the EMU. And third, I'll explore what will be the impact on investments. Let's begin with a quick historic perspective. For your frame of reference, there were five monetary unions in Europe during the late 19th century, but nothing on the scale of the current proposal.

France, Italy, Belgium and Switzerland formed a currency zone linked to silver in the 1860s.

And even the countries of Scandinavia tried to form a monetary union in the late 1800s.

What happened back then was that by the late 19th century, most countries moved onto the gold standard and thus the focal point of their exchange rate policy was a global monetary standard, not a regional one.

Let me make this simple. The current EMU is trying to create a zone of regional monetary stability within an international financial system in which exchange rates will remain flexible.

That's it for the quick history lesson; now let's move on to my second point. Namely, why are countries pushing for EMU and what will the impact be on investments?

There are really four main benefits to the EMU: exchange rate, prices, travel and competition.

First, the exchange rate risk within Europe will be eliminated. That will simplify and promote trade and investment, which in turn will promote growth and employment.

Second, prices in EMU countries can be compared with one another. Third, trade and travel within the EMU will no longer entail currency conversion costs.

And fourth and most importantly, as the country borders disappear, competition will become more intense. Companies and consumers can capitalize on this.

Now that we know why they want it, let's look at the third and final point—What impact it will have on investments.

There will be three major impacts of EMU: first on the bond market, second on the currency market and third on the political markets.

Let's start with the bond market. Along with the establishment of a single European currency, the euro, EMU will create a single broad bond market in which European governments and corporations will issue debt beginning January 1, 1999.

If successful, EMU will create the first liquid, or widely traded, bond market approximating the size of the U.S. market. In fact, large investors, some of whom have shied from the relatively small individual European bond markets in favor of U.S. Treasuries, will for the first time have a choice of venues in which to buy bonds. As an institutional investor, it will be a whole lot easier to invest in all of Europe through EMU than it ever would be to invest in Italy. And the impact on the U.S. Treasury market would increase as the new bond market offered a variety of coordinated maturities and yields. *Issuers* of debt may also choose to go to the EMU market.

Let's now move on to the second point, the currency market impact.

If the euro proves a sufficiently popular currency, international investors, corporations and central banks may see it as a suitable *compliment* to the dollar, if only for *diversification* purposes. While many of these parties already hold substantial foreign-currency reserves, they may increase their holdings if EMU takes off.

And think about this, any diminution of the dollar's overwhelming popularity would likely hurt the demand for dollar-denominated securities especially U.S. bonds.

Now let's move on to the third point, and the one that no one is focusing on, the political impact.

First of all, in order to become eligible for EMU, countries were required to reduce their budget deficits to 3.0% of GDP. This could now serve as the ceiling for the U.S. deficit because in the race for capital it would have to keep it's budget deficit in line with the other EMU countries, with whom they are competing for capital.

And think about this potential political ramification. During a trade or human-rights squabble with the U.S., Chinese and Japanese central banks could threaten to shift investments to the European market. The implication is significant not just for the market, but for the future public policy of our entire country as well.

The EMU will be the single most important development in the U.S. fixed income markets in the next decade.

Let's re-group again. We have explored the baby boomer demographic trends; then we just looked at what's happening in the economies around the globe; now I want to move on to my third and final point. Let's combine demographics with the global economies and see if we can get a peak of what the future may hold. Think of this, my third and final point as Global Demographics.

If any of you have been excited after reading about the investment impact of 76 million baby boomers in the U.S. earlier in this chapter, just wait. An even bigger demographic move has yet to even begin. The single most powerful economic force ever to move through any society in the history of the world has yet to begin to make its true impact on the stock market.

The most influential demographic trend that is looming on the global horizon is what I call Asia's "Roller-blade" generation.

Now you can classify Roller-bladers into two groups. The first group is all Roller-bladers between the ages of 10 to 24. The second group is

276

comprised of everyone else that still acts like they are between the ages 10 to 24. Asia's Roller-blade generation is about the first group.

There is a population bubble about to burst in Asia. In the year 2000, there will be one billion people between the ages of 10 to 24. Asia's Roller-blade generation will be one billion strong by the year 2000.

The desires, tastes and spending habits of this generation will radically reshape the business climate, social fabric and political institutions of Asia and the world.

In order to understand the potential impact of this population bulge in Asia, the crucial point is that Asia's Roller-blade generation was born into a world radically different from the one their parents entered.

Their parents were left largely scared and desolated by World War II. For most of the post-war era rebuilding societies and countries was the primary national goal, requiring hard work, dedication, individual sacrifice, high savings, production, conformity and exports.

These attributes have underpinned the industrial rise of Asia over the past half century and have dramatically reshaped the world that the region's teeming population of youths currently lives in.

Asia's "Roller-blade generation" is by contrast growing up in an era of prosperity, not poverty; and its members have within their grasp opportunities and wealth their parents did not. Shopping is more characteristic of this group than savings. Their parents drank tea, wore sandals, ate rice and bought things with cash. . . . Not the Roller-blade generation.

Think about what they prefer.

- Their parents drank tea, they drink Coke
- Their parents wore sandals, they wear Nikes
- Their parents ate rice, they eat Chicken McNuggets
- Their parents purchased things with cash, they purchase things with credit cards

A by-product of Asia's economic success, this generation is better educated and more willing and able to travel abroad.

Leisure time, convenience, individualism, indulgence, spending and other Western habits (or vices) permeate this group. A radical change in the mind set and actions from previous generations.

Think about this, even if 25% of this population bracket never sees a Coke sign or a Nike swish (two of the most powerful brands in the world) the remaining 75% or 750 million youth represent the largest *consumer* bubble ever in the history of time. To give you a frame of reference at this 75% level, they are still 10 times larger than our baby boomers.

The question to investors is clear . . . Do you own consumer related companies positioned to satisfy the wants and needs of Asia's Roller-blade generation? . . . The most powerful demographic trend in the world.

Think about what products will be hot . . . cigarettes, cars, jeans, fast food, shampoo, beverages, cosmetics, etc.

In order to truly understand the market influence of Asia's Roller-blade generation, which is one billion strong, you need to understand that with our aging baby boomers, we are talking about millions, while with Asia's Roller-blade generation, we are talking a billion. Let me give you a better frame of reference regarding a billion.

If I were to give you one billion inches and you were to line them next to one another, they would stretch all the way from New York to Los Angeles, back to New York, back to Los Angeles, back to New York, back to Los Angeles, with enough inches left over to go all the way to Salt Lake City. Now close your eyes for a minute and imagine a burning cigarette in every one of those inches and you'll see why I don't care about the tobacco settlement in Washington D.C.

As I bring this book to a close, I hope that you now understand the difference between investment blizzards and icebergs.

To briefly recap, I explored three concepts with you. First, we looked at the baby boomer demographic trends; second, we explored what's going on in the economies around the globe; and third, we tied together demographics and the global economies to get a brief peek into the future.

The confluence of these concepts enables me to close this book by giving you a prediction. I am going to predict where the stock market is going to go. Not next week or next year, but rather five years from now, on December 31, 2002.

The DJIA will close December 31, 2002 above 15,000!

Now I know that this prediction may sound outlandish to you, but it's not. In addition to everything else we've already talked about in this chapter, just consider these three events that will turbo charge our stock market:

- Money Market Assets
- Retirement Shift
- Privatization of Social Security

Let me briefly touch on all three of these turbo chargers. Let's start with Money Market Assets.

Currently there is over $1 trillion sitting idle in taxable money market accounts.

Add to that the amount sitting in savings accounts, tax-exempt money market accounts and other liquid assets, and the amount goes to over $3 trillion.

That's currently more than ⅓ of the almost $10 trillion currently invested in U.S. equities.

Which direction do you think the market's going to head when some of that money makes its way into the stock market. Oh, and it will get into the stock market. You see, currently everyone that remembers the stock market crash of the 1920s, has their money in money markets. As they pass away and "will" their money to their boomers, the boomers who inherit that "transfer of wealth" will turn around and put that money in the stock market.

Let's move on to my second point: what I refer to as retirement shift.

You see, corporate cash is migrating from defined-benefit pension plans toward 401(k)s and other defined contribution plans, not just in the U.S. but around the world as well.

Like it or not, people are being forced to become investors in the stock market because employers no longer want to take responsibility for managing retirement assets.

I know that much has been written trying to explain the importance of the retirement shifts from "defined benefit" to "defined contribution." I am now going to take my stab at it. Instead of using the term "defined benefit system," substitute the term "I don't care about the stock market." You see, that is what really was happening under a "defined benefit system." Ten to fifteen years ago you would simply go to work, do your job and your employer would take care of your retirement for you. They would "define" what those benefits would be. At lunch time people read the sports pages not the stock tables to see how their 401(k) was doing. In other words, a "defined benefit" retirement system really means: "I don't care about the stock market." Well, when you move from a defined benefit system to a defined contribution system, we need to substitute a term for "defined contribution" as well. Instead of using the term "defined contribution," substitute it with the term: "I am a stock market junkie."

You see, under the defined contribution plan, you no longer can say, "I don't care about the stock market." Under the defined contribution plan, you receive money either every payday or quarterly or annually and you are forced to invest that money. In other words, we are creating a whole nation of stock market junkies. Once we get you into the market and you watch your money grow, you become a junkie.

This shift from defined benefit to defined contribution is the greatest ponzie scheme corporate America ever invented. We will never shift back. I just cannot imagine any business anywhere in the world saying, "Wait a minute, I changed my mind, we want to be responsible again for your retirement."

Perhaps the best way to show you the unbelievable impact that this is having on investors is to relay a story that happened to me last year.

I was scheduled to deliver a luncheon speech at our headquarters in Chicago to a group of financial advisors regarding the state of the economy. When I arrived a few minutes before the scheduled time, there was nobody at all in the room. I come to find out the meeting location was changed to the Westin Hotel and I was now officially late. Lucky for me our headquarters at 222 South Riverside Plaza in Chicago is actually built above the Union Train Station, which means taxi cabs are plentiful. Thus, I dashed out the building into a cab and screamed, "I'm late for a meeting. Get me to the Westin Hotel as quickly as possible."

The cab driver informed me that it would not be a problem. He then said, "I noticed you came running out of the building; you don't by chance work for Kemper Funds, do you?" I confessed that I did. He then immediately said, "If you don't mind, I have two quick questions for you—one about where I see the stock market going and the other about one of the Kemper Funds that I've invested my 401(k) retirement money into?"

Think about what's happening here. Ten to fifteen years ago, if you were fortunate enough to belong to a country club maybe someone would come up to you to chat about the stock market. Today, hop in a cab in downtown Chicago and the taxi driver wants to debate the direction of the stock market. This retirement shift has truly created a nation of stock market junkies. The shift is far from over. In the United States, a little over 50% of the companies have shifted from defined benefit to defined contribution. This trend will not stop until we reach 100%. Globally, less than 20% of the companies have shifted from defined benefit to defined contribution. Again, this shift will not stop until it reaches 100%.

Which direction do you think the market's going to head as more and more corporations in the U.S. and around the world move from defined benefits and force their employees to become stock market junkies?

Okay, we touched on money market assets and the retirement benefit shift; now let's move to my third and final point, the privatization of Social Security.

Social Security will be privatized because it's not about Democrats and Republicans or Conservatives and Liberals; it's about demographics.

Social Security must be privatized because of demographics. Let me explain it to you this way.

When Social Security was first established, life expectancy in the U.S. was 62. Considering Social Security benefits started at age 65, it was a great system; everyone was expected to die before they received their first penny from Social Security.

Now life expectancy is 76. So we went from 62 to 76, which means that we added 14 years of financial liability for every beneficiary in the Social Security system. We currently have over 40 million beneficiaries. Okay, for any of you who were not a math major, that means we added over ½ billion years of financial liability to the system. The best run pension system in the world, which by the way this was never nominated for, could not absorb an additional ½ billion years of financial liability.

Look what's happened to the work force that pays for Social Security. In 1935 when Social Security was established, everything was fine. We had 10 workers for every one retiree on Social Security. Last year that number dropped to 5 to 1. By the year 2010, which by the way is less than 12 years away, the ratio drops to 2 to 1. At 2 to 1, the system cannot work—the system will not work, unless of course the two people supporting you are Madonna and Donald Trump.

Let me give you some idea of the magnitude of this problem. If we were to take the present value of the future benefits to be paid out in Social Security, and subtracted from that amount the present value of the future taxes we are going to collect from Social Security payroll taxes, we are only 11 trillion dollars short.

In order to give you some idea of the magnitude of 11 trillion dollars, if we substituted one second in time for each dollar, we would only be 352,000 years short.

The only answer is to privatize Social Security.

The current recommendation on the table to privatize Social Security calls for taxpayers to be able to divert ½ of their 6.2% Social Security payroll tax into a self directed Personal Security Account. They then can invest the money in the stock market or bond market. In five years, if only ½ the taxpayers opt for this option, these Personal Security Accounts will accumulate over one trillion dollars.

Which direction do you think the stock market is going to head when most of this trillion dollars makes its way into the stock market?

Make no mistake about it, the confluence of

- Money Market Assets
- Retirement Benefit Shifts
- And The Privatization of Social Security

will turbo charge the stock market to 15,000 by the year 2002!

Oh, and by the way, for your frame of reference on this, after the stock market closed at the end of 1997 at 7908 consider this. Since the boomers started focusing on the stock market in 1991 when it closed on December 31 at 3168, the average return for the last six years from 1991–1997, was 17%. To appease all you "bears" out there—let's assume that for the next five years the market will only return 75% of that average return over the last six years. If that's all that happens, the DJIA will be at 14,570 by 2002. I think that my 15,000 might be a little light. Sometimes it's very difficult to see the iceberg through the blizzards.

I want to make a date with each and every one of you that reads this book. I'll see you in the year 2002 at the top of the Boomernomics Iceberg at 15,000!